网络中文教学指南

Teach Chinese Online – An Essential Guide

PHOENIX TREE
PUBLISHING

Teach Chinese Online: An Essential Guide

By Miao-fen Tseng & Yan Gao

ISBN: 978-1-62575-318-2

Library of Congress Control Number: 2021936014

First Printing: January 2021

Printed in the US

Editors: Yao Li, Chao Shi

Phoenix Tree Publishing Inc.

5660 North Jersey Ave, Chicago, IL 60659

Phone: 773.250.0707 Fax: 773.250.0808

Email: marketing@phoenixtree.com

For information about the special discounts for bulk purchases,

Please contact the publisher at the address above.

Find out more about Phoenix Tree Publishing Inc. at

www.phoenixtree.com

Preface

This book is a product of experience and contemplation. It builds on the summative research findings of the successful UVA STARTALK teacher and student academy, ongoing critical analysis and exploration of what it takes to make online teaching successful, and profound self-reflection. Its discussion of virtual F2F teaching begins with STARTALK and extends to a wide range of deliberations and evidence-based practice, all grounded in the encouraging and observable fact that frequent quality interaction can be achieved through online instruction.

I have never imagined that I would be so fascinated by online language teaching. Running the STARTALK teacher and student program catalyzed a shift in my interest from face-to-face teaching to online teaching. After concluding the eight-year in-person STARTALK program, I looked for ways to continue its work, to reactivate it in refreshing and rejuvenating ways. In the summer of 2015, a historical juncture, I restructured my core team and rehired teaching staff. This gave me the opportunity to rethink how the program would be: a continuation with minor tweaks, or something brand-new and inspirational. With Henny Chen, the leading force for innovative technology on our team, I decided to make a big leap and transform the program to online learning in the summer of 2016. We made it! In what seemed a miracle, we achieved a 100% completion rate for the zero-credit online student program, much higher than our goal. We dared to dream big, and we were amazed to find our dreams realized.

When my role was solely a language instructor and researcher of classroom-based empirical studies, I was not technology-savvy — I'd even say I was tech-phobic. And I would have continued on that path if I had not had the honor to serve as the inaugural director of the Institute of World Languages (IWL) at the University of Virginia (UVA) starting in 2014. Leading the IWL introduced me to a mosaic of e-learning and a widening horizon. Through my directorship, I am driven to keep abreast of the newest developments in world language education in relation to the advancement of technology in the United States and around the world. Digital humanities, e-learning, mobile learning, virtual reality, augmented reality — the list goes on, and all these opportunities promise to reshape the language classroom, both present and potential.

I am deeply grateful to those who have helped me to shape ideas about different parts of the book — small or big, directly or indirectly. My heartfelt thanks go to Dr. Yan Gao, who generously agreed to contribute to technology-focused chapters of the book as a co-author. Her extensive experience and expertise in using technology as a facilitating tool to enhance online teaching makes this book possible. I also want to express my deepest appreciation of the UVA STARTALK core instructional team, who inspired me to create a robust combination program for teachers and students. They are Dr. Ziyi Geng and Luoyi Cai, both excellent online Chinese language educators in the United States. UVA STARTALK teaching fellows also were fundamental for the success of the program, and thus of this book. In the process of writing, I was fortunate to be able to interview several other devoted Chinese language educators. Our discussions have re-affirmed my determination to complete this book, particularly at this time. They are Jennifer Jezzi at Oneida-Herkimer-Madison BOCES in New York, Ya-ching Hsu-Kelkis at Chinese American International School in San Francisco, Dr. Haohsiang Liao at Massachusetts Institute of Technology, and Shuishui Long at Pennsylvania State University.

This book includes eight chapters. Chapter 1 introduces a model program for online Chinese language learning, funded by a US STARTALK grant. It highlights the design and structure of the program, well-tested learning outcomes, learners' testimonials, and after-program reflections and recommendations. Chapter 2 provides an overview of delivery modes for online teaching essentials, an analysis of three types of interaction in each delivery mode, and explanations of the elements contributing to online interaction. Chapter 3 summarizes effective principles and strategies for successful online teaching with supporting evidence and includes useful examples to illustrate best practices. Chapters 4 and 5 offer detailed illustrations of student-centered communicative tasks that are implemented synchronously and asynchronously in online teaching. They are described with can-do statements, communicative mode, performance level, technology tools, and step-by-step instructions that are ready for teachers to use in classrooms. Instructional strategies are provided at the end of some tasks to reinforce effective instruction. Chapter 6 introduces a list of technology resources, applications, and tools with high relevancy to the realization of pedagogical objectives introduced in chapters 4 and 5. Chapter 7 lists ten essentials for creating a successful online language course. It emphasizes practicality, applicability, and user-friendliness for online language teachers. To conclude, chapter 8 compiles fifteen frequently asked questions that language teachers have pondered since the emergence of online language teaching and learning; building on the practical guidance offered in the earlier chapters, the answers to these questions should set many teachers' minds at ease. Effective online language teaching is not only possible, practical, and accessible to all, it is exciting, creative, and interactive. With this book as your guide, you can take on this journey of exploration and discovery with confidence, curiosity, and clarity.

To add a final note, this book is largely a reaction to the 2020 global crisis, the COVID-19 pandemic that forced many of us to our homes, eager to do something differently. The pandemic has drastically reshaped what we do and how we think and work. But it has given me a luxury of intensive writing in tranquility, for which I am profoundly grateful. While we are all deep in rethinking how best to respond to this global challenge, I warmly and humbly welcome you to embark on this journey and enjoy reading this book, a heavenly gift of professional and spiritual nourishment I never expected or imagined, and now am honored to share with you.

Miao-fen Tseng
Daniels Family NEH Distinguished Teaching Professor
Inaugural Director of the Institute of World Languages
University of Virginia, USA

About the Author

Daniels Family NEH Distinguished Teaching Professor, University of Virginia

Inaugural Director, Institute of World Languages, University of Virginia

Director, Virginia STARTALK Chinese Teacher/Student Academy, University of Virginia

Albert Nelson Marquis Who's Who Lifetime Achievement Award

Helen Warriner-Burke FLAVA Distinguished Service Award

AP Chinese Consultant, College Board

Academic Advisor/Senior Reviewer for AP Chinese Course Audit, College Board

Miao-fen Tseng 曾妙芬

美国国家人文学科 Daniels Family 杰出教学教授

弗吉尼亚大学世界外语中心创办人暨主任

星谈中文教师培训与学生项目主任

Albert Nelson Marquis 名人录终身成就奖

Helen Warriner-Burke FLAVA 杰出外语贡献奖

大学理事会 AP 中文顾问

AP 中文课程审查资深学术顾问与评审委员

Dr. Miao-Fen Tseng is the Daniels Family NEH Distinguished Teaching Professor and the Inaugural Director of the Institute of World Languages at the University of Virginia (UVA). She has frequently given talks and workshops on Chinese language pedagogy and taught graduate-level courses under the auspices of various collaborative initiatives and professional development programs in the US and globally. Her influential roles include, but are not limited to, Director of UVA STARTALK Teacher/Student Academy, Founder and President of the Chinese Language Teachers Association of Virginia (CLTA-VA), member of the CLTA Board of Directors, member of STARTALK Task Force, College Board consultant in AP Chinese, Academic Advisor and Senior Reviewer for AP Chinese Audit, and Evaluator of K-16 Chinese language programs and teacher preparation programs. She has received many accolades in recognition of her contribution to Chinese language education, among them the Albert Nelson Marquis Who's Who Lifetime Achievement Award (2019), the STARTALK Award (2008-2019), the Jefferson Trust Award (2018), the Helen Warriner-Burke FLAVA Distinguished Service Award (2016), and the Jiede Empirical Research grant (2015) by CLTA. She has written numerous peer-reviewed articles and five books, including *AP Chinese Language and Culture Teacher's Guide*, *Promoting Professionalism in Teaching AP Chinese*（推动专业化的 AP 中文教学）, and *The Handbook of Tasks and Rubrics for Teaching Mandarin Chinese* (Volume I, II, III). Her major interest lies in CFL curriculum design and pedagogy, task-based teaching, teacher training, and online teaching and technology.

（请编辑核对标点符号正确使用）

　　曾妙芬博士目前为美国国家人文学科 Daniels Family 杰出教学教授暨弗吉尼亚大学世界外语中心创办主任。她经常受邀参与海内外演讲及中文教学工作坊，并提供各类中文专业师资培训，担任研究所创新计划课程的教授。她在中文教学界也扮演具影响力的角色，例如担任美国星谈中文教师培训与学生项目主任，维州中文教师学会创始人暨会长，全美中文教师学会董事，星谈线上教学筹备委员，大学理事会 AP 中文顾问，AP 中文课程审查资深学术顾问与评审委员，K-16 中文语言项目与师资培训项目评鉴委员。她曾荣获诸多奖项，包括 Albert Nelson Marquis 名人录终身成就奖 (2019)，星谈联邦政府经费 (2008-2019)，美国第三任总统汤姆逊杰弗逊外语前瞻计划奖 (2018)，Helen Warriner-Burke FLAVA 杰出外语贡献奖 (2016)，全美中文教师学会 Jiede 实证研究奖 (2015) 与 Ron Walton 最佳论文发表奖 (1998)。她的学术论文刊登在诸多专业学术期刊并出版五本专业书籍，包括推动专业化的 AP 中文教学，AP 中文教学指引，中文任务型教学活动与评量手册 (1-3 册)。其研究领域主要为对外汉语课程设计与教学、任务型教学法、师资培训、线上线下教学与科技应用等方面。

About the Author

Dr. Yan Gao teaches Mandarin Chinese at Henrico County Public Schools (HCPS). She is the recipient of ACTFL Distant Learning Award for K-12 education and of the Quest Global Impact Award at the Virginia Commonwealth University in 2017. She is the educational technology coordinator and co-trainer at UVA Startalk Chinese Teacher and Student Academy since 2018. Since 2011, she has been making the Chinese language curriculum "real" by introducing telecollaboration, student blogging, curation projects, and other high-impact learning activities in the online environment. With many years of experience in integrating technology into teaching Chinese, she believes

Yan Gao 高　燕

that technology integration will not only foster language acquisition but also help learners think more critically and boost interest and motivation in language and cultural studies.

高燕博士目前任教于亨利科县公立中学，她是美国 2017 年全美外语教学学会（ACTFL）K-12 远程教学的获奖者，并于同一年荣获维吉尼亚州立大学的 Quest 全球影响力奖。高博士自 2018 年至今在维吉尼亚大学星谈项目担任 UVA Startalk 中文教师和学生项目的教育技术培训师。2011 年至今，通过远程协作、学生博客策展项目以及其他具有影响力的科技教学活动，使网络中文课程能够真正在"真实情境中"进行沉浸式语言教学。高博士根据多年将技术整合到中文教学所积累的经验，相信技术整合不仅有助于语言习得，也能帮助学生进行更深层次的思考，提高学生对语言和文化学习的兴趣与动力。

Contents

Chapter 1
A Successful Online Chinese Language Program

The majority of online courses offered in secondary schools are asynchronous and self-paced, whereas courses at postsecondary settings are mostly synchronous and face-to-face (F2F), either online or in a physical classroom (Barbour, 2017; Hampel & Hauck, 2004). Language learners in K-12 educational settings tend to hold more negative perceptions of online learning than their F2F counterparts despite well-attested benefits of computer-assisted language teaching and learning (Tseng et al., 2018). This poses unique challenges for administrators and language educators in secondary schools, and language faculty at colleges and universities are compelled to think further on the continuity of instruction and student placement. One clear way to meet this challenge is to enable the real-time interaction and engagement that enables and empowers students to practice the target language (Baker, 2011).

An attempt to explore and resolve this issue, the Virginia STARTALK Chinese Student Academy, funded by a federal STARTALK grant, joins a national initiative for increasing the capacity of language teaching and learning in the United States. Its operations and recommendations have evolved from F2F learning in 2008–14, to flipped learning in 2015, and to completely online learning in 2016–19. The program, led by a strong forward-thinking team, resulted in the creation of an online teaching model with versatile technology and innovative pedagogy. It is an exciting and inspirational adventure whose goal is to build an innovative and successful online Chinese language program.

Two Anecdotal Accounts of Online Language Courses

About one year before I was deep in deliberating what the UVA STARTALK online learning program should be like in 2015, my daughter, Regan, warned me not to do it. The following is what she said out loud to me right after she learned of my intent.

Regan: "Mom, don't do it. It's no use at all!"

Me: "The program we have in mind is different from the online courses you took before."

Regan stood still and listened attentively when I raised my voice, trying to enunciate each single word forcefully in the above sentence. I knew very well that she was projecting from several Chinese language courses that she learned painfully online and did not want me to replicate her failing experience. This brings back old memories that she and I both shared together in a three-year period spanning 2012 to 2014 when she was a high schooler.

In her high school years, Regan wanted to continue studying Chinese language and culture after discontinuing lessons in a Chinese weekend school. But her high school did not offer Mandarin Chinese. She then took her school counselor's advice and enrolled in virtual Chinese language courses for Level II, Level III, and AP Chinese. She ended up having lots of complaints and great dissatisfaction although she received a solid A for each course and a score of 5 on the Chinese AP Exam.

Her major dissatisfaction was from the classes' sheer reliance on self-learning; most of the time, she had to seek answers herself, was sort of disoriented, and begged me as her mom to do homework with her very late at night. There were so many nights of co-work between her and me, as I could still recall, that I sacrificed my bed time, sitting on the floor with drooping eyes to read the exercises filled with Chinese characters on the tiny screen of her laptop in her bedroom. She so desperately needed me to be her tutor, or she could not have finished her homework and gone to bed. I do not remember what types of homework she finished on so many late nights. But I do remember that almost all the questions and exercises were just like those in conventional textbooks. Apart from my help, she seemed to do almost everything on her own. She was not motivated to learn but merely did all the work to get a grade and be a student in good standing.

The answer to the problem with her online learning experience is critically clear. She did not get needed help, support, or guidance from her online instructors in time and was left to solve almost all problems herself from the beginning till the end of the course. There was no genuine teaching, and far more importantly, no genuine human interactions at all. Feeling helpless, she counted on my immediate tutorial to save her from frustration and failure.

Her unpleasant learning experience concurs with many others who learn a foreign language in virtual schools. To avoid duplicating the type of learning that Regan had gone through, I was determined to make a change to online learning in Mandarin Chinese.

Another anecdote also makes me think long and deeply about how to envision, frame, and structure an online learning program.

One of my good friends in the school of education did not quite understand why I wanted to convert F2F learning to completely online and train teachers how to teach in the online learning program. At that time, she was the field director of a teacher preparation program supervising graduate students studying and working toward a K-12 teacher license in foreign language teaching. After learning my primary intent, she asked me the following question in a very soft tone, skeptically but meticulously, not wanting to hurt my feelings or challenge my professional judgment, as I could tell then.

My friend: "Some online programs already have online tutors. Why do you want to train teachers to teach Chinese online?"

Me: "We are training teachers to teach online, but not tutors."

Think about how little time it takes to train an online tutor and how long it takes to prepare a language teacher with qualified credentials. There are striking differences between a tutor and a professional language teacher. Commercial companies that invent and market online language learning products are in the profit-making business, and they may not be interested in investing so much time in assisting online tutors to pursue the same level of professionalism as is required to get a teacher certificate in accordance with state and national standards. If we think very carefully about the following questions about the quality of an online tutor, then an answer would be clear.

What does an online language tutor do while tutoring someone online?
What are the responsibilities of an online tutor?
Who is qualified to be an online tutor?
How many hours of training are required before starting online tutoring?
What professional knowledge and expertise are required for an online tutor?

Similar questions can go on to unfold a very long list of requirements that are demanded for certified language teachers in the United States. Obviously, the educational system sets very high standards for professional language teachers, but not for tutors in an online language program.

The status quo of virtual language schools in the United States may call an online tutor an instructor, but their role is more like a coach, as they are not responsible for developing teaching materials. They only grade assignments and answer students' questions. This type of virtual language school, program, or course is not what I am pursuing. I am looking for an online learning model that resembles F2F learning in a four-walled classroom and that has great potential to produce high-performing learners.

With these central questions lingering for quite a while, I consulted several leading experts in Second Language Acquisition to ask them about my hypothesis, which they strongly supported and confirmed. This gave me the momentum to turn my floating ideas into action and increased my confidence in the structure of the online learning program that I was imagining. Since the summer of 2015, we started to frame a program for online learning and an intensive training model to best prepare teachers to teach online. The two programs partnered with each other and were in place in the summer of 2016, continuing for four consecutive summers until 2019.

The following two assumptions have guided me and my teammates to shape the fundamental mechanism of the design of the program.

Assumption 1:
Complete or heavy reliance on self-learning is doomed to little success for online learning.

Assumption 2:
Frequent quality interaction is key to success for online learning.

The above two assumptions speak the same thing on two reversed sides. As the first assumption indicates, complete or heavy reliance on self-learning yields little success in online learning. The opposite of reliance on self-learning is the frequent quality interaction that happens in real-time learning. This is not possible without live teaching by a professional, well-trained language educator. Even though computer-assisted learning can be interactive, that interaction can only partially mimic human interaction; it can never replace genuine interaction between human beings. Keeping frequent and quality interaction as a core guiding principle, we adopted a virtual F2F learning mode with a human-oriented approach to create online language learning for UVA STARTALK.

Overview of an Online Program

Every summer from 2016 to 2019, the UVA STARTALK team designed and implemented a 12-day immersive online Chinese language course featuring daily synchronous learning in an active online community. The courses placed special emphasis on meaningful, communicative, and authentic interactions and relied on technology-mediated tasks. Sessions followed a three-stage learning cycle: pre-class flipped learning, in-class learning, and post-class review. This streamlined process had proven effects that helped learners achieve learning goals and make desirable progress in language performance.

1. Pre-program Logistics

Students submitted their online application package, including an application form, agreement form, parental consent form, transcript, and an uploaded video of self-introduction in Chinese and English. After a rigorous review process, a group of students was chosen for the program. Recruited students were required to do the following prior to the onset of the program:

1. Sign the agreement letter
2. Complete a survey on learning style and individual needs
3. Complete a language performance assessment for placement
4. Complete a survey on character learning
5. Read the student handbook
6. Participate in pre-program technology camp individually and in small groups
7. Post a first response to prompts in Facebook
8. Communicate with the program assistant and receive timely help via email

2. Pre-program Technology Camp

Students were required to sign up for a technology virtual camp and develop familiarity and readiness skills in technology tools and applications. In the technology camp, they learned how to navigate Canvas or Google Site, logged in to the online platform, through WizIQ or Zoom, and learned to use different tools required for pre-class, in-class, and after-class synchronous and asynchronous learning. The camp also fostered the skills of character typing and conversion between traditional and simplified characters. Although students recruited into the program had experience in typing on a word processor, every year a couple of students needed additional training in character typing. The technology camp was a necessary step. It not only provided training that helped students become familiar with and better use technology, but it also created opportunities for online gathering and pre-program team building, so students were connected even before the program started.

The following provides a glimpse of a list of technology tools and applications that students learned through pre-program Technology Camp in the program in 2016–19.

3. Technology Use

Technology tools were selected through a careful and deliberate process, including testing. While curricular and pedagogical goals remained fundamentally the same over the four years, they were slightly adjusted to respond to the availability and accessibility of tools and applications.

Learning Management System: Canvas (2016–18); Google Site (2019)

Online Platform: WizIQ (2016–17); Zoom enhanced by Nearpod (accessed through iPhone)

Technology tools for pre-class, in-class, and after-class learning: Doodle, Quizlet, Interactive video (made possible by Zaption in 2016 and Playposit in 2017–19), Google Form, VoiceThread, Padlet, Flipgrid

4. Creating Welcoming Videos to Build an Online Community

To create a sense of connectivity within the online learning community, the program created two welcoming videos: one was an overview of the program, and the other, completed through Biteable, included special visual, graphic, and animation effects to deliver a sense of humor, playfulness, and vitality. In addition, students saw the faces of all staff members and participating instructors through a video gallery. This added human touches and friendliness and created a sense of belonging and bonding for all involved in the program.

5. Learners

Thirty-six learners were recruited nationwide, 2016–18, and 24 in 2019. The program included 9th–12th graders, with ages ranging from 14 to 17 each year. Target students were non-heritage learners without prior exposure to Chinese language and culture at home. Each year, female students outnumbered male students. Their language proficiency ranged from novice-high to intermediate-low at the entry point according to ACTFL Proficiency Guidelines.

6. Class Size

Class size is extremely small, allowing teachers to individualize instruction. Teachers taught in pairs, each pair teaching two to four students in one-hour synchronous sessions in the morning, every day of the week. The teacher-student ratio was 1:1 or 1:2.

7. Instructors and Instructional Support Team

The online course was taught by experienced teachers who had already taught for three to nine years at secondary and postsecondary levels. Before starting teaching online, all instructors received intensive training for three weeks in a blended training model so they were familiar with effective pedagogy and advanced technologies for online teaching. When they entered the practicum phase or actual online teaching of the accepted students in the last two weeks of the program, the preparation of lesson plans, rehearsals, and online teaching were well guided and supervised by trainers, practicum facilitators, and a technology coordinator. Daily lesson plans and teaching materials were brainstormed in a group of six to twelve and critiqued by the entire group. Rehearsals were a very important step before finalizing instructional plans. Each year there were six teaching pairs, totaling twelve teachers. Each pair of teachers alternated roles as the homeroom teacher and supporting teacher. While the homeroom teacher taught online, the supporting teacher helped with technology troubleshooting, typing responses and reminders in the chatbox, and taking notes and writing comments to complete an observation checklist. The technology coordinator and program assistants stood by all the time to provide immediate help for teachers and students during the practicum.

The instructors in the program were teacher participants who received training to practice online teaching during practicum. Their major responsibilities included creating lesson plans and PowerPoint slides to deliver two one-hour synchronous teaching sessions on a daily basis; giving feedback to students on their daily review assignments and tasks; and responding to students' inquiries in the learning management system, in order to establish a strong rapport with the students. The PowerPoint slides and instructional materials were basically the same across the two daily sessions but were modified to meet diverse needs of learners in each session.

A thematically organized curriculum was created by the core instructional team, with an overarching central theme, accompanying can-do statements, and language components such as vocabulary, word expressions, and structures to achieve the language functions essential for the development of expected language proficiency. The core teammates also collaboratively and consciously designed different types of learning tasks for pre-class and post-class learning. This eased pressure and balanced the workload for teacher participants, who otherwise would have been overwhelmed by the tremendous amount of work.

8. Theme and Content

Students participated in two one-hour online orientations and then embarked on an exciting ten-day US-China Virtual Exchange Program, in which they were immersed in authentic Chinese language and cultural products, practices, and perspectives in Beijing, China. The virtual adventure guided them to engage in authentic experiences in the following five subthemes.

Subtheme 1: Arrival at the airport (Day 1)
Subtheme 2: Visiting Chinese host family (Days 2–3)
Subtheme 3: Visiting a Chinese school (Days 4–6)
Subtheme 4: Exploring Beijing (Days 7–9)
Subtheme 5: Farewell to Beijing (Day 10)

The twelve-day student program featured a two-day online orientation followed by a ten-day immersion experience. Upon completion of the online course, learners were expected to have developed proficiency at the intermediate-low level in listening, speaking, reading, and writing. While formal instruction took place for one hour in the morning, self-paced learning for preview and review was required before and after class every day. Learning materials and tasks were thoughtfully created and organized by the instructional team and uploaded to the central learning management system. The course offered zero credit. Upon completion of the program, learners developed a better understanding of Chinese cultural norms and became more aware of the differences in common cultural values and perspectives between Chinese and American people. Those who successfully completed the online course received a certificate of excellence in learning and a small gift card.

9. Three-stage Daily Learning Cycle

The program offered technology orientations, an opening ceremony involving the entire program, and the first virtual F2F meeting between online instructors and students in the first two days of the program. After that, ten days of the immersive program began, with a daily three-stage learning cycle: pre-class asynchronous flipped learning, one-hour synchronous learning, and after-class asynchronous learning. The three stages were well-connected and sequenced to streamline the learning process and reinforce one another. Learners' performance was closely monitored and recorded with instant feedback, based on which instructors offered remedial instruction whenever needed.

Pre-class Flipped Learning

Before attending each synchronous session, students were required to complete four pre-class flipped learning activities: 1) answer embedded comprehension-check questions after watching two or three interactive videos; 2) read a daily study guide; 3) practice vocabulary through interactive tasks on Quizlet; and 4) watch recorded conversations in the target language. The interactive video allowed students to build their skills and competence in learning grammar, vocabulary, and content knowledge by typing their responses to true-or-false questions, multiple-choice questions, and open-ended questions, and by drawing lines to complete matching tasks. Students received instant feedback and scoring right after they completed the activities. The Quizlet tasks allowed students to use flashcards as a learning tool to reinforce memory and to apply vocabulary in meaningful contexts. Each recorded conversation was taken from the study guide, in the form of either a video recording or an audio recording paired with printed images.

The interactive videos were created by Zaption in 2016–17 and later replaced by PlayPosit, with content being identical in four straight years. Recorded conversations recorded in videos were substituted by VoiceThread interactive tasks through which students posted their typed responses to different types of stimuli, including photos, images, videos, oral recordings, public announcements, and short essays. Another type of preview task was added to flipped learning in 2017–19: students completed lesson-based comprehension questions in Google Forms.

In-class Synchronous Learning

WizIQ, an interactive online delivery platform, was selected to deliver instruction during the synchronous sessions due to its multifunctionality and ability to create a student-centered learning setting in 2016–17. Its user interface featured a built-in interactive whiteboard in support of pedagogical objectives. After experimenting with WizIQ for two years, the team decided instead to select Zoom as the online platform in 2018–19 to increase the stability and smoothness of synchronous sessions. Zoom was very user-friendly and included an embedded interactive whiteboard. It was complemented by Nearpod to empower student-centered pedagogy. Students were advised to enter Zoom from their computer and access Nearpod to synchronously engage in interactive tasks from their iPhones.

After-class Reviews

After attending a one-hour synchronous session, students completed two review tasks: a presentational writing task through Padlet, and a presentational speaking task that involved recording a video on Flipgrid. Padlet is a versatile digital canvas whereby learners share collaborative multimedia projects. The Flipgrid speaking tasks differed in type, ranging from a narrative of personal experience to the singing of a Chinese song, and these tasks could be completed individually or in pairs. Both Padlet and Flipgrid promoted interaction among learners and allowed them to post comments on peers' collaborative work.

10. Group Board

Interactive Discussion Board served as a direct communicative platform to create an online community between the instructor and students. It was very user-friendly and convenient, as it was embedded in Canvas and Google Site. Students used both English and Chinese to communicate in Group Board every day for updates on the class and reminders for pre-class preparation and after-class assignments posted by teachers.

11. Tutorial/Cultural Sessions and Office Hours

Online tutorial sessions were offered during afternoon office hours. Students could also sign up for cultural and review sessions in the afternoon. Each student was required to participate in at least three afternoon sessions for the purposes of tutorials, cultural learning, or review. The afternoon sessions were led by program assistants, who answered questions online, lead students to review daily lessons in Kahoot, Jeopardy, and Polleverywhere, and facilitated discussions on cultural and language topics. The program assistant took daily questions and communicated with students and parents in a timely manner to provide support for learning.

12. Social Media: Facebook and WeChat

A Facebook group was created as a means of social media for the program. It was managed by a program assistant who posted daily news, announcements, and discussion topics, inviting all instructors and students to post their responses and comments. WeChat was another option to engage program participants in online chats and social gathering.

Engagement, Satisfaction, and Learning Outcomes

Every year, the online learning program had a miraculous 100% completion rate. This arose as a big surprise and contrasted with the high dropout rate that was anticipated for online language courses. It is conjectured that online courses that heavily rely on learners' self-paced learning might have higher dropout rates than other modes of online learning. But other online teaching modes do not guarantee a satisfactory completion rate unless they are well-planned and delivered.

The program features synchronous learning that fosters interaction and participation on a daily basis. This is fully strengthened and consolidated by preview and review before and after daily one-hour synchronous learning online. In 2016, a study was launched to examine learners' learning experience in four aspects: 1) effort and time; 2) recommendations for the daily three-stage learning cycle; 3) engagement and anxiety level; and 4) learning outcomes. Thirty-six students were recruited, and thirty-five completed a program survey on their learning experiences and evaluation of their language performance.

The 2016 survey included a set of questions based on 7-point Likert scale, with 1 meaning least agree and 7 meaning strongly agree. The analyses of the survey results are summarized in the following tables (Tseng et. al., 2018).

Table 1.1 shows calculations of time that students spent and effort made to preview and review learning materials before and after synchronous learning.

Table 1.1 Students' Time Spent on Before-class and After-class Asynchronous Learning

Phase	Components	M (minutes)	S.D. (minutes)
Pre-class preparation	Watching interactive videos and completing comprehension-check questions	25.76	19.51
	Reading the study guide	22.35	26.78
	Completing Quizlet	21.40	18.14
	Watching and listening to conversation recordings	15.21	12.27
After-class review	Written task (Padlet post)	30.33	15.86
	Oral task (Flipgrid)	28.01	13.94

The actual time that students spent on different components of pre-class and after-class learning conforms with what was predicted prior to the program. Pre-class preparation included four components, and time distribution varied in different learning components. Students spent less time watching and listening to conversation recordings (15.21 minutes), but spent the most time watching interactive videos and completing comprehension-check questions (25.76 minutes). Time spent reading the study guide and completing Quizlet vocabulary learning was in the middle. After-class review activities had two learning components, and on average each took about 30 minutes. Students allocated equal time to written and oral tasks after class each day. Adding all the components together for pre-learning and post-learning, on average, each student spent a total of 1.5 hours on pre-class learning and a total of 1 hour on after-class learning. This is consistent with the pre-program prediction that students would spend about 3.5 hours each day to complete the three-stage learning cycle: pre-class, in-class, and after-class. Students' full devotion to the program was possible in summer, but this amount of time might be infeasible in regular semesters. Still, the three-stage design offers good takeaways, as each stage of learning connects with and reinforces the others.

Table 1.2 reveals learners' recommendations for each learning task they completed before and after class.

Table 1.2 Students' Levels of Recommendation for Each Type of Assignment

Phase	Component	M	S.D.
Pre-class preparation	Interactive videos	6.26	1.21
	Study guide	6.00	1.44
	Quizlet	5.90	1.68
	Conversation recordings	5.59	1.63
After-class review	Written task using Padlet	6.58	0.72
	Oral task using Flipgrid	6.42	1.12

Of the four components of flipped learning, interactive videos were learners' favorite preview activity (M=6.26). The remaining three types of flipped learning are ranked in order from most to least popular: study guide (M=6.00), Quizlet (M=5.90), and conversation recordings (M=5.59). Each learning component has distinct and reinforcing pedagogical values, each of which is confirmed by high ratings by students.

The averages of after-class review were higher than those in pre-class learning. Either the written task using Padlet or the oral task using Flipgrid received 6.5 out of 7. Students recommended pre-class learning, but they spoke more highly of after-class review tasks with a higher level of recommendation. This might be attributed to the technology tools that were used for assessment. Padlet and Flipgrid are colorful and visually appealing, and completing review tasks after learning from one-hour synchronous learning is helpful and gives learners a sense of achievement. This differs from pre-class learning, which learners did independently and without the attractive visual stimuli in the post-class review activities.

Table 1.3 summarizes perceived helpfulness and overall effectiveness of three stages of learning.

Table 1.3 Perceived Helpfulness of the Program

Statements	M	S.D.
The one-hour synchronous sessions taught by the instructor were very helpful for my learning.	6.77	0.56

Statements	M	S.D.
Post-class asynchronous learning was very helpful for my learning.	5.97	1.56
Pre-class asynchronous learning was very helpful for my learning.	5.84	1.49

Both pre-class and post-class learning were considered very helpful. Aligning with Table 1.2, students gave slightly higher credit to post-class asynchronous learning than to pre-class asynchronous learning. The one-hour synchronous learning received the highest average rating, with a mean of 6.77, close to the full score 7. These ratings re-affirm the value of a highly interactive virtual class that is designed and conducted to engage and interact with learners simultaneously. This simulates learning experience in a F2F four-walled setting in a more humane way. While the majority of K-12 virtual language schools are designed for asynchronous learning, Table 1.3 gives offers evidence that human live interaction in real time seems to be the most favorable learning mode for language learning. This, again, reconfirms the assumptions and beliefs of the UVA STARTALK program.

Creating an online class that mimics real-time learning in a physical F2F setting is necessary but not sufficient. A successful online class always immerses learners in full use of target language. Table 1.4 gives us some clues about how the use of the target language triggers engagement with learners in different ways.

Table 2.4 Students' Engagement During Synchronous Sessions

Statements	M	S.D.
Frequent interactions with the instructor in the target language enhance my engagement.	6.77	0.50
Making efforts to use the target language enhances my engagement.	6.71	0.53
Participation in interactive activities enhances my engagement.	6.68	0.75
Using online interactive tools enhances my engagement.	6.35	0.98
Frequent interactions with my peers in the target language enhance my engagement.	6.29	0.86

As indicated in the table above, the one-hour synchronous sessions fully engage learners in the use of the target language to promote interactions. Indeed, frequent interactions with the instructor in the target language (M=6.77) was the top-rated element for engagement.

Almost equally important to this was making efforts to use the target language (M=6.71) and participate in interactive activities (M=6.68). Although using technology tools (M=6.35) and interactions with peers (M=6.29) do not get ratings as high as the first three, their ratings are still very favorable. Analyzing these results more deeply, it can be inferred that learners credit their online engagement to the instructor more than to their peers. The role of the instructor exerts multi-functioned pedagogical purposes: use of the target language, such as scaffolding learners to help them speak the language, participating in interactive activities, and using online interactive technology tools. These are not easy or straightforward, and can only be achieved by experienced and well-prepared instructors.

Speaking the target language in an online setting can be sometimes frustrating or even frightening. The lack of non-verbal cues and distant learning inherently creates gaps for learning and causes a certain level of anxiety that can exceed what is observed in a F2F regular classroom. This, gratefully, is not an impediment to the online learning environment created for the program under study.

Table 1.5 Students' Anxiety During Synchronous Sessions

Statements	M	S.D.
I feel more nervous in the STARTALK online course than in my F2F Chinese language classes.	2.29	1.70
I feel nervous when I am called by the instructor to answer questions in the target language.	3.26	1.83
I worry about making mistakes in the target language.	4.00	1.97

As Table 1.5 indicates, the means of three items measuring learners' anxiety are much lower than the previous level, and this delivers the encouraging news that no more anxiety is added to their virtual learning in comparison to in-person F2F learning. The development of a comfort zone among learners, and the low levels of fear of making mistakes in the target language, are also cause for celebration. This would not be made possible without instructors' detailed planning for and rehearsal of each step of teaching.

Table 1.6 demonstrates learning outcomes in different language skills, learners' satisfaction level, and improvement in pre-test and post-test language performance.

Table 1.6 Learning Outcomes

Statements	M	S.D.
Perceived progress		
My listening ability improved a lot after the course.	6.29	1.04
My speaking ability improved a lot after the course.	6.29	1.07
My reading ability improved a lot after the course.	6.16	1.21
My writing ability improved a lot after the course.	5.47	1.78
Satisfaction		
I would recommend this course to other students.	6.90	0.30
Overall, I am satisfied with this course.	6.84	0.45
I would take a course like this again in the future.	6.77	0.50
Language performance		
Pre-test scores	12.61	3.40
Post-test scores	16.45	2.63

Overall, learners' perceived progress has very high means in four language skills. The highest rests in listening and speaking (M=6.29), which makes sense, as the one-hour synchronous learning focuses on these two skills that are most needed by non-heritage learners. Reading ability (M=6.16) is rated close to listening and speaking, due to learners' frequent exposure to characters as a medium in the synchronous sessions and asynchronous self-paced learning. Interestingly but not surprisingly, self-perceived improvement in writing (M=5.47) is the lowest among four language skills. Although some interactive activities are aimed at writing characters by typing and mouse clicking, they are relatively few comparing to the performance-based tasks in the other three language skills.

In addition to collecting learners' input in a survey, a language performance test was administered at the beginning and end of the program to assess language gains. The language test included 20 items, most of which were interpersonal in nature, in a question-and-answer format. Each item carries a target language function with an embedded grammatical structure. The results of the pre-test and post-test scores supported learners' self-perceived growth. A *t*-test revealed that the aforementioned 3.84-point difference between the participants' average pre-test and post-test scores was statistically significant, $t(30) = 6.69$, $p<001$. The correlations among pre-test scores, post-test scores, and perceived progress are shown in Table 1.7.

Table 1.7 Correlations Among Pre-test Scores, Post-test Scores, and Perceived Progress

	Pre-test	Post-test	Perceived progress
Pre-test	1		
Post-test	0.463**	1	
Perceived progress	-0.166	0.134	1

**$p < 0.01$

Learners' satisfaction represents their summative evaluation of the course. As Table 1.6 shows, an extremely positive rating indicates that students' satisfaction with the course receives the highest means in all tables. Almost all learners would recommend the course (M=6.90) and take the same course in the future (M=6.77). Their high levels of satisfaction and recommendation are an indication of their endorsement and extremely positive evaluation of the course.

The holistic analysis of the data in the tables delivers a very strong message that learners in the program strove to use the target language to spontaneously communicative with the instructor and engage in interactive activities in a linguistically and culturally rich immersive setting. This happened in a low-anxiety expanding comfort zone where learners were able to fully connect with what the instructor guided them to do in a facilitating process. To conclude, students had a very positive experience of the course, felt satisfied with it, and showed statistically significant improvement in their language skills.

Learners' Reflections and Testimony

The online course offered zero credit, and students participated in the program on a completely voluntary basis. This raises the question of what made students want to continue attending UVA STARTALK till the end. In individual interviews, students shared brief comments, which were recorded and transcribed later. The following provides a glimpse of the interviews.

- I really enjoyed the actual classes and the teachers were helpful and kind ... that motivated me to do well.

- I already committed to the program and saw that I was learning stuff, and I was motivated to learn because if I had conflicts, they were very lenient and willing to work with me.
- Going to classes was fun, and it was easy to be motivated to do the pre-assignments because if I didn't, I wouldn't know what teachers would be talking about the next day.
- I looked forward to seeing my teachers and I liked getting stars.
- STARTALK was my biggest priority so I didn't do much besides that. I am a Chinese tutor and I will start doing it again once the program ends.
- I had motivation for myself to get better at Mandarin. Friends in the program also helped motivate me. I enjoyed the assignments.
- Getting into the program was difficult because it was completely online, but my teacher's excitement motivated me and were very supportive. They were very encouraging.
- I was honored to be a part of the program, and I was also rewarded for it. It was a learning experience and I enjoyed meeting other people.

Students were invited to share their overall learning experience at the end of program. Their end-of-program summary of learning experiences complements the above very short feedback and adds more detailed information to enlighten the whole picture below.

- For me, the best thing about the STARTALK program was the homework assignment setup. I really liked the written/speaking platforms (especially speaking) and also think that the pre-class work was very beneficial. I wish that we used interactive videos in my class at school!
- I thoroughly enjoyed UVA STARTALK because I was able to learn more about Chinese culture. After the program, I also noticed that my Chinese (tones and pronunciation) improved a lot! I really enjoyed the oral assignments because I personally think that speaking is the most difficult part when learning a new language. My teachers were awesome, patient, and I could tell that they had a genuine interest in teaching my class. STARTALK has definitely made me more confident in speaking Chinese, I just wish the program lasted longer! :)
- I loved the program because it helped me understand more than I have already learned. I loved learning how to give directions, and places to go in Beijing. My favorite part was making new friends during class.
- I enjoyed being a part of a fully immersed Chinese classroom which I felt helped me learn the most. I also feel that the lessons that teach practical things that you would do in and say in China was really well done. I also liked the video responses that

allowed for everyone to see their classmates.

- I loved the program! I was able to meet and interact with so many new people from across the country. Through Twitter I learned about the similarities and differences between my life and those in different states. The social media platforms helped me know my classmates better outside of learning material while still using Chinese. Overall, it was a fun program that I looked forward to attending online every morning because my teachers were so sweet and helpful!

- I am very glad I participated in this program because I feel like it boosted my confidence in my Chinese skills and made me want to get better. I had great teachers who were willing to help answer any of my questions, and I wouldn't recommend having classes bigger than 3 people. I enjoyed making videos every night for my oral homework and watching others' videos as well as the small journey entry for homework. I would definitely recommend this program to a friend!

Recommendations for Creating a Successful Online Course

The UVA STARTALK program recruited students nationwide through a robust review and selection process. A course offered at school does not involve such national wide-scaled recruitment, advertisement, and logistics coordination. An instructor, therefore, does not need to invest an enormous amount of time in this regard and can focus on the design of content and online delivery. Reflecting on learners' overwhelmingly positive feedback and evaluation, we share a list of recommendations for creating a successful online course.

1. Form an instructional team with experts in pedagogy and instructional design.

Keep curricular objectives and pedagogy upfront, and technology supplementary. Let instructional needs guide decisions on technology. An instructional designer can add needed value to the team and contribute to the decision-making process. An overarching principle is that pedagogical goals cannot be at the expense of technology.

2. Recruit motivated and independent learners.

Online learning needs to hold learners accountable. A group of motivated and independent learners makes satisfactory learning outcomes readily achievable. High-performing teachers know how to motivate students but might have some difficulty with less independent learners. Still, teachers can foster learners' independence with patience, constant reminders, and a clearly established class routine.

3. Pre-course welcoming messages give a head start for human online connections.

Greetings and welcoming messages can be delivered via email communication. These, however, are static and flat. Create a video to warmly welcome the learning group, so learners can see your face and hear what you say before the course begins. This shows that you care and makes you approachable to them even earlier.

4. Synchronous learning is strongly favored by students.

Online synchronous learning mirrors in-class F2F learning more than other delivery modes do. Learners' testimony to synchronous learning is validated in UVA STARTALK. Whenever possible and feasible, create more opportunities for synchronous learning to take place. Exposure to synchronous learning, of course, is best when it is mediated and balanced with other courses to avoid too many hours of static learning in front of the computer. This is an issue that is of particular importance for young learners.

5. Pre-class preview and post-class review are highly recommended.

Post-class review is more common than pre-class preview for language courses. The latter has proven value and functions as flipped learning; consider adding it and making it as interactive and interesting as possible. A study guide and conversation recordings are necessary despite not being as highly rated and interactive as Quizlet and Interactive videos. Adding playfulness to fulfill the educational goal is possible but takes time for design and planning. The invention of 3D virtual learning and artificial intelligence are evolving advanced technologies that help bring the playfulness of gaming into language learning.

6. Building an online community enhances bonding and a sense of belonging.

Overemphasis on self-paced learning is likely to create a feeling of isolation. No one wants to live on an isolated, socially disconnected island. To avoid this, it is essential to build an authentic online community, which offers community members (learners) bonding experiences and a sense of belonging. Strategies for creating an interactive online community will be discussed in later chapters.

7. Always provide immediate support and assistance in a timely manner.

It goes without saying that online learning needs more support that is timely and often immediate. Learners expect to get support through interactive discussion boards, email, and any built-in online devices. Live chats and real-time meetings are favored by most learners. Whenever possible, it is best to offer individual meetings and consultation with students earlier than later.

8. Needs for individualized instructions become salient for online learning.

Learners vary in learning style and needs, and differences become more noticeable online. Sensitivity to different needs is even more critical in the online environment, and they should be taken care of with gentility and agility. Always handle issues within the learner's comfort zone. This can be complicated when it interacts with learners' academic capacity, affective and psychological needs, communication and social patterns, and many other factors. To be concise, keeping learners' self-esteem and autonomy central is fundamental to maintaining positive relationships and a good atmosphere between instructor and students.

9. Organize details for materials and instructional planning.

Online teaching requires teachers to do more careful preparation and be organized in detailing each step of instruction. Due to a lack of sufficient physical and visual clues to facilitate online learning, PowerPoint slides that show on the computer screen become even more pivotal. Therefore, clarity, logics, and cognitive load need to be well-thought-out before class. Guidelines and techniques for creating effective PowerPoint slides can be found in Chapter 7.

10. Test technology before class and have backup plans in mind.

Always test technology before class, every time. Sometimes a lesson does not go as predicted and may get interrupted with technology. Even seasoned online teachers have faced challenges and had to troubleshoot. At least come up with a backup plan beforehand. As you accumulate more experience, it will be easier for you to come up with more alternatives.

In sum, teaching online follows the same principles as traditional in-person language teaching. The teaching goals are paramount; learner's individual needs must be addressed in a kind and timely way; authentic, immersive interaction in the target language is most effective and rewarding for students; class organization leads to a smooth experience for both instructor and students; and most importantly, a class should be a true community of learners, with a welcoming atmosphere and accessible instructors. It is key to becoming familiar with various kinds of technology, indeed familiar enough, especially with interactive tools, to simulate the experience of togetherness. But the teaching and learning should always be the focus; the technology just enables them. The goal is for the experience to be paramount, and for the online aspect of that experience to be simply the medium through which community, cultural and linguistic immersion, and learning can happen.

References

Barbour, M.K. 2017. K-12 online learning and school choice: Growth and expansion in the absence of evidence. In R.A. Fox & N.K. Buchanan (Eds.), The Wiley handbook of school choice (pp. 421–440). Hoboken, NJ: Wiley Blackwell.

Blake, R. 2011. Current trends in online language learning. Annual Review of Applied Linguistics, 31, 19–35. https://doi.org/10.1017/S026719051100002X

Hampel, R., & Hauck, M. 2004. Towards an effective use of audio conferencing in distance language courses. Language Learning & Technology, 8, 66–82.

Tseng, M., Lin, C., & Chen, H. 2018. An immersive flipped classroom for learning Mandarin Chinese: design, implementation, and outcomes. Journal of Computer-assisted Language Learning. https://doi.org/10.1080/09588221.2018.1440603.

Chapter 2

Online Delivery Modes and Teaching Essentials

In recent years, online language courses have become more prevalent and increasingly accessible, and the search for the best online teaching model has grown correspondingly urgent. This chapter begins with an overview of delivery modes for language teaching, outlining the distinct and shared features of each mode and comparing three ways of interaction: teacher-student, student-student, and student-content. Additionally, it introduces four key elements essential to satisfactory interaction and engagement in language teaching.

Delivery Modes

Language teaching takes place through three types of delivery modes, depending on the proportional distribution of classroom time allocated for face-to-face (F2F) and online learning. The three types of delivery modes include F2F teaching, blended or hybrid teaching, and online teaching. The following categorizes and explains each type of delivery mode.

1. F2F Teaching

F2F teaching is in-person and occurs in regularly scheduled sessions in one or more four-walled classrooms. Learners have real-time interactions with the instructor and their peers on a regular basis throughout the entire course. Technology, if used, is supplementary. With the ongoing and rapid advancement of multifaceted technologies in the era of digital humanities, almost all language educators now have experience in incorporating different types of technologies to support and enhance learning before, during, and after class. The learning management system (LMS) for a given class is mostly predetermined based on instructional policy and decisions. The LMS is a central site where learners study and download learning materials that the instructor has organized and uploaded for the course. An online platform is not necessary since all teaching is completed in the F2F mode, with the instructor and students meeting in person during regular class time, as well as during office hours (except for special circumstances that are substituted by online F2F meetings).

2. Blended Teaching

Blended teaching, sometimes called hybrid teaching, has a combination of F2F and online modes. Approximately 20% to 80% of the course occurs in the F2F mode. This proportion is determined by factors such as fiscal budget, the instructor's teaching load, classroom space, enrollment numbers, learners' needs, course design, and proficiency level, among others.

The F2F proportion can be teacher-led or student-centered learning, including, but not limited to, lectures and discussions, student-centered communicative tasks, formative and summative assessments, and cultural events. It can be as creative and diversified as desired, in order to meet curricular objectives and needs as determined by learners' backgrounds. The online proportion is mainly conducted in one of the following two ways.

Asynchronous Learning

Students complete self-paced learning and required assignments, mostly individually or in pairs and groups online without the instructor's presence. They access the LMS to complete what the instructor asks them to do. No online platform is required, but students may be given opportunities to use online video-based conferencing tools to participate in online tutorial sessions on a one-on-one basis or in pairs or groups.

Synchronous Learning

While asynchronous learning in blended models may feature interactions between and among learners during any type of pair or group work, synchronous learning happens when students interact with an instructor, an assistant, or a tutor for real-time learning and live interaction. It can involve the entire class or small groups. The latter is more beneficial for learners, as they are better able to practice using the target language and thus make progress in both quantity and quality. An online platform is needed to proceed with the entire-class synchronous teaching or small-group interactive sessions. Learners can gain an understanding of the course structure, requirements, and materials online through the LMS. Technology is partially mediated in this delivery mode. Office hours can be held in F2F meetings and possibly online.

3. Online Teaching

Online teaching is a very broad term that can apply to different realizations of course design. When this term is brought up for discussion, it is always necessary to define and clarify it. In general, online teaching can refer to three types of online instructional delivery: non-F2F online teaching, F2F online teaching, and a combination of the two. A major distinction lies in whether the instructor and students can see each others' faces and interact synchronously online. Non-F2F features asynchronous learning, which learners complete, for the most part, independently and on a self-paced schedule, without the instructor's virtual presence. By contrast, F2F online teaching places great value on synchronous learning, in which students can see their instructor's face and interact with their instructor and their peers in real time, online, during class. To be easily understood, a traditional F2F class, as outlined above, is situated in a four-walled classroom, and an F2F virtual class is mediated and made possible through a video-conferencing online platform. The last is a combined mode, including both F2F and non-F2F online teaching. A certain proportion is done synchronously, and the remaining proportion is done asynchronously. The following provides more explanation of these three types of online teaching.

Non-F2F Online Teaching (Asynchronous)

Non-F2F online teaching features individual asynchronous learning without the teacher's presence. Learning is self-paced and independent. The entire course is mediated by technology. A highly accessible LMS becomes crucial, as it is likely the central site at which learners view and upload learning materials and post their questions. An online platform, independent of or separate from the LMS, is needed if online F2F tutorials and meetings are included. Very few F2F meetings, if any, are held. If F2F meetings are held, they are typically limited to orientation or capstone events. The course may include proctored exams that are taken F2F on-site.

Online courses in this category may offer tutorials, coaching, or Q&A sessions, in which an instructor, coach, or tutor works with students, individually or in small groups, to answer questions and practice the language to satisfy individual needs. These happen on a weekly or biweekly basis and can be conducted through regular office hours, with sessions normally ranging from 10 to 30 minutes. Such sessions, if offered, might not be conducted entirely in Chinese; English is permitted especially for questions about assignments, grading, and classroom management.

F2F Online Teaching (Synchronous)

In F2F online teaching, also called F2F virtual, real-time, or synchronous teaching, every class is taught online synchronously. The four-walled classroom is converted to the four edges of the laptop, iPad, or desktop computer, and a series of teaching and learning activities are instructed and directed through the screen in forms including verbal, visual, and auditory. Whatever is shown on the screen becomes the source of core attention and stimuli that guides and facilitates learning. Like other types of teaching modes, an LMS is required as a central site to host the course syllabus and all types of learning materials. It connects with an online platform through which both the instructor and students log in to enter the virtual class regularly. Internet stability and accessibility are necessary for a smooth real-time online course to get running. The course is fully mediated by technology. Office hours are held mostly online.

A Mix of Synchronous and Asynchronous Sessions

The third type of delivery mode for online teaching involves a combination of synchronous and asynchronous sessions. The proportion of the two varies, roughly ranging from 20% to 80% for each. This adds flexibility and variety for the structure and time allotment of the course.

Table 2.1 outlines three types of delivery modes for language teaching.

Table 2.1 A Comparison of Three Types of Delivery Modes

Modes	Percentage of F2F vs. Online	Technology	Office Hours
F2F (in-person)	Teaching occurs 100% on-site in a four-walled classroom.	Technology is supplementary. LMS is required. Online platform not required.	Mainly in-person; online possible.
Blended	20%–80% of teaching occurs in a four-walled classroom, with the rest online in one of the following options: Option 1: synchronous teaching Option 2: asynchronous teaching; self-paced learning	The course is partially mediated by technology. LMS required. Online platform optional.	Mainly in-person; online possible.
Online	Teaching occurs 100% or almost 100% online. Option 1: 100% asynchronous online Option 2: A mix of asynchronous and synchronous sessions Option 3: 100% synchronous online (100% virtual F2F)	The course is fully mediated by technology. LMS and online platform both required.	Mainly online; in-person possible.

In language courses, actual learning requires genuine interaction. Both the quantity and quality of interaction determine the success of language learning. On one hand, learners need ample opportunities and sufficient time to use and practice the target language. On the other hand, they benefit from being fully immersed in a quality learning environment. Quality is achieved through effective course design, instruction, and assessment, or, in other words, application of a set of effective principles and strategies for teaching and learning. Keeping quantity and quality of interaction in mind, F2F learning in a four-walled classroom remains favorable and is recommended by most language instructors and learners. Online asynchronous learning without any virtual co-presence of the instructor and learner is an alternative to language learning, but it is not ideal for achieving proximal interaction. However, interaction is enhanced when it is combined with online synchronous learning. Interactions are more likely and more frequent in blended learning with a combination of F2F in-person and either synchronous or asynchronous online learning and in F2F virtual with a great emphasis on synchronous learning.

Three Types of Interaction

These three delivery modes can also be analyzed from a different angle: the types of interaction. There are generally three types of interaction for language teaching and learning: teacher-student (T-S) interaction, student-student (S-S) interaction, and student-content (S-C) interaction. T-S interaction happens when an instructor meets with students in person or remotely to deliver instruction, as well as when an instructor answers learners' questions via email or in an online meeting. S-S interaction happens between two learners or among a group of learners enrolled in the same course. This happens with or without the instructor's presence. S-C interaction takes place when learners access different types of learning materials to obtain and study information. The level of interaction varies, ranging from browsing or scanning to deep engrossment with the content.

Additionally, a fourth type of interaction, student-platform (S-P), is a useful way to compare the different delivery instructional modes. It mainly deals with the affordances, stability, and accessibility of an online platform and does not involve pedagogical complexity like the other three types of interaction. Therefore, the S-P interaction is not as widely researched and is not included in Table 2.2.

Table 2.2 Three Ways of Interaction and Potential Effectiveness of Teaching

Delivery mode	T-S interaction	S-S interaction	S-C interaction	Total pts.
F2F in-person	Full (4 pts.)	Full (4 pts.)	Full (4 pts.)	12 pts.
Blended (F2F + synchronous online)	Maximal–Full (3–4 pts.)	Maximal–Full (3–4 pts.)	Full (4 pts.)	10–12 pts.
Blended (F2F + asynchronous)	Partial–Maximal (2–3 pts.)	Partial–Maximal (2–3 pts.)	Full (4 pts.)	8–10 pts.

Delivery mode	T-S interaction	S-S interaction	S-C interaction	Total pts.
Online (asynchronous)	None–Partial (0–2 pt.)	None–Minimal (0–1 pt.)	Full (4 pts.)	4–7 pts.
Online (asynchronous + synchronous)	Minimal–Maximal (1–3 pts.)	Minimal–Maximal (1–3 pts.)	Full (4 pts.)	6–10 pts.
F2F Online (synchronous)	Maximal–Full (3–4 pts.)	Maximal–Full (3–4 pts.)	Full (4 pts.)	10–12 pts.

The predicted values in Table 2.2 are based on the assumption that all factors and variables are well controlled across delivery modes. To get a clear picture of the attributes of the three ways of interaction, Table 2.2 includes four levels of graduation to indicate potential effectiveness of teaching: full, maximal, partial, and minimal. To complement these four levels of verbal description, a numerical calculation is added to each level to help project potential teaching effectiveness. Each verbal description goes with a numerical value: full is associated with 4 points, minimal with 1 point, and maximal and partial are in the middle range:

Full = 4 points; Maximal: 3 points; Partial: 2 points; Minimal: 1 point; None: 0 point.

This calculation is by no means intended to attribute any absolute value to each instructional delivery mode in relation to each type of interaction. Instead, it is aimed at applying an analytical tool, i.e., assigning and calculating comparative numerical values, to predict and understand at one glance the overall teaching effectiveness of each type of instructional mode. Furthermore, the four-leveled graduation signals a continuum of potentiality rather than discrete values. In Table 2, some cells have only one numerical value, while others have two values, indicating a continuum from a lower to a higher end, in order to make the table more inclusive and able to encompass a more realistic range of possibility.

The following is a prediction of teaching effectiveness of each delivery mode, presented from a highest potential score to the lowest potential score.

1) 12 points: F2F in-person teaching
2) 10–12 points: F2F Online (synchronous); Blended (F2F + synchronous)
3) 8–10 points: Blended (F2F+ asynchronous)
4) 6–10 points: Online (synchronous + asynchronous)
5) 4–7 points: Online (asynchronous)

The following describes the five ranked teaching modes in relation to three types of interaction. Presumably, each delivery mode has the fullest score attributed to the S-C interaction. The major difference lies in the remaining two types of interaction, T-S and S-S.

1st Rank: F2F In-person Teaching

F2F in-person teaching wins 4 points, the highest possible, in each type of interaction. Its ability to achieve the utmost out of the three types of interaction is irreplaceable and undisputable.

2nd Rank: F2F Online Teaching and Blended Teaching (synchronous)

Second are F2F online teaching and Blended teaching. The former features real-time teaching during regular class time, when an instructor and students meet online with live interaction. The latter features a combination of F2F in-person teaching and synchronous online teaching. Both rank second with a projected score of 10–12 points, indicating their potential to achieve maximal teaching effectiveness at the high end, meaning they both have the potential to be as effective as F2F live teaching in a regular classroom. That said, both methods' effectiveness may also be downgraded, as determined by whether T-S and S-S interactions can reach their highest potential. These two types of interaction may get interrupted due to technology instability and uncertainty. This touches on the issue of the gap between what is theoretical and what is realistic. Ideally, we hold high hopes that virtual F2F teaching and blended learning with synchronous teaching can fully translate the effectiveness and likeability of F2F live on-site teaching. However, realistically this does not happen all the time. Some constraints due to the medium of technology impose upon these two delivery modes. As a result, the interactions between a teacher and students and between students and students are often less frequent and less favorable than in live F2F teaching.

3rd Rank: Blended Teaching (F2F in-person + asynchronous learning)

Adding asynchronous learning to any delivery mode tends to lower its potential for satisfaction. Blended teaching featuring a mix of F2F in-person and asynchronous teaching is likely to achieve lower effectiveness than a mix of F2F in-person and synchronous teaching. As the proportion of asynchronous learning increases, the potential effectiveness decreases, reaching a low of 8 points and a high of 10 points.

4th Rank: Online Teaching (synchronous + asynchronous)

While online synchronous teaching has great potential to achieve maximal T-S and S-S interactions, a combination of synchronous and asynchronous teaching inherently lowers the effectiveness of both types of interaction. This type of delivery mode potentially has different gradual effects in each type of interaction, ranging from minimal (6 pts.) to maximal (10 pts.) depending on the proportion of synchronous and asynchronous learning. The more synchronous meetings, the more likely both types of interaction are to increase. Conversely, more asynchronous time tends to increase the level of dissatisfaction with interaction.

5th Rank: Online Teaching (asynchronous)

Online teaching featuring complete reliance on asynchronous learning ranks last, with the likelihood of yielding the least satisfactory T-S and S-S interaction, scored from 0 to 2 points, indicating possibly none, minimal, or partial interaction. Asynchronous learning heavily relies on the teacher's timely responses to learners' questions through a discussion board or via email. A well-designed online learning course also periodically offers F2F online meetings to facilitate learning and meet different individual needs. Unlike T-S interaction, which is likely to happen online, S-S interaction rarely happens in this mode, which has resulted in much criticism. It is therefore reasonable to say that the chance to yield good S-S interaction looks much slimmer than that for T-S interaction in asynchronous self-paced learning. The total expected value of the three types of interaction ranges from 4 to 7 points, which is the lowest among all types of delivery mode. Online tutorial and advising sessions may be offered as needed to students, but they are not as frequent as desired in most cases.

Key Elements Conducive to Interaction

It is important to also delineate what makes interaction more valuable and effective than others. These features are: nonverbal cues, like body movements; here-and-now adjustments; engagement and participation in the conversation; and the sense of community building. Table 2.3 goes a step further to categorize four key elements that are conducive to frequent quality interaction.

Table 2.3 Four Key Elements Conducive to Interaction

Delivery Mode	Nonverbal cues	Here-and-now adjustments	Engagement and participation	Community building
F2F in-person	Yes, always	Yes, always	Yes, most likely	Yes, most likely
Blended (F2F + synchronous)	Yes, for F2F proportion	Yes, for F2F proportion	Yes, for F2F proportion	Yes, for F2F proportion

Delivery Mode	Nonverbal cues	Here-and-now adjustments	Engagement and participation	Community building
Blended (F2F + asynchronous)	Yes, for F2F proportion	Yes, for F2F proportion	Yes, for F2F proportion	Yes, for F2F proportion
Online (asynchronous)	No	No	Possible	Possible
Online (synchronous + asynchronous)	Yes, for synchronous proportion	Yes, for synchronous proportion	Yes, for synchronous proportion	Yes, for synchronous proportion
F2F Online (synchronous)	Yes, but not always	Yes, always	Yes, but not always	Yes, but not always

These four elements are elaborated and defined as follows.

> 1) Nonverbal cues: students can see the instructor use body language, gesture, facial expressions, physical movement, contextual clues, and realia such as objects and tangible teaching aids during class.
> 2) Here-and-now adjustment: the instructor can immediately and synchronously modify activities, instructional flow, PowerPoint slides, and step-by-step instructions in response to learners' needs during class.
> 3) Engagement and participation: students can fully engage and actively participate in interactive discussion before, during, and after class.
> 4) Community building: students can build relationships, bond with their peers, and be well-connected to the entire group before, during, and after class.

These features of interaction can be classified according to type of interaction and delivery mode; the more online teaching can incorporate or approximate these critical elements of human interaction, the more effective it will be.

F2F In-person Teaching

F2F in-person live teaching is the only delivery mode that fully embraces the four key elements of interaction during class. Nonverbal cues are easily observed and noticed by students in class, and the instructor can readily adjust many aspects of teaching by observing learners' performance and needs. This inherently fosters engagement and community building more readily. Real-time in-person interaction tends to yield better results in the four elements than real-time virtual interaction.

F2F Online (synchronous)

Conversely, F2F virtual teaching can embody the four key elements in a remote setting, but not as completely or fully as F2F in-person teaching. Some clear and full contextual cues become invisible, and body language and physical movement can be only partially observed. In a F2F virtual class, here-and-now adjustment is completely possible. An instructor can orchestrate the entire class and make adjustments to teaching materials and PowerPoint slides as needed, on the spot, as in F2F live teaching. Other aspects of here-and-now adjustment seem comparably feasible, such as adjusting instructional activities and flow. Engagement and community building in a F2F virtual setting are also likely to happen though less so than in F2F in-person teaching in part due to learners being getting off track and inattentive. In general, an instructor can adjust many things in a virtual F2F class but may not do so as well as an in-person class.

Blended Teaching (F2F and synchronous or F2F and asynchronous)

The two types of blended teaching are distinguishable by the addition of either synchronous or asynchronous sessions to the F2F in-person sessions. Whether the functionality of the four elements can be fully exerted in the two types of blended teaching rests in the proportion of F2F in-person live teaching. The higher the proportion of F2F live in-person teaching, the more likely it is to keep the integrity of the four key elements to fully engage learners and build connection.

Online Teaching (asynchronous)

To make a sharp contrast, online asynchronous learning is the weakest in keeping the four elements alive. The major criticism lies in the fact that learners cannot see the teacher's presence online, and real-time nonverbal cues are missing, as is any adjustment in a here-and-how setting. Since most, if not all, work is done through independent learning, engagement and community building become difficult.

Online Teaching (synchronous + asynchronous)

Online teaching with different proportions of synchronous and asynchronous learning varies in the effects of the four elements. In principle, the more synchronous online sessions, the more likely the class is to bring about satisfactory outcomes. Conversely, the more asynchronous learning, the less desirable the learning outcomes will be. The full functionality of the four elements depends on the proportion of synchronous sessions for online teaching.

In sum, three ways of interaction and four key elements relate to potential teaching success in each type of delivery mode. Online teachers strive to mimic and mirror the experience of a F2F live class. What deserves further exploration is the question of how to create an online design that resembles a live F2F setting, especially in terms of the key features of interaction. Not only should we compensate for the deficiency of winning features in different types of online teaching, but we also need to think more innovatively about course design and pedagogy enhanced by technology.

The analysis of different delivery modes sheds light on which delivery mode should be chosen when in-person live teaching, whether full or partial, is impossible, and the class needs to go online. Of the three online delivery modes, it is hypothesized that virtual real-time teaching stands out to the most recommended. It wins over both a combination of synchronous and asynchronous teaching and completely asynchronous learning, considering different types of interaction and elements contributing to engagement and community building. Virtual F2F teaching thus instills confidence and can be the driving force for the development of an online learning program.

Chapter 3

Effective Principles for Online Teaching

Language educators are always trying to figure out what makes for an effective language course. Given the complexity of the criteria that define effectiveness, this has been difficult even for in-person classes, and they have been far less explored in the arena of online teaching. In UVA STARTALK program surveys that teacher participants completed at the outset and closure of the program in 2016–19, all teacher participants reported that effective principles for teaching in a traditional class are equally applicable for online synchronous teaching. This chapter addresses five essential questions that can be used to evaluate the effectiveness of an online language class. It further elaborates and illustrates three effective principles for online synchronous teaching, each of which is highly relevant to the five essential questions and particularly salient to issues in language acquisition that may be neglected by many online language instructors. The three principles for effective online teaching are identified as requiring the greatest effort in order to focus attention and enhance online teaching.

Five Key Questions to Assess the Success of an Online Class

No matter what teaching approaches and materials an instructor chooses, the following five key questions are of paramount importance for assessing the success of online teaching. They are outcome-driven and put learner performance front and center. The first two questions are pivotal, and the remaining three further the analysis of the first two. Metaphorically, the first two questions are like a forest, and the latter three are trees that stand out, elect and high. Instructors need to see the wholeness of a class, as well as the pivotal specifics contributing to that wholeness.

Question 1: Were instructional objectives fulfilled?
Question 2: Did students generate expected language output?

Question 3: What was the total amount of time for students' talk?
Question 4: What was the total amount of time for teacher' s talk?
Question 5: What was the total amount of time for student-centered activities?

With limited class time, how to use that time to achieve the most is always key to all types and levels of language classes. To be clear, the above five questions are created for and applicable to language classes that meet the following two preconditions:

Precondition 1: Learners are non-heritage with no or little prior knowledge of Chinese language and culture learned from a home setting.
Precondition 2: Listening and speaking are foremost; and reading and writing are secondary.

As experienced teachers know, a class created for non-heritage learners differs in significant ways from a class targeted at heritage learners. Teaching materials, instructional strategies, and time allotment for the development of each types of language skill, to name a few, should be redesigned to meet the needs of these two different groups of learners. Non-heritage learners should be given more time to practice listening and speaking in class since their home environment and social network lack easy exposure to the target language. This does not devalue the importance of reading and writing in a non-heritage class. It is indeed a matter of in-class time allocation and deliberations of the balance between in-class learning and out-of-class learning, among four language skills in listening, speaking, reading, and writing. In other words, of the three communicative modes — interpretive, interpersonal, and presentational — it is more productive to keep interpersonal in class, and interpretive and presentational outside of class.

Even for heritage language classes, the above first two questions and the last question are still overarching. Only the third and fourth questions should be answered differently depending on whether learners are heritage or non-heritage. In other words, in a heritage class where learners have prior exposure to listening and speaking, it is likely to decrease in-class time allocation for teacher' s talk and students' talk in favor of collaborative reading and writing.

Question 1: Were instructional objectives fulfilled?

This question overrides any other questions that surround it; it guides lesson preparation and instructional delivery. Instructional objectives can be off-track or diluted in the process of planning. Constantly revisiting or revising them is at the heart of lesson planning. The development of teaching materials and sequence of instructional activities, whether teacher-led or student-centered, along with how assessment is done and what is assessed, are integrated to fulfill instructional objectives. Well-thought and careful planning should be in concert with backward design.

Question 2: Did students generate expected language output?

The fulfillment of learning objectives is evaluated based on learners' ultimate language performance. In other words, predetermined can-do statements serve as a blueprint for assessing language performance by the instructor, peers, and learners themselves. Vocabulary, formulaic expressions, structures, and cultural elements are integral to the mastery of language functions and need to be clearly sequenced in the coverage of each lesson or unit. Students appreciate clear guidelines defining both the core components that need to be learned and the marginal ones that are optional and additionally credited. The instructor needs to predetermine and then clearly describe the expected language output based on the scoring guidelines or rubrics prior to assessment.

Question 3: What was the total amount of time for students' talk?

It is enormously helpful to measure the amount of time that students speak the target language from the beginning to the end of class. When a class ends, tally it to add up the total. In an immersive class, students speak the target language as much as they can and as well as they can. They make the greatest effort to use communicative strategies to fully engage and get their meaning across. In a student-centered class, students talk more than the instructor does. If this is impossible, strive for at least an equal amount of talk in the target language between the instructor and students. Avoid unnecessary silent time and be respectful of any learnable moments that arise through students' talk. Of course, students' talk should occur in communicative and authentic contexts where students are fully immersed in the target language and culture.

Question 4: What was the total amount of time for teacher's talk?

This is the other side of Question 3. The more the students talk, the less the teacher talks. An experienced teacher communicates the information learners need in a time-effective manner. Too much teacher's talk is not only a waste of class time, but it also deprives learners of opportunities to learn and practice the language. To improve the quality of teacher's talk and avoid talk that has little or no pedagogical value, an instructor needs to prepare in advance to deliver the teacher-led part of the communicative discussion and introduce the student-centered activities. Effective scaffolding and elicitation techniques are crucial to make this happen. A successful class relies on these techniques.

Question 5: What was the total amount of time for student-centered activities?

Student-centered instruction continues to prevail in communicative language classes. Set the goal of allotting 50% of class time for student-centered activities in the first several contact hours of class, and incrementally increase this percentage toward the last class of each theme or unit. Student-centered activities should be well-planned beforehand and carefully carried out in class to ensure the best use of class time. The total amount of time can be easily calculated and noted by observing a class from the beginning to the end and taking notes in the observation form.

Three Principles for Effective Online Language Teaching

In close alignment with the above five questions on evaluating an online class, the following three effective principles, from the STARTALK principles for effective teaching and learning, are identified as of high relevancy and strong impact. These three core principles are:

Principle 1: Implementing a standards-based and thematically-organized curriculum
Principle 2: Facilitating a student-centered class
Principle 3: Using the target language to provide comprehensible input and generate productive output

They provide a professional path for achieving the best learning outcomes. Table 3.1 matches the key questions on the left column with effective principles on the right.

Table 3.1 The Five Key Questions and Related Principles

Questions (Q)	Principles (P)
Q1: Instructional objectives	P1: Implementing a standards-based and thematically-organized curriculum
Q2: Expected language output	P2: Facilitating a student-centered class P3: Using the target language to provide comprehensible input and generate productive output
Q3: Time for students' talk	P2: Facilitating a student-centered class P3: Using the target language to provide comprehensible input and generate productive output

Questions (Q)	Principles (P)
Q4: Time for teacher's talk	P2: Facilitating a student-centered class
	P3: Using the target language to provide comprehensible input and generate productive output
Q5: Time for student-centered activities	P2: Facilitating a student-centered class

While the three principles on the right column in Table 3.1 are considered the most connected with essential questions, the following four remaining principles interconnect with the three core principles and support the successful implementation of an online course.

Principle 4: Integrating culture, content, and language
Principle 5: Adapting and using age-appropriate authentic materials
Principle 6: Conducting performance-based assessments
Principle 7: Incorporating instructional technology tools to achieve instructional objectives

These principles will be addressed and integrated in the remaining chapters of the book, as they are inseparable from one another and can be better illustrated through a wide variety of sample tasks created for the purposes of online teaching and assessments, synchronously and asynchronously. Technology is useless if it is devoid of instructional contexts. Therefore, we discuss technology use along with pedagogical goals and instructional design. In recent years, technology has gained influence in facilitating instructional design and achieving learning objectives. Undoubtedly it adds significance and complexity to online teaching more than F2F settings, and will be fully discussed in the following chapters wherever relevant.

Principle 1: Implementing a Standards-based and Thematically-organized Curriculum

The five national standards created by the American Council on the Teaching of Foreign Languages (ACTFL) provide governing guidelines and principles for curriculum and course design in world languages in the US. The standards that follow are indicative of the planning that occurs prior to the development of an individual lesson plan.

Communication
Interpersonal   Interpretive   Presentational
Cultures

Practices of cultures	Products of cultures
Connections	
Making connections	Acquiring new information
Comparisons	
Language comparisons	Cultural comparisons
Communities	
School and community	Lifelong learning

The five national standards have been advocated for over a decade, particularly after the launch of AP Chinese, which is equivalent to a fourth-semester college-level Chinese language course. The following lists answers to frequently asked questions from teachers in professional development workshops and meetings.

Question 1: What are the most important national standards in curriculum design?

Communication and cultures are two core national standards that should be included in any thematic unit. Communication involves three communicative modes, and cultures are embedded and integral to language teaching.

Question 2: Should all national standards be included in a thematic unit?

No. The key is to incorporate the standards that are relevant and crucial to fulfill curricular goals, but not all of them. A thematic unit that includes all national standards is not necessarily better than one with fewer national standards. Do not include national standards simply for the sake of squeezing more in. Analyze a theme and its curricular goals first, and then determine which standards are pivotal for realizing the goals.

Question 3: Are there any national standards that are less frequently incorporated in a thematic unit?

The national standard that is least often incorporated into curriculum design is lifelong learning. A course spanning four months or more does not have this goal added to most thematic units. Strong supporting evidence needs to be gathered along a period of time to help verify a learner' s lifelong passion about Chinese language and culture.

Question 4: Are national standards used solely for the purpose of paperwork?

No. National standards have proven value for curriculum design and course development; they go beyond the submission of paperwork or documentation to be reviewed by top administrators or evaluators. They serve as overarching principles for course design and are applicable and implementable for language courses at all levels of proficiency. The essence of national standards exists in language curricula before they are advocated. Many language professionals have incorporated at least some of them in language courses for long. To put it briefly, the essence of the five goals is not brand new, but the framework that is used to organize essentials is new.

In terms of linkage to national standards, backward design undergoes three stages of planning to connect goals, assessment, and instruction in a well-integrated process. See Figure 3.1 for a graphical representation of this.

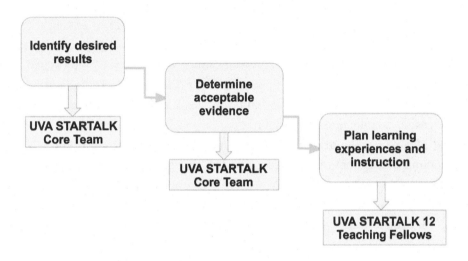

Figure 3.1

The three-stage backward design streamlines the entire planning process for language instruction. It has been widely endorsed and implemented in curriculum design and lesson planning for world language courses and programs.

The first step is identify desired results. This means defining learning objectives, normally articulated and embodied by can-do statements. The can-do statements are devised in accordance with three communicative modes according to projected proficiency levels.

The second step is to determine acceptable evidence. In other words, this step includes figuring out how to access learners' performance and collect evidence of expected learning outcomes through different formats of formative and summative assessments.

After envisioning the likely end products of a lesson or unit through the first two steps of planning, an instructor can then begin to plan for instruction, by creating PowerPoint slides, selecting technology tools, designing student-centered tasks, and selecting instructional materials, including conventionally printed and authentic materials.

In UVA STARTALK, the core instructional team — composed of trainers, practicum facilitators, and technology coordinators — worked collaboratively to complete the first two stages of planning.

The team created a 10-day curriculum with an overarching theme fleshed out by clearly articulated can-do statements in three communicative modes that closely align with ACTFL's proficiency guidelines. Under such a big umbrella, the core team then created daily main texts, each of which included a list of language functions, vocabulary, grammatical structures, cultural notes, and major sources of authentic materials. Teacher participants recruited nationally did not participate in these two stages, in order to ensure timely completion of work required in different stages before intensive training began.

Many language instructors purchase a textbook, and then plan their course according to the lessons of the printed published materials. This has the advantage of saving a lot of time in materials development, and the three-stage backward design still applies. By applying this textbook-based design, teachers will carefully examine the content of the printed materials to define the desirable outcomes, decide how to collect evidence of learning, and finally plan the instructional procedural activities. Even with a textbook at hand, planning for instruction still requires extensive examination and planning.

The central idea of backward design is constantly keeping a goal in mind so that it guides lesson planning, assessment, and instruction. The end goal involves a clear picture of what students need to do and perform at the end of a lesson, theme, or unit. Without backward design, teachers and students may find themselves lost, wandering on a long and slippery trail that leads to nowhere. Backward design helps instructors and learners to head straight toward the destination on a bright and smooth pathway.

As one UVA STARTALK teacher participant summarized,

> The logic and sequence play an essential role in designing a lesson. Backward designing helps teachers to stay focused on the goals when planning a lesson. It is very important to bear in mind with the teaching objectives all the time. This also helps teachers to design engaging activities and tasks.

The following reflective lines resonate with many teacher participants' reshaped mindset after they experienced the power and efficacy of backward design from the training program.

> Before coming to the program, I usually prepare a class from vocabulary, text, to grammar drills and communicative activities. But now, I look at the can-do statements and daily assignments first, and then design activities, and meanwhile considering their types (interpretive, interpersonal or communicative). After finalizing the objectives and framework of a lesson, the following steps are working on details and making them flow better. I will continue to use this strategy to design my class. Additionally, I also learned that we need to figure out and highlight key points for teaching. Especially when the course

is intensive, we need to tailor the study guide for our students. Sometimes emphasizing everything means emphasizing nothing.

Admittedly, it is not uncommon that instructors begin planning a lesson with vocabulary, text, and grammar drills based on selected conventional materials, and then create communicative activities to conclude a lesson. The danger of this is that it may become directionless; the plan may not see the whole but capture pointless details. Wandering among trees without a compass at hand in a big deep forest, it is easy to get disoriented. If instructional planning keeps to predetermined can-do statements with achievable language functions, teachers will be able to lead students toward the right path. The above concluding remark "emphasizing everything means emphasizing nothing" echoes the "less is more" principle as a worthy reminder for all.

Principle 2: Facilitating a Student-centered Classroom

World language researchers and educators have long advocated student-centered instruction, and many Chinese language educators are quite familiar with it. It is realized through analyzing students' diverse needs in curriculum design and carrying out student-centered activities. Despite technological constraints in virtual learning, an online student-centered course remains manageable and feasible. The following are four key reminders to make sure student-centered instruction is done right.

Reminder 1: The success of student-centered instruction builds on teacher-guided scaffolding.

Student-centered activities do not dominate all class time in each class. They account for a certain proportion of class time and are often preceded by teacher-guided communicative discussion. When a new grammatical structure is taught, the procedure normally starts with a presentation and explanation of the new grammatical structure (present), and continues with learners' engagement and participation in a series of question-and-answer interchanges with the instructor in order to practice the core structure in a communicative context (practice). The final step is assigning students to a student-centered communicative task, such as role play, information exchange, or an oral interview, through which learners individually demonstrate their learned knowledge and skills in one to three communicative modes (produce). This conforms with the three-stage procedural learning: I do (instructor), we do (instructor and students), and you do (students).

The present-practice-produce (3-P) sequence characterizes most Chinese language classes. In the first two steps, the instructor orchestrates the entire class to frequently elicit responses, check for understanding, and monitor learner progress. In the third step, learners are given autonomy and independence to work on their own, facilitated by the instructor. The same cycle can repeat several times in a class. Each time when the cycle repeats, some previously learned key vocabulary and language functions are embedded and integrated to gradually expand the student-centered activities. This allows small chunks of information to get connected into big chunks of information and spiral up to reach what students can do the most.

One STARTALK teacher participant recalled:

> The most useful strategy that I have learned from the UVA STARTALK program is how to efficiently design a lesson. The steps of 小讲→小练→小用→大用 (small presentation and explanation → small practice → small application → big application), combining flipped video and backward design are extremely helpful to create an effective class, which also makes lesson planning much easier.

Another wrote,

> With the goals clearly set, the sequence of the lesson follows the cycle 小讲→小练→小用 →大用 , which helps build up students' vocabulary and structures step by step, gradually scaffolding them to the next level where they need to integrate and apply what they have been learning and practicing in the big tasks (大用).

The 小讲 → 小练 → 小用 → 大用 cycle is consistent with the 3-P process, culminating in a summative communicative task in which learners apply all that they have learned to perform at their utmost. The cycle is guided by the can-do statements that are clearly laid out at the beginning and then rolled out, through detailed planning, at the end.

No learners can skip the first two steps and jump right to the third step, and the success of the third step relies on the instructor's successful scaffolding in the first two steps. While student-centeredness has been widely advocated for years, the significant pedagogical value of teacher-guided scaffolded discussion cannot be ignored or underestimated.

Reminder 2: Distinguish fake from true student-centered activities.

Some may think that communication takes place whenever students work in pairs or in groups. This is not true. Communicative activities are not defined by physical presence or by the layout of seats and desks in class. Instead, they are defined by what students really do. Pair work and group work do not necessarily bring about communication, as they can be mechanical or meaningful in nature.

The following three activities are completed in pairs or groups. One is mechanical, one is meaningful, and one is communicative. Thus, despite being pair or group work, they are not communicative automatically or by definition.

1. Students work in pairs to memorize a dialogue on ordering food in the textbook.
2. Students work in groups to choose an object and say it right.

   Student A grabs a bottle of water, asking: 这是什么东西？

   Student B: 这是一瓶水。

   They repeat the same procedure until they have taken turns to describe all objects on the desk.
3. Students work in groups of 3 to discuss their ideal trip to Chinatown according to self-generated criteria. Each group takes turns to give a presentation and then votes for the best.

Memorizing a dialogue in a textbook and acting out a roleplay with peers is not considered a student-centered activity. The first activity is a mechanical exercise since it does not involve students' own expressions of ideas, thoughts, or creativity in the use of target language. The second activity goes beyond the mechanical level and is invested with meaning. In the second activity, Student A and Student B take turns to engage in a question-and-answer activity, aided by real objects. What Student B does is to give a response based on what he or she sees and then formulates a sentence that begins with 这是 (This is). Meaning is embedded in the context, and the tangible object, as shown in the example, 一瓶水 (a bottle of water), is correctly uttered by Student B. The meaningful activity is undertaken with the aid of visual and contextual clues. This, however, merely demonstrates accurate mapping of the object and vocabulary; it lacks full conveyance of genuine communicative intents in the meaning-negotiation process. In the third activity, students work together to generate criteria for an ideal trip to Chinatown. Communication is genuine and invites all learners to participate in the decision-making process by voting in the target language. They develop critical thinking and analytical ability, coupled with cognitive elasticity. All learners have opportunities to bring up what they want to talk about and express their ideas and opinions. Therefore, it is a true communicative student-centered activity.

The following labeling can clearly indicate the differences of the three activities.

1. Student-centered mechanical
2. Student-centered meaningful
3. Student-centered communicative

A genuine student-centered activity cannot be mechanical. Being meaningful is fundamental but not sufficient. It is only through a truly communicative activity that students express, interpret, and negotiate meaning. The three key elements of a communicative activity — express, interpret, and negotiate — can be accomplished in online synchronous learning, but "breakout room" activities (virtual small rooms) need to be carefully planned beforehand. On-site student-centered activities differ from online grouping and group work. Certain strategies can be applied to get the activities completed smoothly and productively. Effective strategies, such as giving instructions in speaking and writing, providing sufficient visual prompts during actions, and ensuring students receive needed feedback, will be addressed later.

Reminder 3: Use the target language most of the time.

Teachers strive to provide comprehensible input in the use of the target language as exclusively as possible. Students are also encouraged to do so. There is no exception to this principle in student-centered activities. It is key to make this rule of thumb clear and transparent at the right start of class and conform to it all the time. The following is a sample rubric (Tseng, 2014, 2018) that teachers can use to constantly monitor the use of the target language and give reminders in the early stages of the habit-formation process. As the class proceeds, students also need to be equipped with circumlocution and communicative strategies, so they can get out of their comfort zone and take risks to negotiate meaning in different types of activities.

Sample Rubric

5: Exceeds expectations (exceptional effort)

Speaks Chinese with ease and confidence whenever required and possible, speaks quality Chinese, speaks no English, frequently willing to step out of comfort zone

4: Meets expectations (satisfactory effort)

Speaks Chinese whenever required and possible, satisfactory target language, speaks minimal English, speaks with some ease, willing to step out of comfort zone

3: Approaching expectations (recognizable effort)

Attempt to use Chinese but speaks with pauses and hesitations, occasionally uses English, occasionally reluctant to step out of comfort zone

2: In progress (minimal effort)

Speaks with guided assistance, sometimes uses English, reluctant to step out of comfort zone

1: Need great improvement (No or almost no effort)

Little attempts to try, complete reliance on frequent guided assistance, frequent use of English, unwilling to step out of comfort zone

0: Absent

Reminder 4: Preparation and clear scoring guidelines lead to better language performance.

Pre-class preparation results in more satisfactory learning than no pre-class preparation. It not only increases students' confidence, but is also beneficial for the smoothness of collaboration and the productivity of language output. When pre-class preparation is required, consider including a presentational communicative mode in speaking or writing. The pre-class preparatory work can be as short as 10 minutes. Avoid busy work or labor-intensive projects. A simple task may serve the purpose well, such as posting a couple of sentences on Padlet, responding to several questions by typing, or writing a small proportion of an essay on Google Forms. When students come to class after having done an activity like this, they will be prepared to present what they want to say or write and engage in interpersonal communication more confidently during class. The essence of language learning is largely in how learners negotiate meaning in the target language. So reserve class time for interpersonal activities and leave interpretive and presentational activities outside of class. Be sure to share rubrics or scoring guidelines with students before assessment, so students are fully aware of your expectations and know exactly what and how much to do to meet and exceed expectations.

It is impossible to create a successful student-centered class with the teacher's effort alone. Effort is mutually beneficial, and students' collaboration is crucial. Use the following guidelines and checklist to plan and conduct student-centered activities.

What teachers should do to deliver a good lesson:

1. Good time length/management
2. Clear instructions
3. Modeling prior to pair/group work
4. Opportune assistance/monitoring
5. Strategic grouping

What students should do and perform:

6. Engagement and participation
7. Satisfactory language output
8. Learning objective achieved

The following checklist has 20 statements for teachers reflect upon as they make plans. The items are created in three aspects to plan, observe, and evaluate the success of student-centered activities: curriculum, implementation, and assessment. They are appropriate for both in-person and online teaching.

Instructions: Reflect upon your teaching and choose the most appropriate answer for each statement. Items 1–3 pertain to curriculum; items 4–14 refer to best practices for implementation; and items 15–20 involve assessment.

	Best practices	Always	Frequently	Sometimes	Never
1	I set instructional goals to meet learners' diverse backgrounds and individual differences.				
2	I take into consideration students' feedback for instructional planning.				
3	I differentiate instruction based on learner needs.				
4	I create a friendly environment for students to work in their comfort zone.				
5	I manage time well while conducting activities.				
6	I use culturally responsive strategies to welcome comments and invite questions from learners.				
7	I employ a variety of grouping techniques.				
8	I create a variety of age-appropriate communicative activities.				
9	I give clear instructions and model activities by providing comprehensible input "i + 1" in the target language.				
10	Learners use the target language during activities.				
11	Students engage in cooperative learning in a reciprocal learning community.				
12	Students take responsibilities for classroom management and behavior.				
13	I use a variety of authentic resources to connect learners to real-life experiences.				
14	I use consistent and effective attention getters.				

	Best practices	Always	Frequently	Sometimes	Never
15	I allow flexibility and freedom for students to choose types of assignment or assessment.				
16	I set instructional goals to monitor and assess learners' progress.				
17	I adjust my teaching based on learners' performance and progress.				
18	I elicit students' input to create rubrics or scoring criteria.				
19	I give opportunities for students to assess their peers' learning.				
20	I give opportunities for students to self-assess their learning.				

Principle 3: Using the Target Language to Provide Comprehensible Input and Generate Productive Output

The use of the target language plays a pivotal role in generating comprehensible input for language learning. The ACTFL Position Statement requires language instructors to use the target language as exclusively as possible in language classes across all levels of instruction. Students are strongly encouraged to strive to use the target language for at least 90% of class time. Comprehensible input is necessary but not sufficient for language learning. It needs to be complemented and reinforced by comprehensible and productive output. Reliance on reading and listening without constant practice in speaking and writing results in better receptive skills but stagnating production skills. The process of receiving meaning-bearing input and generating comprehensible and productive language output brings about two-way interaction, which is optimal for language learning. The roles of input and output are essentially interconnected and interrelated and reinforce each other. The golden rules are stated as follows.

Comprehensible Input

Learners need to be frequently exposed to the target language in meaningful communicative and authentic contexts.

Comprehensible Output

Learners need to be given ample opportunities to perform and produce the target language in meaningful communicative and authentic contexts.

The following five implications (Van Patten, 2002) serve as practical guidelines for dealing with language input and output in a language class. Brief explanations are provided below each implication.

Implication 1: The more input, the better.

The more comprehensible input, the better. Learners should be immersed in meaningful input flood in an immersive setting.

Implication 2: The more interaction, the better.

The process of interaction is manifested by the alternation of input and output. The more opportunities to engage in interaction, the better.

Implication 3: All learner production should be meaning-based, or communicative.

Keep meaning and communication at the heart of instruction to help learners generate proximal language output. The more language output, the better. Learners are given ample opportunities to try to produce "pushed" output that goes slightly beyond what they can do each step and each time.

Implication 4: Focus on form (or grammar instruction) should be meaning-based and tied to input or communication.

Teaching vocabulary and grammar puts meaning, communication, and interaction in a central place while catering to the form of structure. Achieving fluency should not be at the expense of accuracy.

Implication 5: We should watch out for what we expect of learners.

Set reasonable expectations of students and make them clear to ensure students' accountability. To apply the above pedagogical implications in class, instructors can use a set of strategies in accordance with the "i + 1" principle to make meaning comprehensible to learners in contexts.

Strategies for Making Language Comprehensible

1. Body Language, Gesture, and Facial Expressions

Nonverbal cues, including body language, gestures, and facial expressions, are sometimes even more effective than words. They are widely used in a F2F class to facilitate the understanding of meaning conveyance. Although some constraints are imposed upon virtual learning, they are still applicable and valuable if used appropriately and creatively. When body language, gesture, and facial expressions show on the full screen of the computer, they can be even more powerful and appealing than in a traditional class. With careful planning ahead of time, a swift switch from PowerPoint slides to a full screen allows everyone to see one another very clearly and can help learners stay more attentive. Full functionality can be executed in such activities as singing a song, showing directions by physical movements, demonstrating eye protection massage exercises (眼保健操) or radio gymnastics (广播体操), or imitating sports actions. Better effects can be achieved by playing a video to go with the actions to be done right in front of a webcam with a right angle.

2. Language Modification and Simplification

Language use should be level-appropriate to meet learners' comprehension. Formal expressions can be modified and simplified to get learners to comprehend the meaning easily through circumlocution strategies. The following pairs show good examples of formal versus informal word expressions. Instructors can formulate their expressions purposefully and substitute formal word expressions with informal sayings to explain meanings. Pedagogically, a matching comparison of both formal and informal words is very helpful for vocabulary retention.

饮料 (beverage)：喝的东西 (something to drink)
食物 (food)：吃的东西 (something to eat)
绘画 (painting)：画画 (drawing)
摄影 (photography)：照相 / 拍照 (taking pictures)
作曲 (compose)：写歌 (writing songs)

With daily observation and monitoring of learners' progress, instructors know very well what is learned well and what is not learned well, so that they can recycle learned words to explain the unknown and unlearned through comprehensible language use.

3. Contextual Clues

Contextual clues help input to be comprehensible by learners. The following lists four ways to explore contextual clues that instructors can take advantage of to provide comprehensible input.

1) Visual Aids and Realia

A regular classroom has many contextual clues such as visual aids, realia, tangible objects, and photos, flyers, maps, and posters on the wall. While many items can be placed on the desk or other places inside a physical classroom, they cannot be presented all at once on the computer screen in a virtual class. This requires teachers to show items one by one, sequentially, or to resort to other options such as photos and images. Indeed, realia and tangible objects can be shown in front of the webcam very clearly and catch learners' full attention. Besides, teachers can show drawing, numbers, characters, or any visual clues on a piece of paper in front of the webcam to fulfill certain pedagogical objectives. Instructional objectives are still achievable online; it just takes a quick tweak of mindset and creative thinking.

2) Total Physical Response

The Total Typical Response technique is applicable in an online classroom but needs to take into account some limitations and requires careful planning ahead of time. For example, in a spacious classroom, it is quite easy for a teacher to act out the following phrases while teaching *Ba* structures. But when it switches to online synchronous teaching, some are feasible and others are not.

> a. 把书打开，把书翻到第二十八页
> (Open the book, turn to page 28)
> b. 把书放在地上，把考卷放在椅子上
> (Put the book on the floor, put the exam sheet on the chair)
> c. 把门打开，把门关起来
> (Open the door, close the door)
> d. 把书拿起来，把书放下
> (Pick up the book, put the book down)

In the above four sets of expressions that can be easily taught by physical actions, only the first and fourth are conveniently doable online. The second and third sets of expressions cannot be done within the scope of a webcam unless the instructor adjusts the angle or move the laptop somewhere so that students can see the actions that the teacher demonstrates. Even this can be done remotely, but it takes more time to transition into the targeted instructional context and get this done online than it would in a F2F physical classroom. To save time and keep a good instructional flow, the second and third expressions may be better taught with videos or pictures on PowerPoint slides. Language functions pertaining to directional complements can be taught in similar ways, such as 坐过来 (sit closer), 坐过去 (sit farther), 跑进教室 (run into a classroom), 走出教室 (walk out of a classroom). Only a few are mentioned in this section. There are many other examples to continue to experiment online.

3) Here-and-now

The here-and-now strategy does not require teachers to invest too much time or make extensive preparation before class. It is a practical and easy-to-use strategy, based on which teachers can make full use of what is available in class and its surroundings, whether on-site or online, as immediate resources to trigger interesting discussions. When appropriately used, these resources can connect a topic with learners' personal background information and immediate life experience to elicit and compare comments, preferences, opinions, and so on. Describing the color and style of the clothes that students wear can be readily done with visual clues on the computer screen in a virtual class. Many grammatical structures can be taught by using this strategy and engaging students in active learning. For example, inviting learners to talk about a sport activity that almost all love to do except one single student perfectly fits into the practice of the target structure 除了……以外，我们都…… (We all ..., except for someone). The structure indicates a function of exclusiveness in the first clause.

T: 你们喜欢走路吗？
   Do you all like walking?

S1: 喜欢，我常常走路。
   Yes, I often walk.

S2: 我也喜欢，我每天都走路。
   Me too, I walk every day.

S3: 我也喜欢，走路对身体有很多好处。
   I like walking, too, I think walking is very good for our health.

T: 你们都喜欢走路吗？
   So you all like walking, right?

S1-3: 我们都喜欢走路。
   Yes, we all like walking.

S4: 我不喜欢走路，因为……
   I don' t like walking, because ...

T: 好，告诉我们为什么你不喜欢走路？
   OK, please tell us why you don' t like it?

S4: 因为我最近 got hurt，走路不方便。
   Because I got hurt recently, so walking becomes a bit inconvenient ...

T: 哦，最近受伤了，所以走路不方便。
   Oh, recently "got hurt" (correct term in Chinese), so walking becomes a bit annoying.

S4: 对，我最近受伤了，所以走路不方便。
   Yes, I got hurt recently, so walking becomes a bit inconvenient.

T: 好，告诉老师，谁不喜欢走路？

Alright. So now please tell me, who doesn't like walking?

S2:（学生的名字）不喜欢走路。

(A student's name) doesn't like walking.

T: 只有他不喜欢走路，但是你们都喜欢走路。所以我们可以说，除了他以外，我们都喜欢走路。好，大家一起说……

If it's only him who doesn't like walking, but all the rest of you enjoy walking, then we can say — except for him, we all like walking. OK, please say it together …

Ss: 除了他以外，我们都喜欢走路。

Except for him, we all like walking.

In the above dialogue, the teacher chooses walking as a very common exercise that most may favor to do daily. The teacher begins with a simple question 你们喜欢走路吗? (Do you like walking?) and continues to ask other students until one student expresses his or her dislike of this exercise and explains why. At the end of the dialogue, the teacher then concludes by producing the target structure 除了他以外，我们都喜欢走路 (We all like walking except for him). This shows one round of spontaneous "here-and-now" discussion to elicit the target structure, demonstrated by the teacher. To follow up with the entire-class production of the target structure, the teacher would continue to center upon the same thread of discussion to explore students' real experience and elicit expected output of the target structure from more students.

Experienced teachers know how to ask a string of questions that are meaning-bearing and communication-based to help learners get to the target structure in accurate form and with meaning appropriately expressed. To generate the target structure emphasizing "no little kids at all in a classroom", such as "教室里一个小孩子都没有", a teacher can start asking beginning learners a very simple question — Are you college students or little kids? — and then ask if they see any little kids attending their class, and finally lead to the expected target structure.

T: 你们是大学生还是小孩子?

Are you college students or kids?

Ss: 我们是大学生。

We are college students.

T: 教室里有小孩子吗?

Then are there any kids in this classroom?

Ss: 教师里没有小孩子。

There are no kids in the classroom.

T: 所以我们可以说……

So we could say …

Ss: 教室里一个小孩子都没有。

There is not one kid in the classroom.

Admittedly, online teaching poses some constraints with the use of here-and-now resources and on-the-right-spot relevancy conducive to effective live teaching in a regular classroom. Teachers should identify potential constraints ahead of time to plan for alternatives.

4) Meaning-inferring Contextual Clues

The fourth strategy differs from the previous three, which are more straightforward. Although visual aids and photos remain the main source for providing comprehensible input, this strategy requires instructors to create additional meaningful contexts in which learners can guess, infer, and predict to learn the target vocabulary or structures. To avoid using English in speaking and writing, the following three pairs of antonyms that are usually included in a topic on shopping can be well taught through a series of turn-taking between a buyer and a seller. If guided well, learners can get to the meaning from teacher's step-by-step scaffolding with clear and rich visual aids.

买 vs. 卖 (buy vs. sell)
贵 vs. 便宜 (expensive vs. cheap)
够 vs. 不够 (enough vs. not enough)

While teaching a unit on shopping, a virtual background showing a Chinese street market or shopping mall creates an authentic context that preconditions the learning. The online platform, Zoom, has a built-in function that allows instructors to change the virtual background in just seconds before and during an online session. This helps to concretize the immersion context and is highly welcomed by language instructors. Compared to in-person teaching, this sometimes adds better effects for authenticity in learning settings in just seconds.

Teacher Scaffolding for Comprehensible and Productive Output

As stressed earlier, only providing comprehensible input is insufficient for satisfactory language performance. Input needs to partner with comprehensible output, so that learners have ample opportunities to be frequently exposed to target vocabulary and structures and to produce as much language output as possible. This is to say that perception skills in listening, reading, and viewing are not sufficient for successful language learning. They need to be followed and strengthened by production skills in speaking and writing of whatever form.

The following offers a list of strategies to help achieve desirable language output.

1. Meaning and Communicative Drills

As communication continues to be the primary goal for language learning, language professionals have looked for the most effective ways to help learners develop communicative competence. The development of communicative competence needs to be realized and undertaken through teacher-guided discussion and student-centered activities, both of which go hand-in-hand to support and reinforce each other. Even though student-centered instruction has been advocated for long, the importance of teacher-guided discussion can never be overstressed. Paulston (1970) defined three types of elicitation techniques for grammatical instruction: mechanical drills, meaningful drills, and communicative drills. Communicative drills are really what we want to see happening in a truly communicative class. Meaningful drills are required to build a solid foundation for language development before moving into communicative discussion. The most fundamental are mechanical drills that do not carry too much meaning or communicative intent. In a communicative-based class, this type of drill should happen only when vitally necessary.

Following are examples that illustrate the three types of elicitation techniques.

1) Mechanical Drills

A very common type of mechanical drill involves completing a sentence by substituting vocabulary in a certain part of speech, for example, substituting a verb, a noun, and so on. In the following sentence, the teacher guides students to substitute an object in a *Ba* structure involving a subject' s disposal of an object.

    T: 老师把书放在书架上。
        The teacher put the book on the shelf.
    T: 老师把 (   ) 放在书架上。
        The teacher put _____ on the shelf.
    S1: 词典
        Dictionary
    S2: 小说
        Novel
    S3: 历史课本
        History textbook
    S4: 参考书
        Teacher' s handbook
    S5: 功课
        Home assignment
    S6: 卡片
        (Vocabulary) cards

What students need to do in the substitution exercise is replace 书 (book) with a different noun to fill in the blank. The reconstruction of the *Ba* structure, in this way, can be done very quickly by having students taking six turns to say the above six commonly used nouns in class. Syntactically, it can never go wrong by finishing up the mechanical exercise. But criticism is due for its lack of a communicative purpose. While students fill in the blank with a different noun, they might not pay attention to the meaning that they create and merely treat it as an easy-to-pass drill. Such types of drill are not meaning-based or communicative-oriented.

The second category of elicitation technique is meaningful drill. It goes beyond the mechanical drill and creates meaning in the learning process. An example is provided below.

2) Meaningful Drills

Action：老师把手机放在书上。
           The teacher put the cell phone on the book.
Question：老师_____?
          The teacher _____?
a. 老师把什么放在书上
   What did the teacher put on the book
b. 老师把手机放在哪儿 / 那里
   Where did the teacher put the cell phone
c. 老师刚才做什么
   What did the teacher do just now

The teacher first puts a cell phone on the book in the classroom, either four-walled or virtual, and then asks students (a) what he or she put on the book and (b) where he or she put the cell phone. One more question to ask is (c) what the teacher did just now. Guided by the instructor, students respond to the question in a meaningful way. They see the instructor's action and movement of the object first and then respond based on contextual clues provided.

All three questions elicit a sentential response, but they differ in the trigger of lexical items in the meaning-shaping process. While (a) requires students to add an object 手机 (cell phone) based on what the instructor does in the here-and-now setting, (b) directs students to construct the *Ba* structure by filling in a place, i.e., 在书上 (on a book). The question that the teacher asks has exactly the right word order that students need to come up with in the needed sentence. Slightly different from (a) and (b), question (c) does not indicate lexical items needed for construction of the target sentence. Nor does it deliver a clear clue for accurate word order to ensure the accuracy of the target structure. The expected sentential output for (c) is a bit more complicated than those for (a) and (b) due to the lack of lexis and word order required in the sentential response. The questions illustrated by (a), (b), and (c) are good examples of what an instructor can do to vary questions to elicit similar responses in order to make sure that students master both the structural and semantic elements. The alternation of the three questions in this category is necessary for the mastery of target language functions.

The third type of elicitation technique is communicative drill, which is grounded in the shaping and reshaping of meaning and the fulfillment of a communicative intent.

3) Communicative Drills

老师问:
Teacher asks:
a. 你昨天回家以后做什么?
 What did you do after going back home yesterday?
b. 你去过哪些国家旅游? 最喜欢哪儿? 为什么?
 Which countries have you visited? Which do you like the best? Why?

Meaningful drills normally have contextual clues, such as a certain action or movement done by the instructor or students on the right spot. Photos or other visual aids can provide contextual clues as well. An extended dialogue can go from questions geared toward meaningful drills and then to communicative drills, scaffolded by the instructor.

The two questions in the example above indicate communicative drills. The teacher asks a question in (a): What did you do after going home yesterday? Students do not know exactly how to respond to the What-information question, as responses can be as diverse as possible. In (b) there are two Where-information questions and one Why-question: Which countries have you visited? Which do you like the best? and Why? They are open-ended questions, with certain target structures or word expressions that the teacher may have in mind and expect students to express in their responses. To answer these questions, students need to think more deeply, including recalling what they themselves have done, in order to provide information, opinions, explanations or thoughts that go beyond simple facts. A simple turn-taking involves the instructor and one student; further dialogues in the communicative mode can include more than one turn-taking, inviting more students to talk about their experiences and comment on what their peers have said. This does not necessarily involve long turn-taking, but the interactions can go on for longer and produce more output in strings of connected sentences that are all oriented to true communication.

The major differences between meaningful and communicative drills lie in the nature and predictability of the information provided. In meaningful drills, the answer includes information that listeners see and know on-site, immediately, so they can easily distinguish the correct and appropriate answer. Therefore, whether the answer is right or wrong, appropriate or inappropriate, can be easily judged by learners. Conversely, communicative drills embrace information that is new and unpredictable, exerting the purpose of communication. In this regard, communication can be considered as an action in which one interlocutor asks a question and the other answers by offering new and unpredictable information. Both meaningful and communicative drills are frequently employed in a communicative-based class as they achieve different communicative functions.

A simple way to look at communication can be understood through three key elements that construct communicative competence. First, the speaker expresses what he or she wants to say; second, the listener interprets what he or she hears; and third, both the speaker and the listener engage in the meaning-negotiation process, going back and forth to explore what one does not know and wants to know until needed information is gathered and any communicative intent is completed (Savignon, 1983). The three key elements — express, interpret, and negotiate — interact with one another to construct the complexity of communication, which is either regarded as a means or an end for language learning.

In a class where communication is the primary goal, mechanical drills are not without value. They are sometimes used by experienced Chinese language teachers to help students practice pronunciation and repeat core structures to raise their awareness. Whenever used, mechanical drills are regarded as a means to achieve the end goal, being able to communicate. Therefore, whenever feasible, mechanical drills should be transformed to meaningful and communicative drills. For example, leading the entire class to repeat pronouncing the syllable "chi" (吃; to eat) is considered a mechanical drill. After calling on several students to pronounce and make sure most students can do so correctly, the instructor then smoothly switches to meaning-based communication by asking students to talk about their real-life experience, asking questions such as "你喜欢吃中国菜吗？ (Do you like to eat Chinese food?)" . The purpose of practicing pronunciation is thus to support the meaning-shaping process, in order to communicate what one wants to express. Similar questions that center upon the key syllable *chi* can go on and on to engage more students to express their food preferences and dietary habits. This, on one hand, consolidates accurate pronunciation of the syllable, and on the other hand, places communication at the center of the discussion, making genuine learning happen. A successful class can be evaluated based on the time allocation and distribution of the three types of drills. The more communicative drills, the better. Whenever possible, meaning-based and communicative-based discussion should substitute for mechanical drills.

2. Frequent Invitations of Students' Response

A productive language class is high-energy, featuring quick turnings and constant recycling of the question-and-answer process. Teachers' frequent invitations of learners' responses are vital for comprehension checks. When a class fully engages learners, there are always a good number of students who volunteer to answer questions and share their thoughts in the target language. This ideal setting, however, is not exactly what happens in a language class all the time. Without self-initiated responses, calling on students to respond is a good strategy, regardless of delivery mode. Making the expectation of participation crystal clear at the outset of class certainly helps generate a good amount of language output.

Still, it is important to avoid asking the following short questions to check learners' understanding, especially without any follow-ups.

明白吗？
知道了吗？
懂了吗？
懂不懂？
听懂了吗？
All the above mean "do you understand/have you understood?"

When students are asked any of these questions, most of them may simply nod unconsciously and keep silent. Although the questions may be meant to be genuine invitations of learners' responses, from the learners' point of view, they may seem superficial. Those who do not understand and find the flow hard to follow would not know what to say or respond. Unless immediately followed by specific questions that are directly relevant to what is being taught, these short questions often end up being purposeless, redundant, thus a waste of time. Effective comprehension checks, on the other hand, help teachers identify what students have learned well and what they have not yet grasped. These checks can be accomplished through appropriate use of error correction and elicitation techniques to be discussed in the following.

3. Appropriate Error Correction

Six types of error correction strategies (Lyster & Ranta, 1997) are frequently observed in world language classes.

1) Explicit Correction

The teacher clearly points out something that a student says inappropriately or incorrectly and provides explicit correction and explanation.

S: 他不跑得很快。
   *He run doesn't fast.
T: 不 cannot occur before the verb. It should occur after "得".

2) Recast

The teacher provides an accurate utterance based on an inappropriate or incorrect sentence that a student says.

> S: 你喜不喜欢吃饺子吗?
>   *Do you like or not like eating dumplings yes?
> T: 你喜不喜欢吃饺子?
>   Do you like or not like eating dumplings?

3) Clarification Request

The teacher asks students to clarify what is unclear, incorrect, or misunderstood and to repeat or reformulate the original utterance. This is commonly followed by a recast provided by the teacher.

> S: 我有三狗。
>   * I have 3 dog.
> T: 我听不清楚。请再说一次。（Clarification request）
>   I didn't hear clearly. Please say it again.
> S: 我有三狗。
>   * I have 3 dog.
> T: 我有三只狗。（Recast）
>   I have 3 dogs.

4) Metalinguistic Feedback

The teacher provides comments, information, or questions to help a student reformulate his or her original utterance.

> S: 我看书在图书馆。
>   * I read book at the library. (Incorrect in Chinese sentence order)
> T: Where should the verbal phrase and prepositional phrase occur in the sentence?

5) Elicitation

The teacher says something to directly elicit a correct utterance from a student.

> Example 1:
> S: 我爸爸住在日文。
>   *My Dad lives in Japanese.
> T: 你爸爸住在……?
> T: Your Dad lives in _____ ?

Example 2:

S: 我的 sizhuo 是新的。

   *My sizhuo is new.

T: 怎么说 "desk"？

   How to say "desk" in Chinese?

6) Repetition

The teacher repeats what the student says, then often follows that repetition with a recast to provide the correct utterance.

S: 他在厕所吃饭。

   *He eats meals in the bathroom.

T: 厕所？(Repetition) 厨房。他在厨房吃饭 (Recast)。

   Bathroom? Kitchen. He eats meals in the kitchen.

To encourage use of the target language, instructors should avoid error correction strategies that rely on English to get to the point, especially explicit correction (1) and metalinguistic correction (4). The explicit correction strategy can easily be delivered exclusively in Chinese, with a hand gesture pointing to the target component of the structure on the blackboard, whiteboard, or in a PowerPoint slide to get the intent fully understood. Another option is to show key explanatory notes in English on a PowerPoint slide and explain them orally in Chinese. It is always best to be creative, and to replace English with understandable marks or symbols when necessary.

In the above examples, a recast is commonly mingled with another strategy, such as clarification request (3) or repetition (6). This conforms to the frequent occurrence of recasts observed in Chinese language classes, where instructors offer accurate and appropriate input to help catch learners' attention and model target language output. Let's consider the repetition strategy. In the 6th example, the teacher does not simply repeat the wrong word; the goal is to create space and pause there to give time for the student to think about what is said. It is always more effective for teachers to give accurate input than to repeat learners' inaccurate or inappropriate language output. Indeed, repeating learners' mistakes may create a psychological barrier for learners. Immersing learners in a Chinese-speaking setting relies on accurate and appropriate input, and too much inaccurate input, whether speaking or reading, may also delay or interfere with the acquisition of the accurate form and meaning.

The following three transcribed excerpts are selected from a YouTube teaching video (https://www.youtube.com/watch?v=ui7zfVViM2E) on the topic of learning experience in Mandarin Chinese at the elementary level. In the following three excerpts, recast is the most frequently used strategy in shaping and reshaping the language output produced by learners. It is used in combination with at least one more strategy to reinforce the accurate use of the target structure and ensure its integration in further spontaneous communication.

Excerpt 1

T: 你今天累不累?
　　Are you tired today?
T: 你今天很累，为什么?
　　Oh, you' re tired today. Why?
S1: 因为我昨天晚上四点……
　　Because I … 4 am last night …
T: 四点……(Repetition)
　　4 am …?
S1: 再……再睡觉?
　　Go to bed … again …?
T: 才睡觉 (Recast)。他昨天晚上四点才睡觉 (Recast)，你昨天晚上做了什么?
　　Didn' t go to bed until … He didn' t go to bed last night until 4 am. What did you do last night?
S2: 不知道。
　　I don' t know.
T: 你昨天晚上几点睡觉?
　　When did you go to bed last night?
S2: 我昨天……我今天早上三点才睡觉。
　　Last night I … this morning I didn' t go to bed until 3 am.

In Excerpt 1, the instructor begins with a very brief warm-up greeting by asking if students feel tired and why. One student responds in an incomplete sentence without a verb, 因为我昨天晚上四点 (because I ... 4 o' clock last night). The teacher then repeats 四点 (4 o' clock) to stimulate a follow-up response in a complete sentence. The student does fill in the remaining part of the sentence by offering the needed verb 睡觉 (sleep), but preceded by 再 (again), which is inaccurate. The teacher catches the teachable moment right away by offering the accurate use of the adverb 才 followed by the same verb 睡觉 , indicating something that happens earlier than expected.The use of the recast strategy that first occurs with a simple verb is then repeatedly used to extend to a complete sentence 他昨天晚上四点才睡觉 , with the reoccurrence of 才睡觉 to reinforce the learning of the target structure. To recycle the same structure, the teacher asks another student when he or she went to bed last night. Here comes an "Aha!" moment: the student produces a complete sentence with the right usage of 才 before 睡觉 .

The second excerpt shows a teacher' s intent to help learners master the structure "subject +

verb + *De* + verb + adverb", a structure that always requires extensive practice in teacher-guided communicative drills.

Excerpt 2

T: 你今天怎么样？你今天累不累？

   How are you today? Are you tired today?

Ss: 我很累。

   I am tired.

T: 你今天很累，为什么？

   Oh, you are tired today. Why?

S: 因为我昨天晚上……我……我昨天……我昨天晚上睡觉很晚。

   Because last night, I ... I ... I went to bed very late last night.

T: 他睡觉睡得很晚 (Recast)，来我们一起说，睡得很晚 (Recast)。

   He went to bed very late. OK, please say it together – go to bed late.

Ss: 睡得很晚。

   Go to bed late.

T: 睡得很晚。

   Go to bed late.

Ss: 睡得很晚。

   Go to bed late.

T: 睡觉睡得很晚 (Recast)。

   Go to bed late. (Chinese *De* structure)

Ss: 睡觉睡得很晚。

   Go to bed late. (Chinese *De* structure)

T: 你们昨天都……来，一起说……

   You all did what ... OK, say it together ...

Ss+T: 我们昨天都睡觉睡得很晚。(Recast)

      We all went to bed very late. (Chinese *De* structure)

Again, the teacher starts with a warm greeting and asks why a student feels tired. The student makes efforts to express what he wants to say and finally gets to a complete sentence in 我昨天晚上睡觉很晚, which is missing the "verb + *De*." The teacher immediately uses a recast strategy to offer accurate input in a complete sentence 他睡觉睡得很晚.The target phrase and structure are then followed by several rounds of repetition by individual learners (独唱 ; literally solo singing) and the entire class to reinforce the learning of the target component. The repetition of the structure culminates in an expanded sentence with an added time adverbial 昨天 (yesterday), which is collaboratively said out loud (齐唱 , literally choral singing) by the entire class, scaffolded by the teacher. The repetition here is of the accurate stimulus, but not inaccurate output. Since it combines with a meaningful recast in a communicative context, the repetition does not sound too mechanical and instead fulfills its purpose: to catch learners' notice. By combining 独唱 and 齐唱, the teacher makes sure that they constantly reinforce each other, so that the target structure takes root in students' brains and allows them to process information more smoothly. This excerpt shows a good example of how an input flood is created that ultimately will help learners arrive at satisfactory output.

The following excerpt reveals a common error in a prepositional phrases that should occur before a verbal phrase in elementary Mandarin Chinese.

Excerpt 3

T: 这个星期有周考吗？

Is there any weekly test this week?

S: 这个星期没有周考在中文课，可是这个周末有一个周考。

*This week no weekly test at Chinese class, but this weekend there is one.

T: 这个周末有周考，非常好，很长很长。来，在 some place 在 do something 的前面 (Explicit Correction)，对不对？好，来我们一起说，这个星期在这里有周考吗？这个星期在这里有周考吗？来，我们一起说……

This weekend there is a weekly test. Very good. It's a long sentence. OK, "*Zai* some place" precedes "*Zai* do something", is it correct? Let's say it together, "Is there a weekly test here this week?"

Ss+T: 这个星期在这里没有周考 (Recast)

There is no weekly test here this week.

T: 可是，可是我们得……可是我们得……在哪里周考？

But … But we are supposed to …? But where are we supposed to take the weekly test?

S: 在家。

At home.

T: 很好，来，一起说……

Good, let's say it together …

T: 我们得……

We are supposed to …

Ss+T: 我们得在家考周考 (Recast)。

We are supposed to take the weekly test at home.

In Excerpt 3, a student utters a sentence with inappropriate word order in 没有周考在中文课. The teacher uses an explicit correction strategy to explain the right word order, then proceeds with a question that has the same word order as in a response, a linguistic clue that helps learners make the accurate utterance. Without waiting for a response from the students, the teacher then recasts the response by leading the entire class to repeat it with her altogether. A follow-up short question with the target component 在哪里周考 again includes sufficient modeling in the question itself to lead to the corrected utterance 我们得在家考周考 produced by the entire class and the teacher collectively. The use of recast in the form of collective say-out-loud seems to be more effective than a recast by only the teacher.

Research findings indicate mixed results, and it remains unclear which strategy most effective (Ortega, 2016). The best thing to do is consult with students, assess each local situation, and experiment within reason. Error correction is not just about language. Non-language factors such as identity, agency, and affect should be at the front. The teacher needs to take full account of these factors and proceed with error correction within learners' comfort zone. Most important is to help students to set a positive mindset and treat mistakes as opportunities to nurture and foster learning.

4. Effective Elicitation Techniques

Language output relies on teachers' appropriate scaffolding and effective elicitation techniques built on a deep understanding of structure, meaning, and function. The nature of the information provided in discussion can be divided into two categories: information relevant to a printed text, and information relevant to learners' individual expressions and thoughts in connection with their real-life experience. Although the information relevant to predetermined texts is meaningful, it is fixed and bears little resemblance to genuine communication. Spontaneous discussion with a focus on learners' self-expression and various communicative intents is more valuable for its resemblance with native-like social contexts. Additionally, it is likely to generate more language output in terms of the length of discourse, the number of turn-takings, and the quality of language use (Jin, 2019). Class time should be devoted to more discussion of real-life experience than what is stated in the textbooks. This brings in authentic experience and makes the class come alive.

In terms of question types, closed-ended questions are more suited for novice learners. Yes/No questions, alternatives questions, and WH-questions (what, where, when, who, and why) are level-appropriate for learners striving to build complete sentences based on word levels. As language proficiency increases, more open-ended questions should challenge learners to arrive at longer and better utterances. Questions beginning with how, why, and statements such as "tell me more about something" or "describe something in more detail" are strategies frequently used to help learners connect a string of sentences at the intermediate level and beyond. For learners to move away from the novice level and transition to the intermediate level, they need ample opportunities to practice asking and responding to questions in a variety of language functions, so they can make conversations sustainable in different social contexts.

Asking the right questions to lead to target language output requires pre-class planning and on-site adjustment and reinforcement. Teachers of all experience levels normally follow these steps to reach this end:

Before Class:

1. Analyze the target grammatical structure and language function.
2. Formulate a series of questions in alignment with structure and function.
3. Rehearse the questions one by one and take notes as self-reminders.

During Class:

4. Ask the pre-formulated questions and reformulate them according to learners' output.
5. Engage learners in purposeful communication that sounds like spontaneous chats.
6. Recycle and reinforce target structures and functions to get them internalized by learners.

None of the above steps can be skipped, and no shortcuts can be taken. The major differences between inexperienced and experienced teachers are in the time spent planning and in whether target grammatical structures can be smoothly taught and successfully reformulated on-site in immediate response to learners' output, whether expected or unexpected. It takes time for language instructors to build competence and maturity. When teachers have accumulated enough experience, guided by research-supported best practices, they will internalize these elicitation skills so that these steps unfold naturally and effectively. The following structure on the use of 不是……而是…… (is not ... but is ...), which is a bit more formal than "是 …… 而不是……" (is ... but not ...), well illustrates how a target language function can be progressively taught in a carefully sequenced, well-planned process (Bai, 2009).

T: 现在学中文的人越来越多了，你们为什么学中文？
   More and more people are learning Chinese nowadays. Why are you learning Chinese?
S1: 为了了解中国文化。
   To know more about Chinese culture.
T: (Pretends not hearing clearly and turn to asking another student) 她学中文是为了在中国找工作，对吗？
   (Pretends not hearing clearly and turn to asking another student) She is learning Chinese because he wants to work in China, right?
S2: 不对，她说她学中文是为了了解中国文化。
   No. She said she is learning Chinese because she wants to know more about Chinese culture.
T: (Points to the written structure on the blackboard) 所以你们可以说……
   (Points to the written structure on the blackboard) So you can say …
Ss: 她学中文不是为了在中国找工作，而是为了了解中国文化。
   She is learning Chinese not because she wants to work in China, but because she wants to know more about the culture.

After completing the above short teacher-and-student dialogue, the teacher then asks students to fill in the blank at the sentential level in meaningful and communicative contexts.

1. 小王不是去年毕业的，而是……

   Little Wang didn' t graduate last year, he graduated _____ .

2. 他不是……，而是我的朋友。

   He is not _____ , he is my friend.

3. 这张图不是用电脑画出来的，而是……

   This picture is not made by computer, it is made by _____ .

4. 广告的目的不是……，而是为了推销产品。

   The purpose of commercials is not _____ , it is to promote products.

Another round of the question-and-answer scaffolding practice consolidates the learning of the target structure and function:

1. 中国大陆用的是繁体字吗？

   Is Mainland China using traditional characters?

2. 在美国赚钱最多的是老师吗？

   Is teacher the most profitable profession in the US?

3. 世界人口最多的国家是印度吗？

   Is India the most populated country in the world?

4. 美国的首都是纽约吗？

   Is New York City the capital of the US?

The following two excerpts illustrate how a sentence with "verb + 过", indicative of past experience, meaning "have done something or did something", can be learned through responding to a series of questions that keep both structure and function at heart. The verbal phrase "verb + 过" is one of the fundamental structures that must be learned in elementary Chinese and frequently revisited in intermediate courses. The two excerpts are transcribed from a recorded video in the UVA STARTALK online learning program. The teacher uses visual aids, particularly photos in PowerPoint slides, to scaffold learners' output of the target structure in meaningful and communicative contexts.

Excerpt 1

T: 好，刚才我们说了 "吃过" 和 "没吃过"，你们吃过豆腐脑吗？

   OK, just now we were on "have eaten" vs. "have not eaten", so have you ever eaten bean curd jelly?

S1: 从来没吃过豆腐脑。

I have never eaten bean curd jelly.

T: 非常好，我们一起说，从来没吃过。

Good. Let' s say it together … "have never eaten" …

S2: 从来没吃过。

Have never eaten …

T: 很好，你吃过蛋饼吗？吃过吗？

OK. Have you eaten egg quiche?

S1: 嗯……我吃过蛋饼。

Hmm, I have.

T: 嗯，陈敏吃过吗？

OK, Chen Min, have you?

S2: 嗯，我没吃过。

No, I haven' t.

T: 很好，所以你可以说什么？

Good. So you can say …

S2: 从来没吃过。

Have never eaten …

T: 什么？

… Eaten what?

S2: 嗯？

Yes?

T: 蛋饼。

Egg quiche.

S2: 蛋饼，从来没吃过蛋饼。

Egg quiche … Never eaten egg quiche.

T: 很好，还有什么你从来没吃过？

Very good. So is there anything else that you have never eaten?

……

T: 扣德？

Kou De?

S1: 我也从来没吃过油条。

Also, I have never eaten fried bread stick.

T: 真的啊？你问……你问陈敏。

Really? OK, so please ask Chen Min.

S1: 陈敏你呢？

How about you, Chen Min?

S2: 嗯……我也从来没吃过豆腐脑。

Yeah, I have never eaten bean curd jelly.

T: 豆腐脑，很好。

Bean curd jelly, very good.

After briefly explaining the usage of "verb + 过", the teacher engages two learners in simulated real-life conversations, prompted by photos on the computer screen. She begins by asking if the two students have eaten bean curd jelly: 你们吃过豆腐脑吗? Without any further hint, the first student immediately responds 从来没吃过豆腐脑 (I have never eaten bean curd jelly). She then invites the second student, who is not as advanced as the first student, to repeat the same utterance. Next, she puts the cursor on a photo of egg quiche, eliciting the two learners' responses. As expected, the first student responds before the second student again. The first student has eaten egg quiche; the second student has not but is able to use the target structure 从来没吃过 by herself this time. With the teacher's further prompting, the second student adds the object at the end of the sentence to extend the previous utterance and make it structurally complete. In the next round of practice, the teacher intentionally gives more autonomy to the two learners by asking a more open-ended question: 还有什么你从来没吃过? (What are some other foods that you have not eaten?). Following the response provided by the first student, the second student produces a complete sentence all at once by herself, responding 我也从来没吃过豆腐脑 (I have never eaten bean curd jelly either).

Reflecting on the second student's progress, we see genuine learning is taking place after three rounds of evidence as follows.

1st Round:

从来没吃过（Repetition with the teacher）

2nd Round:

1) 没吃过 (Immediate utterance; I have not eaten)

2) 从来没吃过 (Guided by teacher; I have never eaten)

3) 从来没吃过蛋饼 (Guided by teacher; I have never eaten an egg quiche)

3rd Round:

我也从来没吃过豆腐脑 (Immediate utterance; have never eaten any bean curd jelly)

The third round of practice yields a desirable evidence-driven outcome indicative of the second learner's spontaneous production of the target structure, "从来没 + verb + 过 + object". The learning process starts with repetition with the teacher in the first round, gradually building up to a complete sentence structure guided by the teacher, and finally to independent production, without any assistance, of a new sentence that achieves her own communicative intent. The teacher asks and sequences questions purposefully and continues to check for students' understanding and mastery of learned structures, while giving them increasing autonomy, independence, and freedom. These techniques apply to the scaffolding of all other types of target structures and functions in student-centered communicative classes. They are highly recommended.

Contrary to the above example, which demonstrates effective use of techniques to successfully elicit learners' output, the following teacher is off-track and out of focus and fails to keep pedagogical objectives in mind.

Excerpt 2

T: 好，那我们来看一下，我们中国人，我们学习的时候，我们有文房四宝……

S1&3: 文房四宝。

T: 对，文房，就是你学习的地方，四宝，就是你有四个宝贝，来我们一起来说，这个是什么？这是什么？

……

S1&3: 砚。

T: 砚，对，那什么是宝？什么是……我们管他叫四个宝，也叫四个宝贝，什么是宝贝？谁知道？什么是宝贝？

S1: 嗯……都是宝贝。

T: 都是宝贝，他们都是宝贝，那……我们说宝贝是……对你很重要的东西，或者是人，那……你们的爸爸妈妈非常爱你们，你们就是你们爸爸妈妈的宝贝，那你们喜欢的东西比如说计算机，你们觉得计算机很重要，计算机就是你们的宝贝，好，那，来，(a student name) 你最喜欢什么？什么对你最重要？

S2: 我的计算机最重要。

T: 所以计算机是你的……

S2: 所以计算机是我的宝贝。

As indicated in the above excerpt, the key objective is very clear and simple: to guide students to know what 文房四宝 (four treasures) are in Chinese heritage. The teacher does show intentions to keep the thread of central discussion, but a mention of 宝贝 (treasure, loved stuff) emerges as a turning point that leads students to focus on something else that does not fall within the learning objectives. The key learning point is not to apply the concept of 宝贝 in learners' daily lives, but simply to get the concept of what it means by being able to identify the four treasures 笔墨纸砚 (brush, ink, paper, and ink stone), four significant inventions symbolic of cultural heritage in ancient China. The PowerPoint slide on the computer screen has clear photos and Pinyin to help learners easily capture the meaning, and the teacher could have stayed focused on the discussion of these four treasures by asking, for example, 你看过笔吗？ (Have you seen brush?) 你用过纸吗？ (Have you used paper?) 你什么时候用过墨？ (When did you use ink?) These questions would recycle the use of the four key words and integrate learned structures "verb+ 过" in the discussion of four treasures. Apparently the teacher does not do so and creates an unplanned additional learning objective, 什么是我的宝贝？ (something is my treasure), which is not only redundant but wastes time and dilutes the focus of learning. Although a student is able to come up with a sentence that the teacher wants him to say, the amount of time that the teacher spends on scaffolding is much more than the time students spend speaking.

The following excerpt continues the discussion on the off-track pattern that requires students to identify what treasures are in their daily life. This is again irrelevant to the learning objectives of the four traditional treasures in Chinese civilization.

Excerpt 3
T: 那 (a student name) 你呢？你最喜欢什么？什么是你的宝贝？
S3: 嗯……我最喜欢……嗯……（not intelligible here）的宝贝。
T: 什么的宝贝？什么的宝贝？你再说一遍好吗？
S3: 嗯……我最喜欢小吃的宝贝。
T: 小吃的宝贝，喔，你喜欢小吃？所以呢，你认为小吃是你的宝贝是吗？
S3: 嗯……
T: 所以……你喜欢计算机吗？计算机是你的宝贝吗？
S3: 嗯……我喜欢计算机的宝贝。
T: 喔，你说，我喜欢计算机，计算机是我的宝贝。计算机是你的宝贝，来，再说一遍，来，再说一遍。
S3: 嗯……我喜欢计算机是我的宝贝。

Unlike Excerpt 2, the student in Excerpt 3 is not able to produce the target vocabulary. At the beginning, the teacher asks a student the same question on 你最喜欢什么？ (What is your favorite?) and 什么是你的宝贝？ (What is your treasure?) The student does not respond clearly, possibly due to the lack of the vocabulary, and as a result, there is a communication breakdown. After not understanding what the student wants to say twice, the teacher fails to fill in the needed vocabulary and abruptly jumps in to say 小吃的宝贝, suddenly switching to another structure, 什么的宝贝？ instead of keeping the same thread of discussion by asking "What is your treasure?" 什么是你的宝贝？ The student is thus misguided to use "……的宝贝" as the new core pattern, as he attempts to say what the teacher wants him to say. Toward the end of the conversation, the teacher says three sentences relevant to the newly created core pattern and confuses the student again. Since the teacher says 我喜欢计算机，计算机是我的宝贝 (I like computers, computers are my treasure), and then asks the student to repeat one more time, the student does follow the instruction, saying "我喜欢计算机是我的宝贝" by combining two sentences into one.

This teacher violates all six steps for effective elicitation techniques. Even if the teacher analyzes the target grammatical structure and function before class, she does not stick to the predetermined learning objectives and regretfully deviates from the can-do statements. Pre-class rehearsals of elicitation questions and alternatives should have prevented the above off-track dialogue. This is a very important step for pre-class preparation. Without rehearsal and mindfulness of consistent and purposeful formulation of questions, the teacher will fail to scaffold learning, and students will not be able to generate the expected language output, which otherwise is completely achievable and uncomplicated. This results in unwise use of class time and unfulfillment of the pre-planned learning objectives.

Backward design of an online language course follows a procedure identical to that of a course taught in a traditional class. Online or on-site, it is crucial to streamline the planning process, start with abundantly clear goals in mind, transition to the development of formative and summative assessments, and devote oneself to instructional planning with the confidence that all is on the right track. The principles for effective online teaching provide specifics on the implementation of student-centered instruction and the use of the target language to create comprehensible input and productive output in immersive settings. The interconnection and interrelation of comprehensible input and productive output have many nuances and subtleties that are interwoven intrinsically. A teacher who is both observant and reflective is able to tackle these details discretely and relate to things holistically. Because the fundamental principles are the same for online and on-site teaching, teachers should be encouraged by the fact that experience in applying these principles in a typical F2F classroom is by and large transferable to an online class. In this regard, a teacher who successfully teaches a F2F class can transform his or her experience to online teaching without painstaking effort. The transition to online teaching requires only adjustment to new technologies and factors associated with them. There are abundant opportunities for discovery in this domain in the ensuing chapters.

References

Bai, J. 2009. Chinese Grammar Made Easy: A Practical and Effective Guide for Teachers. Yale University Press.

Jin, H. 2009. 课堂互动与教师提问技巧 (In-class interaction and teachers' questioning techniques). Retrieved from https://www.academia.edu/10063877/Dr_Jin_presentation09192009 on July 15, 2020.

Lyster, R., & Ranta, L. 1997. Corrective feedback and learner uptake: Negotiation of form in communicative classrooms. Studies in Second Language Acquisition, 19(1), 37–66.

Paulston, C. 1970. Structural pattern drills: A classification. Retrieved from https://files.eric.ed.gov/fulltext/ED044701.pdf.

Savignon, S. 1983. Communicative Competence: Theory and Classroom Practice. Reading, Mass.: Addison-Wesley.

Ortega, L. 2016. Best Practices for Error Correction in Second Language Classrooms, a PowerPoint presentation given for the Speaker Series at the Institute of World languages of the University of Virginia.

Tseng, M. 2014. The Handbook of Tasks and Rubrics for Teaching Mandarin Chinese (Volume I). Beijing Language and Culture University Press.

Tseng, M. 2018. The Handbook of Tasks and Rubrics for Teaching Mandarin Chinese (Volume I with added e-version). Beijing Language and Culture University Press & Phoenix Tree Publishing Inc.

Van Patten. 2002. From Input to Output: A Teacher's Guide to Second Language Acquisition. McGraw-Hill Company.

Chapter 4

Synchronous Teaching and Technology

Although online synchronous online instruction can be very different from F2F onsite instruction, teachers can make it as successful as the F2F live classroom experience by implementing effective teaching principles and strategies. Of the different online delivery modes, synchronous virtual teaching most resembles F2F live teaching. Since online teaching involves a certain level of uncertainty in coping with technology, detailed planning and careful preparation are necessary to ensure effective use of class time and the fulfillment of instructional objectives. With appropriate use of technology tools, teachers can respond directly to questions and discussions, provide instant feedback, and conduct interactive activities to ensure instructional quality and achieve outcomes. To fully demonstrate how to make this work online, this chapter presents and illustrates a series of student-centered tasks in three communicative modes for synchronous online teaching. Some of them have been field-tested in UVA STARTALK, and others were created based on STARTALK's principles; all are designed to enrich the diversity of task design, authentic materials, and technology use to create an interactive online class.

Selecting a Video Conferencing Platform

Choosing an appropriate video conferencing platform is always the first step for synchronous online teaching. Most schools or institutions already have an institutional subscription to an online meeting platform. Whenever given the freedom to make platform decisions, teachers are strongly advised to carefully choose a video conferencing platform whose features will maximize instructional effectiveness. The following discussion summarizes the four video conferencing platforms that are mostly frequently used for online language teaching: Zoom, Google Meet, Blackboard Collaborate Ultra, and Microsoft Teams. Features that teachers should consider include participant capacity, meeting time limits, screen-sharing, audience control, virtual background, polling, whiteboard mode, annotation, and recording. These capabilities will be most helpful in achieving language teaching goals.

As Table 4.1 shows, Zoom has the greatest number of features useful in language teaching. Teachers should know that video conferencing platforms change rapidly, so it is important to stay up to date on advances. Although Blackboard Collaborate Ultra, as compared to Zoom, is missing only the capability to create virtual backgrounds, its built-in annotation and whiteboard modes are not as diverse, user-friendly, or multifunctional as they are in Zoom. Neither Google Meet nor Microsoft Teams offers the annotation function during the screen-sharing time, as Zoom does, though teachers can consider adding the annotate software from another screen. For example, creating multiple Google Meet links is an option for making group activities in breakout rooms possible. The combination of Google Jamboard and Microsoft Whiteboard can be a great alternative to the interactive whiteboard in Zoom. Considering the close linkage of Zoom' s built-in functions with the pedagogical needs for language teaching, the majority of the tasks discussed in this chapter are conducted through the Zoom video conferencing platform, enhanced and bolstered by auxiliary technology tools to maximize instructional effectiveness.

Table 4.1 A Comparison of Four Video Conferencing Platforms

Features	Zoom	Google Meet	Blackboard Collaborate Ultra	Microsoft Teams
Affordable	Free	Free	Paid	Paid
Participants limit	100	100	250	250
Meeting time limit	40 minutes	60 minutes (unlimited until Sept. 30, 2020)	24 hours	4 hours
Multiple participants on a single screen	Yes	Yes	Yes	Yes
Screen sharing	Yes	Yes	Yes	Yes
Recording support	Yes	Yes	Yes	Yes
Grouping	Yes	No	Yes	Yes
Annotate	Yes	No	Yes	No
Virtual background	Yes	No	No	Yes
Poll	Yes	No	Yes	Yes
Attendance	Yes (Pro)	No	Yes	Yes
Whiteboard	Yes	No	Yes	Yes

Setting Synchronous Class Routines and Rules

It is pivotal to set up class routines and rules upfront for synchronous online teaching, so students are clear about teachers' expectations. Routines and rules ensure fairness and equity, and free teachers and students from the stress associated with unwanted noise and chaos. They are fundamental to creating a positive learning online community. Additionally, handling this well in the initial stage of class enables teachers to focus on teaching itself and avoid hassles in classroom management that can otherwise be unpleasant, dissatisfying, and even painstaking for online language teaching, particularly in K-12 educational settings.

It is best to keep class rules simple and positive. Simple rules are easy for students to remember; rules that foster positive reinforcement are more welcome and more likely to encourage motivational and cooperative learning. Adjust class rules to fit students' age, personalities, and proficiency levels, and consider factors pertinent to learners' cultural backgrounds and individual needs. An ice breaker activity on Day 1 is a great way to model classroom routines and rules. Showing pictures, creating a video, or playing an interactive and communicative game are viable options. It is ideal to set up a comprehensive and inclusive class protocol on Day 1, but more can be added later, when relevant and applicable, after teachers closely observe learners' behavioral patterns. The key is to make them clear and agreeable and then consistently adhere to them as class moves along.

The following three screenshots show how class routines and rules are procedurally reinforced in the first week of class in UVA STARTALK. On Day 1, the teacher sets up a class rule by requiring students to mute their cell phones. On Day 2, the requirement to fully charge computers is added. On Day 3, the teacher adds the requirement to regularly check chat box for instant responses and questions. As indicated in the screenshots, the Day 1 teaching slide includes a "no cell phone" image at the left-bottom corner. On Day 2, a "full battery" icon is added besides the "no cell phone" image. On Day 3, a third icon, "chat box reminder" , is added to the teaching slide to remind students to post questions and responses and look for additional instructional resources in the chat box during class. The first two days focus more on classroom behavior management; only on the third day does the first mention of an online language learning strategy appear. In sum, it is advisable that teachers explain a set of predetermined class routines and expectations on Day 1 and then adjust and remind students constantly in response to different scenarios and situations (See Figure 4.1).

Day 1

Day 2

Day 3

Figure 4.1 Class Routines or Rules

Always Having a Plan B

Since there is always the possibility that technology will fail, it is important to have a Plan B in mind for synchronous online teaching. Devise at least a backup plan in case certain technology tools malfunction before starting the class. Tell students what that Plan B is and what to do if the online meeting is disconnected. It is suggested to create a second place for students to go whenever either teachers or students have problems attending the video conferencing meeting. Below are some suggestions for teachers to consider:

1) Create a discussion board at the LMS for Q&A, which enables everyone to help each other solve problems quickly.
2) Send emails to teachers or students if there is a connection issue with a conference meeting.
3) Always have an alternative activity ready before teaching.
4) Share a second collaboration platform while teaching online, such as Padlet or Google Slides, where teachers and students would be able to communicate by typing messages.
5) Create a group chat for each class to allow teachers and students to communicate, such as WeChat or Group Chat.

If the first video conferencing platform does not have certain needed functions, teachers can achieve the same effects by adding a second screen with Nearpod, Pear deck, Jamboard, or similar. If they have more than one device, students and teachers can use their computers to log into a video conferencing platform, which will be used as the "home screen" of the classroom, and use their tablets, smartphones, or another web browser from the same computer to set up the "second screen", where they can open a page prepared by the teacher in advance. This allows students to participate in classroom activities using both "home screen" and "second screen", so online learning is not interrupted and can proceed as planned.

The effectiveness of interaction is especially critical in synchronous online classrooms. One of the major challenges that teachers encounter in online teaching is how to transform the meaningful experiences that occur in a four-walled classroom, both student-teacher and student-student interactions, to an online virtual classroom. In this process, online platforms offer some built-in tools that can help ensure the interactive quality of online teaching. As indicated in Figure 4.2, teachers can directly use the different embedded functions of a video conferencing platform such as video camera, virtual background, sharing-screen, annotation, chat box, nonverbal icon, whiteboard, and others.

Sharing & Annotate

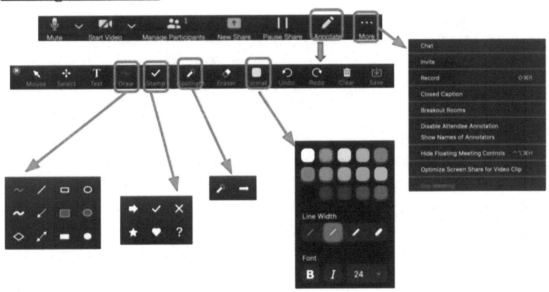

Figure 4.2 Zoom Sharing and Annotate

In the rest of this chapter, we offer a series of tasks in three communicative modes that make full use of the built-in functions of a video conferencing tool to achieve pedagogical objectives. These tasks demonstrate effective teacher-guided instruction and student-centered tasks that are completed synchronously while keeping can-do statements in mind all the time. Considering constraints with existing built-in functions within any video conferencing platform, technology tools and applications outside of the platform are added to help accomplish instructional goals in some tasks.

Task 1: Body Parts 身体部位 (老师说)

Communication Mode: Interpretive
Performance Level: Novice-high
Can-do Statements:

>   Students can understand words and phrases about body parts.
>
>   Students can ask the question "Where is + body part?" and respond to it.

Technology Tool: Zoom with a webcam

Instructions:

Step 1: Students turn on the web camera and adjust it in order to show their whole body while participating in the activity.

Step 2: Students check the speaker and microphone before the activity. Ask students to type 1 if they can hear the teacher and 2 if they cannot.

Step 3: Begin the task on "老师说" . Students point to that part of the body with their hands when they hear "老师说 + body part in Chinese" . Continue until time is up.

Step 4: Any student who does not follow with the task as expected plays the role of what the teacher does in Step 3 by saying "Student Name in Chinese 说 + body part" .

Step 5: Students add oral responses in addition to pointing to the body part as directed. When they hear "老师说 + body part in Chinese + 在哪儿？" , they point to the body part with their hands, saying "body part in Chinese + 在这儿" . Any student who does not follow with the task plays the role of what the teacher does.

词汇与语法：

>   老师说……
>
>   身体部位：头，头发，眼睛，鼻子，耳朵，嘴，牙齿，手，胳膊，肩膀，腿，膝盖，脚

Instructional Strategies:

1. The above interpretive task in Steps 3–4 is interesting, engaging, and very easy to follow. When students touch any body part after hearing what the teacher says, it is completely doable and very useful to also ask students to say a complete sentence, for example, "眼睛在这儿" by responding to a question such as "眼睛在哪儿？" .

2. Another appropriate sentence to replace the simple question "body part + 在哪儿" is "这是什么？" . Similarly, when students touch a body part, they can also respond orally by saying " 这是 + body part" . This seizes a teachable moment to go beyond the "word" level and guides students to come up with short complete sentences within their comfort zone.

3. Guiding students to generate "pushed" language output by adding oral responses in short complete sentences complies with the "i + 1" strategy. This helps students

to go one small step beyond their current level. Novice learners should be given ample opportunities to produce short simple sentences in the first several weeks of a beginning class.

Task 2: **You Act, I Guess 你比我猜 (Hobbies 爱好)**

Communication Mode: Interpretive
Performance Level: Novice-high
Can-do Statements:
    Students can comprehend and interpret facial expressions and body language about hobbies.
Technology Tool: Zoom with a webcam

Instructions:
Step 1: Students turn on the web camera before the activity.
Step 2: The teacher uses a random team generator tool to pair up students.
Step 3: The teacher sends five sentences to each individual student privately through chat box. The other student in the same pair does NOT have access to the five sentences. This makes a total of ten sentences in each pair.
Step 4: The first pair starts to act and guess, while all other students watch them perform, Student A acts out the sentences, and Student B makes a guess as to what they are. Repeat the same procedure up to five times to finish up all the sentences. Then Students A and B switch roles and act out five different sentences. This makes a total of ten sentences in five minutes. The teacher keeps track of the score for right and wrong guesses for each pair.
Step 5: The remaining pairs follow the same steps, and the teacher continues to keep track of the score that each pair wins.
Step 6: The teacher announces the winning pairs with the three highest scores.

词汇与语法：
    一边……一边……
    虽然……，可是／但是……
    听音乐，唱歌，跳舞，画画，看电视，跑步，看电影，踢足球，打篮球，游泳，打橄榄球，打乒乓球，打网球，弹钢琴，拉小提琴
Examples:
    我喜欢一边画画一边听音乐。
    虽然我喜欢打篮球，可是／但是我不喜欢打橄榄球。

Instructional Strategies:
    1. The teacher should send five typed sentences to each student privately in the chat

box. Make sure to prepare enough various sentences about hobbies in a Word document beforehand, so that the pre-typed sentences can just be copied and pasted from the Word document, saving a lot of in-class time. Pre-class preparation makes the task run smoothly.

2. Before class, the teacher should configure the chat box so it is "host only" (see Figure 4.3). This means that only the teacher can type in the chat box, and students can only receive and read information sent from the teacher. Students cannot type in the chat box, meaning they also cannot send the sentences that they receive from the teacher to their partner. This ensures that it is a fair game, as no one will get any hints and steal answers from their partner before acting and guessing. However, the teacher also should remind students that they should not send any message to each other, which would be considered "Breaking the Rule" , such as text messages, or sending emails.

3. The game requires students to act and guess full sentences. This is a recommended strategy for upgrading learners' language performance to the sentential level, avoiding stagnation at the word level and constantly employing strategies for generating "pushed" language output.

4. The design of the interactive game can be framed in a one-to-all context. Namely, instead of pair competition, each individual student can take turns to act out and guess in the main room.

Figure 4.3 Zoom Chat Box Settings

Task 3: Pictionary 猜成语

Communication Modes: Interpretive and presentational
Performance Level: Intermediate-low to Intermediate-mid
Can-do Statements:

  Students can understand Chinese idioms.

  Students can tell a short and simple story about Chinese idioms.

Technology Tool: Zoom Interactive Whiteboard

Instructions:

Step 1: Students test the function of the interactive whiteboard to make sure they can draw on it comfortably.

Step 2: Each student receives a Chinese idiom from the teacher within the chat box privately.

Step 3: One student plays the artist role and on the interactive whiteboard draws the story related to the Chinese idiom, orally explaining the drawing in Chinese while drawing. Other students see the drawing while listening to the story and guess what the Chinese idiom is (see Figure 4.4).

Step 4: The student who guesses the Chinese idiom right gets one point. The teacher keeps track of the points.

Step 5: Repeat Steps 2–4 until everyone finishes.

Instructional Strategies:

1. This activity involves drawing for comprehension. But be warned that beautiful drawing is not key to the success of this activity. Instead, the narration of a short story indicating the meaning of the idioms is the focused learning point. If teachers are concerned about taking too much time for in-class drawing, a wise decision is to ask students to draw on a piece of paper before class and hold it in front of the webcam during the activity. Another option is to ask students to upload their drawing into a designated folder and show one by one during the activity. This saves lots of in-class time and makes the class more time effective.

2. To enter the interactive whiteboard, the teacher does the following: 1) click "share screen" at the bottom of the computer screen; 2) click "whiteboard" ; and then 3) click "share" .

3. Just as in the second instructional strategy for Task 2, the teacher disables the chat box setting to be "host only" (see Figure 4.3), so students are not able to send the message to their partners. Teachers should announce that students should not send any information to each other using other devices.

4. Teachers can use prepared tools (like ClassDojo) or spreadsheets for mark the points for each round.

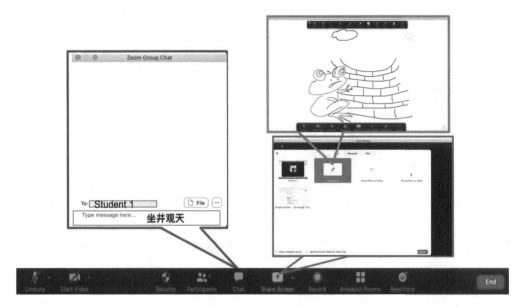

Figure 4.4 Zoom Whiteboard

词汇与语法：

Suggested Chinese idioms

从古至今，一石二鸟，耳熟能详，家喻户晓，众所周知，对牛弹琴，画蛇添足，井底之蛙，盲人摸象，骑虎难下，水滴石穿，三心二意，一干二净，眉来眼去，年年有余，白头到老，一见钟情，望子成龙，走马观花，将错就错，如诗如画，察言观色，各式各样，红红火火，黑白分明

Task 4: **True or False 真真假假**

Communication Mode: Interpersonal

Performance Level: Intermediate-low

Can-do Statements:

Students can talk about their past experience by using the "verb + 过 + object" structure.

Students can ask and respond to questions about past experience to sustain a simple short conversation.

Authentic Materials: Photos

Technology Tools: Chat box, Stamp in Annotate, or symbols and icons chosen from "Participants" and "More" in Zoom

Instructions:

Step 1: The teacher says a sentence with the "verb + 过 + object" structure to describe his or her past experience. A student guesses if it's True (真) or False (假). The teacher releases the answer. Repeat the same procedure for several rounds.

Step 2: After the teacher talks about his/her past experiences, students are paired up and take turns to talk about their own past experiences. Student A says a sentence to describe his/her own past experience with the same structure. Student B responds to the question with "真的，我觉得你……过……" or "假的，我觉得你没……过……" Student A then tells Student B if what he/she says is right. Repeat the same procedure for several rounds.

Step 3: Students start a conversation asking and responding to questions about their past experience based on given pictures with verbal actions provided by the teacher.

词汇与语法：

V+ 过 + object：去过，看过，听过，唱过，吃过，玩过，做过……

A：我 V 过……。

B：真的！我觉得你 V 过……。or 假的！我觉得你没 V 过……。

A：你 V 过……吗?

B：我 V 过……。or 我没 V 过……。你呢?

A：……

Instructional Strategies:

Consider the following options to indicate True (真的) or False (假的) in combination with oral expressions:

1. Use Zoom Annotate to type the character "真的" or "假的" or put a check or cross on the screen.

2. Click "Participants" and choose the green yes or the red no. Or click "more" to choose a nonverbal icon, for example, a thumbs-up or thumbs-down to indicate yes or no for a true or false statement (see Figure 4.5).

3. Use the Stamp icons in Zoom Annotate to show True (真) or False (假) (see Figures 4.6 and 4.7).

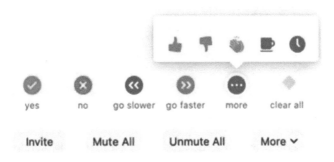

Figure 4.5 Zoom Nonverbal Icons Chosen from "More"

Figure 4.6 Stamp in Zoom Annotate

Figure 4.7 Activity for True or False

Task 5: **Class Schedule 课程表**

Communication Modes: Interpretive, Presentational

Performance Level: Intermediate-low

Can-do Statements:

Students can comprehend and interpret a typical class schedule in a Chinese high school.

Students can present the schedule of a typical school day.

Authentic Materials: Daily class schedule

Technology Tools: Zoom annotate and animation in PowerPoint

Instructions:

Step 1: Students listen to the audio about a typical class schedule in a Chinese high school.

Step 2: After listening to the audio file, students use the type function in Annotate to type school subjects in Chinese characters in the appropriate time slot of the class schedule table.

Step 3: Students direct the teacher to put the textbooks indicative of the school subjects into the book bag in a correct order, using sentence structures "上 完 …… 课 以 后，我 上……课" and "先上……课，再/然后上……课". The teacher follows students' direction to click the PowerPoint slide and activate the embedded animation effects for selected textbooks to fly into the book bag (see Figure 4.8).

Step 4: The teacher shows the class schedule table with accurate information about school subjects and schedule, so students can double-check their comprehension.

Step 5: Students orally present the schedule of a typical school day by including time, school subjects, and activities.

词汇与语法：

门，节，数学，课，化学，教室，操场，课间操，广播体操，眼保健操，体育，美术，音乐

每天 + time + 上 + subject

上完……课以后，我上……课

先上……课，再/然后上……课

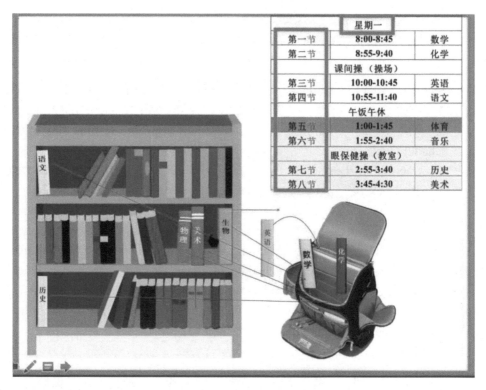

Figure 4.8 Activity on Class Schedule

Task 6: **How to Write a Chinese Home Address? 中国的住址怎么写？**

Communicative Mode: Interpretive
Performance Level: Intermediate-low
Can-do Statements:
> Students can identify the order of different pieces of information about Chinese home address.
> Students can identify the differences between home addresses in China and the United States.

Authentic Materials: Chinese postcards
Technology Tools: Zoom annotate or Nearpod draw

Instructions:
Step 1: Students read different pieces of information about the home address on a Chinese postcard.
Step 2: Students organize the information in order by writing A, B, C, D, E, and F, using Zoom Annotate to reflect the accurate order.

Step 3: Students talk about the order of different pieces of information in home addresses in Chinese and American cultures (see Figure 4.9).

词汇与语法：

国，市，小区，楼，层，号

Noun1 跟 Noun2 一样 / 不一样

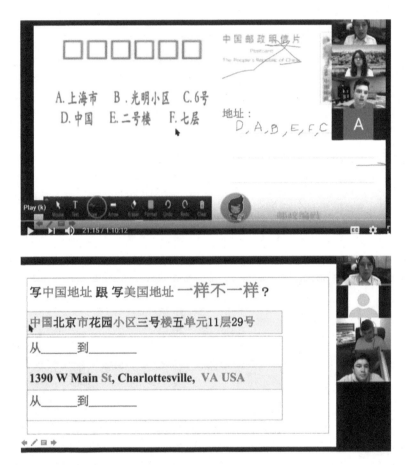

Figure 4.9 Address on a Chinese Postcard and Language Comparison

Task 7: Buy Steamed Buns 买包子

Communicative Mode: Interpretive

Performance Level: Intermediate-low

Can-do Statements:

Students can comprehend a short video on a traditional Chinese cuisine 包子 (steamed bun) and identify its ingredients and flavor, and how to pay for it in China.

Authentic Material: Video on 庆丰包子铺 *Special Street Food in Beijing China* (https://www.youtube.com/watch?v=o5KPdceMGe8)

Technology Tool: Zoom poll

Instructions:

Step 1: Students watch the video for the first time and answer the following questions.
  1) 你们看到了什么?
  2) 你吃过包子吗?
  3) 想不想尝一尝? 为什么?
  4) 包子的味道怎么样?
  5) 根据学生兴趣点,加入其他问题。

Step 2: Students watch the video a second time and focus on the following three questions that show on screen. If necessary, students may watch the video two to three more times to better comprehend its content.
  1) 客人买什么肉包子?
  2) 客人用什么付钱?
  3) 包子的味道怎么样?

Step 3: Students answer three questions in a Zoom Poll (see Figure 4.10).

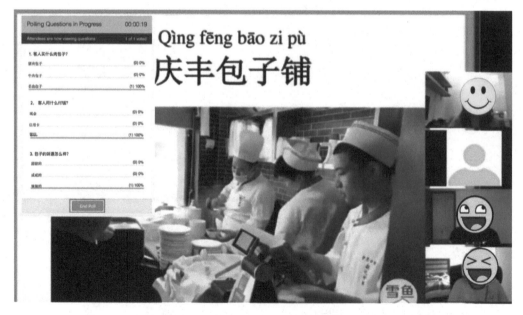

Figure 4.10 Watch a Video and Answer Questions in a Zoom Poll

Video Source: *Special Street Food in Beijing China* (https://www.youtube.com/watch?v=o5KPdce MGe8)

Step 4: The teacher shows the poll results, leads the entire class to discuss the results, and then explains, clarifies, and reinforces understanding.

The following dialogue is transcribed based on the content of the video segment.

A: 你好！

B: 那个……猪肉大葱和茴香鸡蛋各来二两，再来一份大份的炒肝。

A: 在这儿吃吗？

B: 对。

A: 48 元。

(Screen shows "猪肉大葱 7 元 /3 个" and "刚出炉的包子 3 个 7 元")

B: 我的是微信的。

A: 微信扫这里，带走还是在这里吃？

B: 带走，谢谢。

(买包子的人坐下以后……)

B: 看这个包子，皮薄大馅儿，汤汁浓郁，看起来，汤汁和肉馅要冲破包子皮，吃起来微微的咸味。

Instructional Strategies:

1. A video maybe longer than what needs to be taught for predetermined pedagogical purposes. Teachers should watch any selected video before class and decide which part to focus on for listening comprehension practice. Note the length of the selected part of the video, identify the start and end point, and play only the selected segment in class.

2. Zoom's embedded Poll function allows polling up to a maximum of three questions. The selected video segment is conducive to more questions to check for understanding, such as how many buns the guest bought, how much a bun cost, and so on. Poll Everywhere is more appropriate for a survey with more than three questions. Both Zoom's embedded Poll function and Poll Everywhere allow the screen to display the results immediately after students complete the survey.

Breakout Rooms for Grouping Activities

Group work in online breakout rooms allows interaction and negotiation of meaning. The purpose of group work is to get students to talk to their group members, put their Chinese skills to good use, and engage in collaborative work to complete diverse communicative tasks. Using breakout rooms is a recommended alternative to in-person grouping in a regular classroom. It is especially needed and important in large classes. Both Zoom and Blackboard Collaborate Ultra have breakout room functions, and teachers can divide students into groups automatically or manually within these two platforms. If the chosen video conferencing platform lacks the breakout room function, teachers can still use other tools or extensions to group students in different ways. For example, teachers can open several Google Meet rooms, and post each room's hyperlink on the second screen, so students could click to join the assigned room immediately (see Figure 4.11).

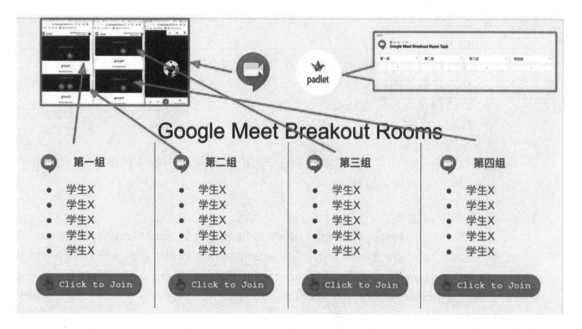

Figure 4.11 Create Groups in Google Meet

Task 8: Which House Would You Like to Pick? 你会选哪个房子？

Communicative Modes: Interpretive, Interpersonal, Presentational
Performance Level: Intermediate-low to Intermediate-mid
Can-do Statements:

    1. Students can describe the interior layout of houses and their surroundings.

    2. Students can compare houses, share their comments, and justify their preference.

    3. Students can ask and respond to questions about the descriptions of the houses.

Authentic Material: Airbnb 爱彼迎 (https://zh.airbnb.com/)
Technology Tools: Breakout rooms and Padlet

Instructions:

Step 1: The teacher shows two houses selected from the Airbnb website.

Step 2: The teacher explains the task as follows.

Task: you are going to take a trip to a foreign city with your classmates in summertime. Compare the two houses selected from Airbnb, choose one that you prefer, and explain why you made such a choice.

Step 3: Divide the entire class into several groups by using the Breakout Rooms function.

Step 4: Students enter the assigned breakout rooms, discuss and compare the two choices based on the following guided questions, reach to a consensus on which house they prefer, and explain why.

1) 这个房子有几个卧室？

2) 这个房子有几个卫生间？

3) 除了卧室和卫生间以外，还有什么？

4) 这个房子可以住几个人？（住得下几个人？）

5) 这个房子看起来怎么样？（大，小，干净，漂亮，新，旧，老，凉，暗，舒适，时尚）

6) 这个房子附近的环境怎么样？

7) 这个房子一个晚上多少钱？贵不贵？

8)（学生自己再加上自己的问题。）

Step 5: Each group of students type their discussions and summative responses on Padlet in their own breakout room.

Step 6: Students return to the main room and present the description about the house they have chosen and explain why. After presenting their choice, each group asks the entire class three comprehension questions based on the content of the presentation (see Figure 4.12):

1) 这个房子有几个卧室和卫生间？还有什么房间？

2) 房子的附近有什么？

3) 说一说你为什么喜欢这个房子？

词汇与语法：

A 比 B (更) + adjective

A 比 B + adjective + 多了（得多）

A 比较 + adjective

A 在 B (的) 左边 / 右边 (location word)

附近，超市，公共汽车，站，地铁，方便，走路，好像，厨房，餐厅，旁边，卫生间，左边，右边，前边，后边，书房，卧室，对面，干净，房子，客厅，院子

Instructional Strategies:

1. To fully engage students, ask them to search on their own and find two to three Airbnb houses they would like to compare and describe.

2. The teacher should create a Padlet link and share it with students before they join the breakout rooms. Nearpod Collaborate is a good alternative that can achieve the same pedagogical functions.

3. To keep learners attentive while listening to their peers' presentations, require each group of students to ask comprehension questions at the end of their presentation. Consider this as part of the daily participation grade.

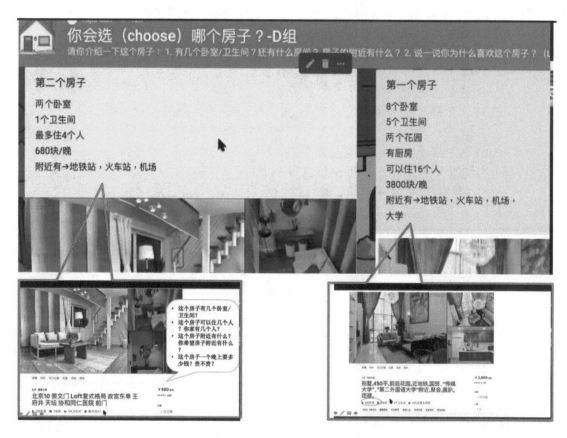

Figure 4.12 Choosing an Airbnb House

Task 9: **Which Chinese Restaurant Would You Like to Recommend?** 你推荐哪家中餐馆？

Communicative Modes: Interpretive, Interpersonal, Presentational
Performance Level: Intermediate-low to Intermediate-mid

Can-do Statements:

Students can exchange information about a Chinese restaurant.

Students can exchange information about the interior of the restaurant and services.

Students can describe the dishes and comment on the flavors and prices.

Students can present and summarize their experiences in eating at a Chinese restaurant.

Students can explain and justify their recommendation for a favorable restaurant.

Authentic Materials: Menu, Pictures of Chinese dishes, and many other objects in a Chinese restaurant

Technology Tools: Breakout rooms and Padlet

Instructions:

Step 1: Pre-task 1

Students eat Chinese food at a local Chinese restaurant and take at least five photos or film different scenes inside the restaurant.

Step 2: Pre-task 2

Students answer the following questions based on their real-life experience.

1) 这家餐馆叫什么名字？餐馆离你家远吗？

2) 你经常去这家餐馆吗？你多久去一次这家餐馆？为什么？

3) 这家餐馆的室内装潢怎么样？

4) 服务员是中国人还是美国人？他们会说中文吗？服务员的态度怎么样？

5) 这家餐馆的拿手菜是什么？味道怎么样？

6) 你经常去这家餐馆吗？你最爱吃什么菜？

7) 这家餐馆的价钱怎么样？

8) 你会推荐这家餐馆给你的朋友吗？为什么？

9) 你觉得你去的这家餐馆比其他的餐馆好吗？为什么？

10) 其他问题。

Step 3: Breakout rooms during Class

1. Students are divided into different groups and join the assigned breakout rooms to show the photos they have collected or the video they have created. They share their experiences verbally while showing the photos or video with their peers.

2. Each group chooses one Chinese restaurant to recommend to others after the discussion and then posts photos and descriptions on Padlet (see Figure 4.13).

Step 4: Main room during Class

All students return to the main room, introduce the recommended restaurant, and explain why they have made the decision and recommendation.

Instructional Strategies:

Teachers should allow students to have options to collect information about the restaurants they want to recommend considering some lower income students may not be able to go to restaurant.

Option 1: Go to restaurants and take photos or videos.

Option 2: Search online and collect photos or videos from restaurants they like.

Option 3: Choose photos or videos of the restaurant from the folder provided by the teacher with materials they can use.

词汇与语法：

餐馆，服务员，态度，室内装潢，整洁，干净，明亮，拿手菜，味道，色香味俱全，咸，淡，酸，甜，辣，点菜，价钱，便宜，贵，推荐

……离……远 / 近

……比……

Figure 4.13 Showing Chinese Restaurants on Padlet

Task 10: Entry into the Customs Area 入境过海关

Communicative Mode: Interpersonal

Performance Level: Intermediate-low

Can-do Statement:

Students can ask and respond to questions by a customs officer at the airport.

Authentic Materials: Photos taken at the airport

Technology Tools: Zoom annotate or Nearpod draw

Instructions:

Step 1: Students take turns to ask and respond to questions in two rounds. Key words needed to respond to the questions appear at the bottom of the teaching slide. The teaching slide shows one question at a time, followed by a blank space for students to fill in a complete sentence as a response (see Figure 4.14).

Step 2: Students take turns to ask and respond to questions in an extension of five rounds. Incomplete sentences are provided at the bottom of the teaching slide with key information left blank. As in Step 1, the teaching slide shows one question at a time to avoid too much information processing.

Step 3: Students create their own questions and responses and negotiate meaning without seeing any language clues on the teaching slide. They take turns to complete a role-play activity in their own words.

Instructional Strategies:

1. While teaching a dialogue, avoid presenting the entire dialogue all at once on the teaching slide. Instead, present one question first and wait for students to come up with their own response. Then show the accurate response on the screen, after students have made efforts to look for the language resources on their own. This allows students to think and process information first, in an active learning process.

2. Follow the three-stage sequence to present information (present), practice with students (practice), and create opportunities for students to work in pairs or groups to complete the conversation (produce). The process starts with the teacher's full control over the learning setting, transitions to a semi-controlled context, and concludes with little or no control from the teacher. The progressive learning process needs to be carefully thought-out and planned before class.

3. The sequence of language clues and information presented on the teaching slides should be well-organized and sequenced with logics and coherence. The combination of the three teaching slides above shows a good instructional flow with needed information provided progressively in each step. This sample activity demonstrates that visual language clues and the teacher's verbal expressions appropriately scaffold learners to meet learning objectives.

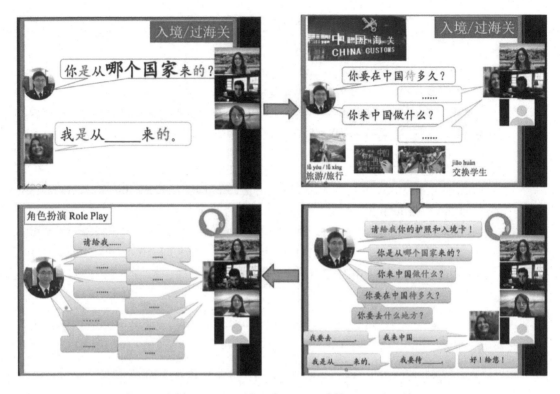

Figure 4.14 Interact with a Customs Officer at the Airport

Task 11: Role Play on Airport Pickup 机场接机

Communicative Modes: Interpersonal and Presentational

Performance Level: Intermediate-low

Can-do statements:

Students can ask and respond to questions with a host family upon pickup at the airport.

Students can present the role-play dialogue at the airport pickup.

Technology Tool: Nearpod collaborate

Instructions:

Step 1: Students work in pairs to complete the role play. Student A plays the role of a host family, and student B plays the role of an exchange student.

Step 2: Students ask and respond to questions aloud while typing the questions and responses on Nearpod Collaborate, according to the scenario provided.

Step 3: After creating the dialogue, students A and B take turns orally presenting the completed dialogue (see Figure 4.15).

词汇与语法：

Scenario: 明年暑假李明要去美国做交换学生，在你家住一年，你去机场接他，你们会说什么？

可以用的词：欢迎，帮，拿行李，睡觉，verb＋过，……从……到……，多长时间，小时，累，吵，高兴，地道

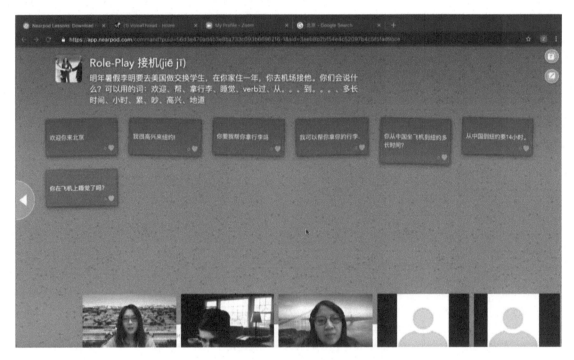

Figure 4.15 Nearpod Collaborate for a Role Play

Task 12: **School Life in China and the US 中美学校的异同**

Communicative Modes: Interpretive, Interpersonal, Presentational

Performance Level: Intermediate-low

Can-do Statements:

Students watch and interpret a YouTube video describing high school student life in China and the United States.

Students discuss the differences of high school student life in China and the United States.

Students can describe and compare the differences of school life in China and the United States.

Authentic Materials: YouTube video

Technology Tool: Breakout rooms in Zoom

Instructions:

Step 1: Students describe what the schedule of a typical school day is like in the United States.

Step 2: Students watch the YouTube video, *Chinese High School Student VS. Western High School Student* (https://www.youtube.com/watch?v=PNZ-u21kVCI)

Step 3: The teacher divides students into different breakout rooms and ask them to discuss the following questions:

1) 中国学生上课以前做什么？美国学生呢？

2) 看到考试成绩 (chéngjì)，中国学生跟美国学生有什么不一样的反应 (fǎnyìng =reaction)？

3) 中国学生周末做什么？美国学生呢？

4) 你的高中生活和电影里那个美国男孩子的一样不一样？

5) 在视频里，中美高中生活还有什么一样的地方？什么不一样的地方？

Step 4: Students return to the main room and share the summary of differences between high schools in the United States and China (see Figure 4.16).

词汇与语法：

Structure 1: 节

节 is a measure word to be used to describe the number of classes in a daily schedule at school such as 一节课. It differs from the usage of 门, which is used to describe how many classes are taken during one semester.

Structure 2: ... 在 + place + do something (verb phrase)

Structure 3: ... verb 1 完 object (or verbal phase) 以后，... verb 2

Structure 4: ……和 / 跟……一样 / 不一样

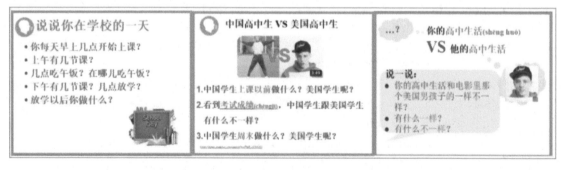

Figure 4.16 Activity About the Discussion of School Life

Video Source: *Chinese High School Student VS. Western High School Student* (https://www.youtube.com/watch?v=PNZ-u21kVCI)

Task 13: **Same or Different?** 一样还是不一样?

Communicative Modes: Interpretive, Interpersonal, Presentational
Performance Level: Intermediate-low
Can-do Statements:

   Students can describe pictures and compare observed differences.

   Students can ask and respond to questions related to the pictures.
Authentic Materials: Pictures for Finding Differences (找不同)
Technology Tool: Breakout rooms in Zoom

Instructions:

Step 1: Students are divided into groups A and B, and each student in group A is paired with a student in group B.

Step 2: Information Gap

   Each student A gets a picture from Google Slide, and each student B gets a different picture from Google Slide.

Step 3: Each pair of students is assigned to a breakout room. Students A and B take turns describing to their partner the picture they have and circling the differences from their partner' s picture on their own picture. Students ask and respond to each other' s questions to confirm the information they discuss.

   1) 这张图有几个人，他们是谁?

   2) 他们长什么样子? 穿什么衣服? 衣服是什么颜色的?

   3) 他们在什么地方? 他们在做什么?

   4) 墙上一共有几件衣服? 衣服是什么颜色的? 衣服上有什么?

   5) 这张图片里还有什么东西?

Step 4: Students compare their pictures, mark the differences, and present their findings to the entire class (see Figure 4.17).

Figure 4.17 Spot the Differences

Image Source: https://kknews.cc/zh-my/game/jrbjr8q.html

Communicative Mode: Presentational (writing and speaking)
Performance Level: Intermediate-low to Intermediate-mid
Can-do Statement:

Students can introduce cultural products, practices, and perspectives of a traditional Chinese festival.

Technology Tool: Text in Zoom annotate

Instructions:

Step 1: The teacher leads the entire class to discuss traditional Chinese festivals and choose one festival they would like to talk about.

Step 2: Students pick their own favorite annotation color and type their name in a self-chosen cell in the following table.

Step 3: Simultaneously, all students type their responses about cultural customs and practices on a traditional Chinese festival. Then they take turns to orally describe and elaborate on what they have typed.

Instructional Strategies:

1. Inviting all students to type simultaneously enhances full engagement. This strategy is time-effective and appropriate for the typing of key phrases and short sentences.
2. Students type first and then describe and elaborate what they type afterward (see Figure 4.18).
3. The design of the table is appropriate for many topics covered at the novice and intermediate levels.

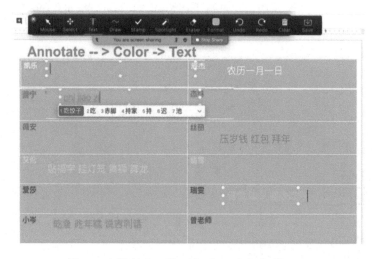

Figure 4.18 Using Text in Annotate in Zoom

Communicative Mode: Presentational (speaking)

Performance Level: Novice-high

Can-do Statements:

> Students can describe what they wear by using appropriate verbs, measurement words, and adjectives.
>
> Students can give comments on different aspects of clothes.

Authentic Materials: Chinese music

Technology Tool: Virtual background in Zoom

Instructions:

Step 1: Pre-task

> Students prepare for a fashion show according to the following instructions.
>
> 1) Determine the outfit to wear "on the runway".
>
> 2) Choose a virtual background photo and show it as the stage set for the fashion show (see Figure 4.19).
>
> 3) Select background music and play it during the fashion show.
>
> 4) Add any pops and accessories whenever appropriate.
>
> 5) Tell your partner what you plan to wear before the show, so he or she can practice how to describe your outfit during the show.

Step 2: Students work in pairs and take turns to complete the show. While Student A runs the show in front of the webcam, Student B describes what he or she wears in as much detail as possible. Then Student B does the same.

Step 3: The remaining students comment on the outfit the student wears after the show.

Step 4: Students vote for the superstar of the fashion show after they all finish the performance.

Figure 4.19 Fashion Show Using Virtual Background

Instructional Strategies:

1. Tell students to be as creative as they can on what they wear for the show. It is totally fine to pick "crazy" outfits that they normally would not wear. But make sure to comply with school policies.

2. Remind students to play the background music at a good volume, so other students can hear the description given by the other student in the same pair.

3. This task requires students to adjust their laptop and webcam before the class, so they can walk around and move freely in front of the webcam. The same concept also perfectly applies to a unit on 做眼保健操 or 做广播体操. Both types of tasks use culturally appropriate authentic materials and involve physical movements that require adjustment of the distance between the webcam and where a student sits, stands, or walks around (see Figure 4.20).

Figure 4.20 Doing Eye and Morning Exercise Using Virtual Background

词汇与语法：

Verbs: two different verbs meaning "wear" that go with different clothes and accessories in Chinese.

穿 wear clothes

戴 wear accessories

Measure words:

件：衣服，衬衫，T恤衫，上衣，外套，大衣，西服

条：裤子（西裤，长裤，短裤，牛仔裤），裙子（长裙，短裙），项链

双：鞋子（皮鞋，运动鞋），袜子，靴子

顶：帽子

Adjectives: 漂亮，好看，大，小，贵，便宜，流行，时髦，时尚，长，短，合适，合身

Required expressions:

因为……

看起来……

我觉得……

Task 16: How to Eat a Hotpot? 怎么吃火锅？

Communication Modes: Interpretive, Interpersonal, Presentational

Performance Level: Intermediate-low

Can-do Statement:

Students can describe the procedure of eating a Chinese hotpot and their experience eating food in a Chinese hotpot.

Authentic Materials: Video of 我们一起吃火锅啊啊啊 *Eating a Hotpot* (https://www.youtube.com/watch?v=xqj-lajSsAI)

Technology Tool: Zoom annotate

Instructions:

Step 1: Students watch the video of eating a hotpot to comprehend the steps of how Chinese people eat a hotpot.

Step 2: Students talk about the ingredients that they would choose（选菜）from the teaching slides and then practice introducing the order in which to put different ingredients into the hotpot (see Figure 4.21).

Step 3: Students describe the procedure by using connectors and time adverbials indicative of sequence that show in the teaching slide, guided by the teacher: 先……，然后……，再……，最后…….

Step 4: Students pick a color, use the "draw" function in Zoom annotate, and use the mouse cursor to write numbers 1, 2, 3, 4 on the teaching slide to indicate the procedure of eating a Chinese hotpot.

Step 5: The teacher plays to video again and ask students to introduce the procedure of eating hotpot in a string of connected sentences (see Figure 4.22).

Figure 4.21 PowerPoint for the Procedure of Eating Hotpot

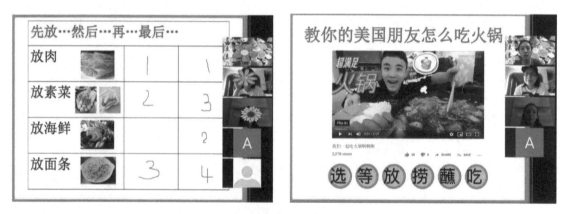

Figure 4.22 Eating a Hotpot

Task 17: **Where do You Want to Go? 你想去哪里？**

Communicative Modes: Interpretive, Interpersonal, Presentational
Performance Level: Intermediate-low
Can-do Statements:

Students can identify locations and facilities on a school map.

Students can introduce school locations and facilities.

Students can ask and respond to questions about school activities and after-school activities.

Technology Tools: Zoom annotate or Nearpod draw

Instructions:

Step 1: The teacher guides students to connect school's facilities with the corresponding activities by using the draw function selected from Zoom annotate, such as "操场",

"游泳池", "篮球场", and so on (see Figure 4.23).

Step 2: Students connect two to three activities by using time adverbial-related devices that indicate action sequence to describe what they want to do after the class: 先……，再……，最后…….

Step 3: Students work as student guides to introduce "Beijing No. 4 High School" to an international exchange student who comes to visit the school. Repeat the process until all students in the class have practiced introducing the high school.

Step 4: The teacher asks students to mark the location names of the corresponding school venues and facilities on the school map using the text or draw function selected from Zoom annotate.

Step 5: Assign students to pairs in which one student plays the tour guide, and the other student plays the exchange student. The "tour guide" starts to introduce the facilities and what students can do at them according to the information just marked. The "exchange student" asks further questions based on the information provided by the tour guide.

词汇与语法：

校园，篮球场，前边，体育馆，放学，有的时候，羽毛球，游泳池，后边，带，游泳衣，操场，真的，橄榄球，墙

Structure 1: 先……，再……

        Subject + 先 + verb 1，再 + verb 2（然后再 verb2）

        Subject + 先 + Verb 1 + 完 + object 以后，再 + verb 2

        Subject + 一 + verb 1 + 完 + object 以后，就 + verb 2

Structure 2: 有的时候……有的时候……

Structure 3: Subject + time+ 就 + verb + 了

Figure 4.23 Using Annotate in Zoom

Task 18: What Did the Teacher Do Last Night? 老师昨天晚上做什么了？

Communicative Modes: Interpretive, Interpersonal, Presentational
Performance Level: Intermediate-low
Can-do Statements:

Students can understand the activities the teacher did last night.

Students can interview the teacher about the activities that he or she did last night.

Students can describe what the teacher did last night by using a string of sentences with appropriate conjunction words and time-adverbials to connect a sequence of actions.

Technology Tools: Annotate draw in Zoom, Nearpod draw, or Poll Everywhere

Instructions:

Step 1: Students guess what the teacher did last night and put a check next to the chosen activities (see Figure 4.24).

Step 2: Students ask the teacher "您昨天 verb phrase 了吗？" to check if their guesses are right and put a check in the parentheses to indicate the activities that the teacher did last night. They erase the check mark for those the teacher did not do.

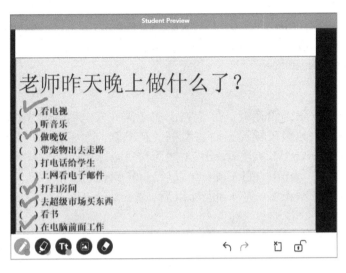

Figure 4.24 Check for Last Night's Activities with Nearpod Draw

Step 3: Students interview the teacher again to get a better idea about the sequence of the activities that the teacher did last night.

Step 4: Students put 1, 2, 3, 4, 5 to indicate the order of actions on the same Nearpod slide. Another option is to use Poll Everywhere to indicate the order of actions (see Figure 4.25).

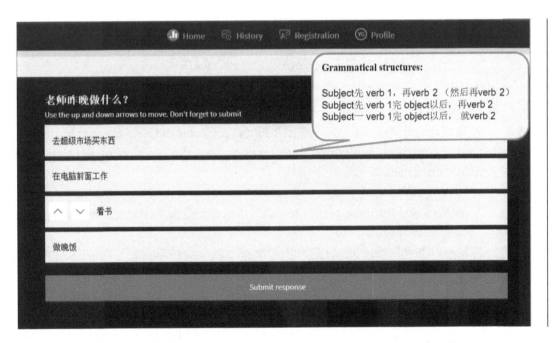

Figure 4.25 Using Poll Everywhere to Indicate a Sequence of Actions

Step 5: Students describe what the teacher did last night in a sequence of actions in order by using appropriate conjunction words and time adverbials to generate a string of connected sentences.

词汇与语法：

看电视，听音乐，做晚饭，带宠物出去走路，打电话给学生，上网看电子邮件，打扫房间，去超级市场买东西，看书，在电脑前面工作

Subject + 先 + verb 1，再 + verb 2（然后再 + verb 2）

Subject + 先 + verb 1 + 完 + object 以后，再 + verb 2

Subject + 一 + verb 1 + 完 + object 以后，就 + verb 2

Task 19: **A Three-day Tour in Beijing** 北京三日游

Communicative Modes: Interpretive, Interpersonal, Presentational

Performance Level: Intermediate-mid

Can-do Statements:

Students can comprehend and interpret information in 3D 全景客，高德地图，大众点评，爱彼迎.

Students can ask and respond to questions after a presentation.

Students can present and describe a three-day Beijing tour with required information.

Students can provide reasons to explain their decisions and choices.

Authentic Materials: 3D 全景客（http://www.quanjingke.com/），高德地图 (amap.com）大众点评 (dianping.com), Airbnb · China（爱彼迎）(https://zh.airbnb.com/s/China)

Technology Tools: Zoom, Google Slides, PowerPoint, or Prezi

Instructions:

Step 1: The teacher helps students frame the task by showing different websites（全景客，大众点评，爱彼迎，and 高德地图）for the project on a three-day tour in Beijing.

Step 2: Students research and collect information about the itinerary of the tour in the following aspects:

1) Choose sightseeing places and specific points of interest for each place. Collect 360° photos for these places from the website 全景客 (http://www.quanjingke.com/).

2) Book a hotel using 爱彼迎 (https://zh.airbnb.com/s/China).

3) Determine where to shop and eat for three meals each day using 大众点评 (dianping.com).

4) Search for transportation means and routes using 高德地图 (amap.com).

Step 3: Students put all the travel information together and organize it according to the following list of "Must Haves" in Google Slides, PowerPoint, or Prezi.

1) A minimum of five sightseeing places in Beijing, with at least three specific points of interest for each site (in a 360° photo) and descriptions of their historic and cultural significance.

2) A hotel and three reasons to justify the choice using 爱彼迎 .

3) At least one store or shop for buying gifts and reasons why (360° photo or regular photos).

4) Restaurants for three meals a day, with at least three authentic dishes to be introduced in color, flavor, and taste (360° photo or regular photos).

5) Transportation means and the routes to go to different locations (screenshot from 高德地图).

6) Estimated cost for each category of expenses and the total of a three-day tour.

Step 4: The teacher hosts a tour information session in Zoom. Each student presents their tour as a tour guide (see Figure 4.26).

Step 5: While each student tour guide gives a presentation, others listen and ask questions to gather more information about the tour.

Step 6: The entire class votes for the best and most highly recommended three-day tour in Beijing.

Figure 4.26 A Three-day Tour in Beijing

词汇与语法：

　　1. 名胜古迹

　　　　一说到……，……就会想到……

　　　　有名 / 著名，以……闻名

　　　　是……建的

　　　　有……年的历史

　　　　是……住的地方

　　　　要是你到北京，一定要去……

　　　　因为……

　　　　不但……而且……

　　　　又……又……

　　　　古老，雄伟，金碧辉煌，庄严绚丽，气魄宏伟，极为壮观，代表中国文化

　　2. 买东西

　　　　在……可以买到……

　　　　好看，好玩，漂亮，有用，不贵，便宜，讨价还价，物美价廉

　　3. 吃饭

　　　　一到北京，我就想吃……

　　　　地道，流口水，色香味俱全，酸甜苦辣

　　4. 交通

　　　　搭地铁，搭公交车，搭出租汽车，走路

　　5. 花费

　　　　人民币，美金，一共 / 总共

Task 20: **Dub a Film Clip** 电影配音

Communicative Modes: Interpretive, Interpersonal, Presentational

Performance Level: Intermediate-low

Can-do Statements:

　　Students can identify key information about a video on high school student life in China.

　　Students can ask and respond to questions about school activities and after-school activities.

　　Students can narrate a short story for a film segment by dubbing.

Technology Tools: Breakout rooms in Zoom and Loom

Authentic Materials: A short film made by students from Beijing No. 4 High School. (https://youtu.be/Ms5Xz-sxX_c)

Instructions：

Step 1: Students watch the video and answer the following questions:

1) 北京四中的学生上午做了什么?

2) 他们在哪儿吃午饭?

3) 下课以后，他们做了什么活动?

Step 2: Guided by the teacher, students complete the dialogue based on screenshot photos that indicate six different scenarios selected from the film clips (see Figure 4.27).

Step 3: Students enter different breakout rooms and work in pairs to complete the film-dubbing task by using Loom as instructed (see Figures 4.28 and 4.29).

Step 4: Students return to the main room and share their dubbing videos.

词汇与语法：

Structure 1: 先……, 再……

Subject + 先 + verb 1，再 + verb 2（然后再 + verb 2）

Subject + 先 + verb 1 + 完 + object 以后，再 + verb 2

Subject + 一 + verb 1 + 完 + object 以后，就 + verb 2

Structure 2: 有的时候……, 有的时候……

Structure 3: Subject + time + 就 + verb + 了

Structure 4: A 比 B + adjective

Structure 5: 要是……, 就……

Figure 4.27 Role Play for Film Clip

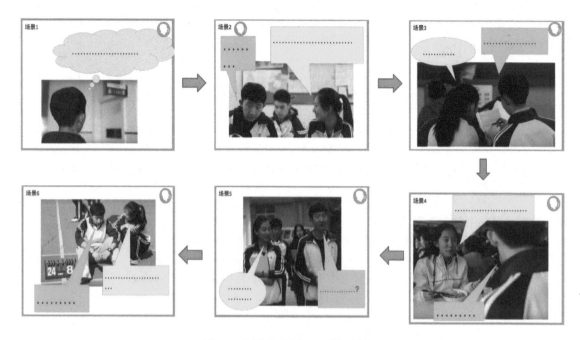

Figure 4.28 Dubbing a Film Clip

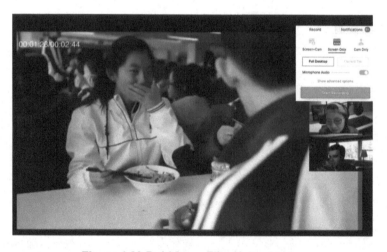

Figure 4.29 Dubbing a Film Using Loom

Task 21: **Narrate a Story** 看图写故事

Communicative Modes: Interpretive, Interpersonal, Presentational
Performance Level: Intermediate-mid to Advanced-low

Can-do Statements:

Students can identify and interpret visual clues in four sequenced photos.

Students can comprehend and interpret stories based on four sequenced photos.

Students can exchange ideas and discuss story lines based on four sequenced photos.

Students can narrate a story with a string of sentences based on four pictures provided.

Authentic Materials: Photos

Technology Tool: Google Jamboard

Instructions:

Step 1: Teacher-guided story writing

1) Each student collects four photos about family or school life and bring them to class. The photos indicate a sequence of four actions and are stored in each student's own Google Jamboard.

2) In class, each student types one to two sentences to describe actions or activities in each of the four photos.

3) The student adds time adverbials and connectors to begin with the story, connect a sequence of actions, and conclude the story.

4) The student adds detailed information about a) adjectives about feeling and mood, and b) adverbial expressions describing unexpectedness.

5) Finally, the student edits the story and submit it to a designated place, so all students in class have access to all stories.

Self-checklist

Name of story writer:_____

Name of editor: _____

Date: _____

The story includes the following required components. Please circle what is included in the list of recommended functions, vocabulary, and structures as follows.

1. WH-information
   1) When
   2) Who
   3) What
   4) Where
   5) How
   6) Why

2. Organization
   1) Beginning, middle, and end
   2) Coherent and progressive development of a series of actions

3. Appropriate language use
   1) Verbs and verbal phrases indicative of a series of actions
   2) Time adverbials and connectors for sequencing a series of actions
   3) Adjectives about feelings, emotions, and mood
   4) Adverbial phrases indicative of surprise or unexpectedness

Overall Rating

Excellent   Very good   Good   In Progress   No submission

Additional Comments:

Signature: _____   Date: _____

Step 2: Peer editing
   1) The teacher assigns partners for peer editing.
   2) Each partner uses copies of the same checklist to give feedback.
   3) Each student shares the completed checklist with their assigned partner(s).
   4) Repeat the same procedure in 1, 2, and 3 to invite learners to get involved in the second cycle of peer editing. The draft story should be edited in at least two rounds.

Step 3: Finalize story writing and peer learning
   1) Each learner receives at least two completed checklists by peers and revises according to the comments.
   2) Each learner uploads his or her final version of the narrated story to a "Story Gallery" where the entire class can view and read them at any time.
   3) The teacher uses a team generator tool to automatically assign three stories for each student to read, appreciate, and comment on.
   4) To comment on peers' stories, each student types two to three sentences at the end of each story.
   These comments should refer to the following adjectives and add move adjectives

and further information:

喜欢，吸引，合理，惊喜，奇怪，有趣，很有创造力，很有想象力……

Sample: 这个故事很吸引人，非常有趣。最特别的地方是他们竟然在烤肉的时候，在后院看到三只兔子跳来跳去，跑来跑去，还给兔子吃红萝卜，真的是太可爱了。兔子是我最喜爱的宠物，我希望今年生日的时候，我的朋友能送我一只兔子。

Step 4: Narrate a story in groups

1) The teacher leads the entire class in taking a quick look at four photos in Jamboard, as depicted in Figure 4.30.

2) The entire class determines the names of the figures in the story and the perspective taken in the story, either the first-person "I" or third-person "third party".

3) Students are divided into several groups and enter breakout rooms to begin to collaborate on story writing. Each group of students sees four pictures in Jamboard and completes the narration of the story.

4) Students return to the main room, take turns reading and editing the stories written by other groups, and finally discuss how to edit their own stories based on peers' comments.

5) Students finalize their stories and submit them to a designated area called "Story Gallery".

Organization and Structures:

1. The beginning of a story

First sentence (when): a sentence with a time adverbial indicative when a certain action took place

Example: 有一天，上个星期六，昨天下课以后

Second sentence (who): a sentence with the names of the story figures and a very short description of a place, a scene, an action, an activity, etc.

Example 1: 我跟小明（约好了）一起 + verbal phrase (a perspective from I)

Example 2: 大生和小明（约好了）一起 + verbal phrase (a perspective from a third party)

2. The middle of a story

Progressive development of a sequence of actions

……的时候……

开始的时候，……

Subject + 先 + action 1, 然后 / 然后（再）+ action 2

一边 + action 1 + 一边 + action 2

1st sentence, 然后 , 2nd sentence

Verb + 完 + object 以后……

一 + 1st verbal phrase, 就 + 2nd verbal phrase

3. The end of a story

最后，结果，结局，终于

4. Expressions indicative of unexpectedness

没想到，突然，忽然，居然，很意外地

5. Expressions related to feeling, emotion, and mood

觉得，感到，看起来

很 / 有点 / 非常 / 十分 / 相当 + adjective

太 + adjective + 了

Adjective + 极了 / 得不得了

Adjectives: 生气 / 紧张 / 着急 / 兴奋 / 开心 / 高兴 / 难过 / 意外 / 惊喜 / 害怕

急急忙忙，匆匆忙忙，不慌不乱，不急不徐，慌慌张张，惊慌失措，欣喜若狂，格外兴奋，惊喜万分，兴高采烈

又 + adjective/verb + 又 + adjective/verb

不但 + adjective + 而且 + adjective

Adjective 得 + 像 + noun + 一样 (急得像热锅上的蚂蚁一样)

6. Others

因为……，所以……

虽然…… 可是 / 但是……

1st sentence, 于是 (= 所以) 2nd sentence

First sample story narration (an estimated score of 4 for story narration in AP Chinese)

今天晚上王星和天一彼此踢足球。王星踢球踢到一个房子的花盆。王星和天一感到很害怕，因为花盆的主人可以很生气。因为王星太害怕了，所以要赶快回家。天一告诉他 "我们一定要说对不起和给他一盆花。" 然后他们一起去买了一盆花和去他的家说对不起。他们看到花盆的的主人说 "你好！ 我们踢足球不小心踢到你的花盆。我们来你的家说对不起，这是我们送你的花。" 花盆的主人很高兴地："没关系！ 你们都是好孩子！ 。"

Second sample story narration (an estimated score of 6 for story narration in AP Chinese)

大生和小明是高中同学，他们约好了这个周末去足球场踢足球。当他们玩得兴高采烈的时候，大生一不小心用力过猛，足球意外地飞出去就砸到了足球场对面一户人家的阳台上的花盆。大生和小明都惊慌失措，因为大生紧张又害怕所以他想马上走人，想逃避砸破花盆的责任。但是这时候小明拉住了他，让他和自己一起去给那户人家赔偿道歉。大生自己也觉得非常惭愧。 他们决定先一起去买一盆花，然后回来赔给这家人。 大生和小明两个人捧着买

回来的新花盆一起找到了那户人家。两个人不但向主人表达了深深的歉意，而且还把新买的一盆花送给他作为赔偿。令人高兴的是花盆的主人不但接受他们的道歉，而且称赞他们是诚实的好孩子。大生看到花盆的主人原谅了他们顿时感到身上轻松了许多。在回家的路上，大生格外开心地对小明说："谢谢你及时拉住了我，让我做了一个勇于面对自己错误的人。"

(Note: The first sample story is at the intermediate-mid level. However, a good story typically reveals language proficiency at the advanced level, as indicated in the second sample story. Although it is rare that AP Chinese learners can reach the advanced level of proficiency, it is completely achievable to develop proficiency levels of intermediate-mid and intermediate-high upon completion of the course.)

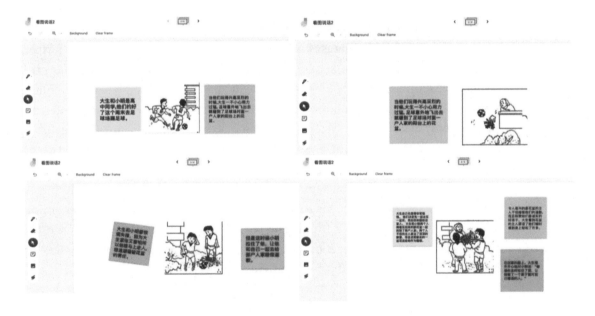

Figure 4.30 Google Jamboard for Story Narration

Image Source: http://www.23book.com/400000/397029.shtml

Instructional Strategies:

1. Narrating a story is a complex process that requires multifaceted language skills. Step 1 involves teacher-guided writing and illustrates step-by-step instructions in accordance with the "i + 1" principle. It begins with one to two simple sentences that describe action verbs in each photo and then connect simple sentences with conjunction words and time adverbials to sequence a series of actions. This is a

very important preliminary stage required for novice learners to move toward the intermediate level. Repeat the procedure to get learners accustomed to the usage of cohesive and coherent devices to organize ideas, thoughts, and sequential actions.

2. Expanding the amount of vocabulary is key to the development of advanced language proficiency. An advanced learner is typically characterized as a storyteller, and telling a story requires a wide range of vocabulary. It is important to expose learners to different scenarios of stories, so students can build the ability to use different types of verbs, actions, and related vocabulary and idiomatic expressions.

3. A story has three parts: beginning, middle, and end. Advise learners to start with a sentence that frames the time element first, and follow with another sentence to identify the characters and setting of the story based on picture clues. The middle part of the story involves appropriately chosen action verbs and vocabulary in accurate responses to the prompts. This is an area that requires more elaboration and detailed description before the end of the story.

4. Mastering time adverbial phrases and connectors moves learners one step further to being able to connect a sequence of actions and spiral up toward the pre-advanced level. The usage of adverbial phrases and connectors indicates the ability to organize and sequence actions, and transition from one to another in a coherent story. Through constant and systematic learning, learners can write a well-organized story by employing coherent and progressive devices to connect a sequence of actions.

5. Using adjectives to describe feelings, emotions, and mood seems subtle but is crucial for story narration. A story normally involves a reaction to something unexpected or unpredicted. It triggers affective change. A story is not well-written without the inclusion of such aspect of detailed descriptions. It is necessary to help learners to go beyond the commonly used adjectives such as 高兴, 快乐 and develop the ability to describe the turn and tweak of 喜怒哀乐 (happiness, anger, and sadness).

Task 22: **Watch a Film and Play Kahoot! 看电影玩 Kahoot!**

Communicative Modes: Interpretive, Presentational
Performance Level: Intermediate-mid
Can-do Statements:

Students will be able to understand the main ideas of the movie clips.

Students will be able to provide detailed information about the movie clips watched.

Authentic Materials: Movie video clips of 和你在一起 *Together 02* (https://www.youtube.com/watch?v=T8sFEazunRo&list=PL5EOtUzsZK5Gqr2xN60XiQ0HoChfzpwec&index=2)

Instructions:

Before Class

The teacher adds five film segments to the Kahoot! site (the section at 11:00 to 14:00) with four corresponding multiple-choice questions and one open-ended question. Note that the video captions have a typo: the main character's name that should be 小春 instead of 小村 (see Figure 4.31).

1. 小春一进门的时候，江老师叫他做什么？ (film segment: 10:54–11:08)

　　1）洗脸

　　2）洗手

　　3）洗脚

　　4）洗碗

2. 小春拉小提琴的时候，江老师叫小春做什么？ (film segment: 11:08–12:30)

　　1）专心拉小提琴

　　2）吃点心喝水

　　3）好好休息

　　4）帮忙做东西给小猫吃

3. 小春从床底下找到了什么东西？ (film segment: 12:30–13:32)

　　1）照片

　　2）袜子

　　3）镜子

　　4）衣服

4. 小春为什么离开老师家，不拉琴了呢？ (film segment: 13:32–13:50)

　　1）不喜欢拉琴。

　　2）老师叫他做别的事情，没教他拉琴。

　　3）想找别的老师教他拉琴。

　　4）老师不知道怎么教学生拉琴。

5. 你觉得江老师是一个什么样的老师？ (open-ended question)

　　请把你的答案打出来。

In Class

1. Watch the film to gather background information.

　　The teacher shows the film before the segment of 11:00–14:00 and leads the entire class to discuss and predict what they will see from the film.

2. Get ready to enter the Kahoot! site.

　　The teacher shows the Kahoot! website link and code on the screen. Students go to https://kahoot.it and enter the code.

3. Watch the film with focused questions.

Remind students that the captions have a typo and that main character's name should be 小春 instead of 小村. Students begin to watch each film segment and answer each corresponding question. The question and answer choices will be visible on the screen while they watch the film segments.

4. See instant results.

    After students answer each question, the Kahoot! site automatically generates the top three winners and will do the same at the end of the game. The teacher and the entire class congratulate the winners to conclude the game.

5. The teacher leads the entire class to discuss the responses to the open-ended question, and the characters, plots, and significant Chinese values relevant to the film.

6. Narrate a story.

    The entire class leaves the Kahoot! site and transitions to the teaching slides that the teacher prepares before class. The teaching slides include all the questions and accurate responses that students can use as prompts to connect a sequence of actions about the film. Students add connectors and time adverbial expressions to complete the story. Refer to Task 21 to see effective strategies for story narration.

Instructional Strategies:

1. Interactive games are fun, interesting, and engaging. After the game is over, proceed with follow-up activities to integrate and consolidate what is covered in the game, so students have opportunities to reflect on their learning and gain the most out of the process.

2. Kahoot! is highly recommended as the platform for this task. In comparison with Kahoot!, interactive videos created on PlayPosit, Edpuzzle, or H5P can achieve several pedagogical functions, but they are created for independent learning, not for team competition involving the entire class. Videos created through these alternatives also do not automatically play live music during the game, and learners cannot see questions until the video pauses. Kahoot! games and interactive videos serve distinctive pedagogical purposes, and teachers can choose the aspects and functions that are best suited for their local classroom.

3. To create a Kahoot! game with a film, teachers need to determine the start and end points of each film segment and set up proper time limits for response time (see Figure 4.32).

4. In addition to multiple-choice questions for a quiz, Kahoot! can also offer true/false, open-ended questions, puzzle, poll, and slide functions that give players additional explanation or contextual information. Each question type can go with or without a film, at the discretion of teachers.

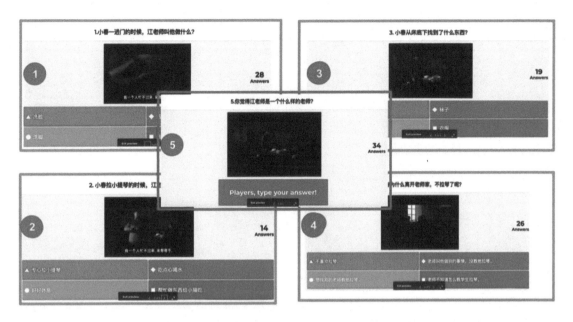

Figure 4.31 Questions for Watching *Together 02*

Figure 4.32 Add Video in Kahoot!

Chapter 5
Asynchronous Teaching and Technology

Asynchronous teaching requires teachers to prepare learning materials ahead of time. Regardless of delivery mode, asynchronous learning provides more flexibility than synchronous learning, as students can learn and complete a variety of tasks at their own pace before and after class time. It helps students to digest and engage in more depth with the learning materials, allowing the synchronous online teaching sessions to be more thought-provoking and interesting. If well designed, asynchronous learning can be as engaging and effective as synchronous learning, as the tasks in this chapter demonstrate. Although asynchronous teaching gives students the opportunity to learn from anywhere and at any time, designing online learning materials can be challenging for teachers. This chapter introduces a list of well-tested student-centered communicative tasks, enhanced by technology tools and effective teaching strategies for teachers to make offline learning meaningful and productive with their students.

Asynchronous Videos

Asynchronous videos offer rich content and create human connections. They are another channel through which students can connect with the course, with the teacher, and with learners in the online community. Language classes are different from subject-based classes, because the development of language skills requires genuine communicative situations and a community of learners with a variety of learning styles, including visual, audio, physical or verbal. In the online setting especially, given these unique needs, asynchronous videos play a powerful role: they enable teachers to save hours of repetitive teaching, give individual feedback on students' work, and satisfy the needs of differentiated instruction. Useful categories of videos for asynchronous online teaching include welcome videos, instructional videos, and videos for giving announcements, instructions on assignments, and feedback.

Welcome videos give students the opportunity to get to know their teachers prior to the start of the class. This creates a social presence, which is so important in an online course. When students are able to know the teachers from the welcome video, they can more easily connect with the teachers emotionally and are more likely to enjoy the online learning experience.

It is easy to embed welcome videos into the LMS for an online class. Teachers can record them easily with a professional camera, smart phone, or web camera. Video editing programs, such as WeVideo, iMovie, Windows Movie Maker, can help make welcome videos more attractive and professional.

The leading instructors in UVA STARTALK created their own individual welcome videos, which not only gave the warmest welcome to the teaching fellows but also demonstrated how teaching fellows can create their own videos (see Figure 5.1).

Figure 5.1 Program Welcome Videos for UVA STARTALK

It may be challenging for some teachers who have never done this, or for those who don' t feel comfortable talking in front of the camera. An alternative is for teachers to record a slideshow with still photos as a welcome or intro video. Animation effects can be automatically added to welcome videos through cartoon figures. The UVA STARTALK Teacher Program also created a video like this through Biteable, a do-it-yourself video making platform (see Figure 5.2).

Figure 5.2 Biteable Welcome Videos for UVA STARTALK

Following are some suggestions for creating a welcome or intro video for your online Chinese language course.

- Make it short: limit it to three to four minutes.
- Show your personality and make yourself approachable. Adding personal information such as your family and hobbies is a plus.
- Create a script or outline to help keep your video brief.
- Make eye contact with your audience by looking into the camera or webcam. Don't stare at the script or watch yourself on the computer.
- Add visual aids whenever possible.
- For an introductory video, teachers may include information about how to start with this course and class expectations on behavior and participation.
- Use the target language to create videos for intermediate and advanced Chinese language classes.

Recording Live Lecture Videos

Flipping the classroom begins with recording live lectures, which all synchronous conferencing platforms would be able to achieve easily using the recording function. (See Figure 5.3 for instructions on the Zoom meeting recording function). Sending recorded lectures to students allows them to pause and watch the video repeatedly if they do not understand it completely or need to skip a class for whatever reason. With recorded lectures, students can pause the video, watch the lesson multiple times according to their learning pace and needs. In UVA STARTALK, each synchronous teaching session was recorded and shared with students and teachers right after teaching ended. Teachers could use video conferencing platforms as recording tools to create the lecture videos. Please note, when recording live lectures, it is important to comply with school policies and ensure no violation of privacy or confidentiality.

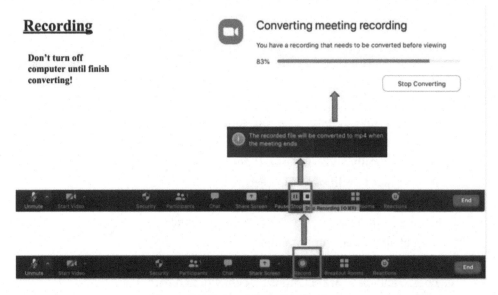

Figure 5.3 Record Function in Zoom

Pre-recorded Lecture Videos

Considering its content delivery method, the pre-recorded lecture video is probably the best alternative to live lectures. Pre-recording a video lesson allows teachers to teach at a time that is best for them and also allows students to learn at a time that works best for them. The pre-recorded lecture video with the teacher's visual image resembles live instruction, enabling students to feel a connection with the teacher. This further supports the social and cognitive presence that is so essential and critical for creating a successful learning experience.

Videos for Giving Announcements, Instructions, and Feedback

Sending class messages to students via email is probably the most common way of communication between teachers and students, in all types of delivery modes. As learning transforms to partially or mostly online, different modes of message delivery need to be considered to offset the absence of F2F live communication. Regular video announcements are a welcome component in online teaching. They are more engaging and effective than sending email messages alone.

While giving instructions and feedback, teachers should also consider creating a short video in lieu of or along with typed textual instructions. This is a thoughtful way to consider the diverse needs of learners in processing information and cognitive load. Being able to see the teacher's face and listen to what the teacher says offers one more channel of information delivery, in addition to reading typed textual announcements in whatever form. In 2019 UVA STARTALK, the instructional team created video assignment instructional videos along with typed textual instructions for after-review tasks in speaking and writing. Information delivery in a combination of different stimuli — visual, audio, and audiovisual — accommodates diverse learning styles and allows learners to process information most suitable for their individual needs and comfort zone (see Figures 5.4 and 5.5).

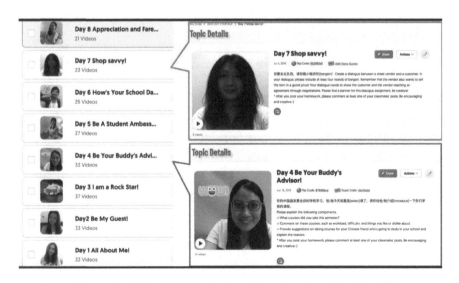

Figure 5.4 Videos Giving Instructions for Speaking Tasks

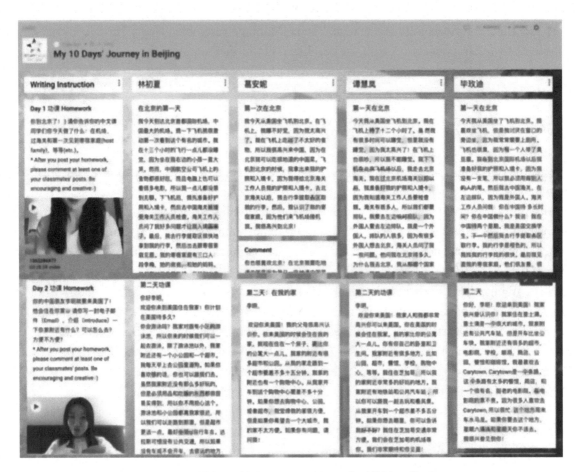

Figure 5.5 Videos Giving Instructions for Writing Tasks

Student-centered Tasks in Three Communicative Modes

Asynchronous learning keeps student-centeredness at the heart of design for both traditional and online learning. There are numerous advantages to adding asynchronous learning to online language courses. Asynchronous learning provides opportunities for students to preview before class and review after class. The former fosters flipped learning and helps learners get well-equipped with needed knowledge and skills, based on which they can apply what they have learned before class and engage in class activities. This not only saves class time but also maximizes learning outcomes. The latter reinforces in-class learning through after-class review work in different forms to consolidate different aspects of learning. Technology tools, when appropriately chosen, can help online language courses create the best possible learning experience for learners.

Following are field-tested student-centered communicative tasks in three communicative modes with recommended technology tools and apps, accompanying strategies, and illustrations. It is impossible to do them all in one class; choose those that you feel comfortable and familiar with. Always put the needs of your local classroom and learners at the center of your consideration.

Task 1: Figurative Meaning of Idioms 成语的喻义

Communicative Mode: Interpretative
Performance Level: Intermediate-mid to Intermediate-high
Can-do Statement:
   Students can comprehend and interpret the figurative meaning of Chinese idioms.
Technology Tool: Quizlet flashcards

Instructions:
Step 1: The teacher decides how many Chinese idioms to be used for a set of flashcards.
Step 2: The teacher creates a new study set for the selected Chinese idioms, clicks "Term" to add the Chinese idioms, and clicks "Definition" to add the figurative meanings of the Chinese idioms (see Figure 5.6).
Step 3: The teacher assigns this set of flashcards to students to study by sending a shareable link.

Figure 5.6 Quizlet Digital Flashcards for Chinese Idioms

Image Source: quizlet.com

Task 2: What is in the Study Room? 书房里面有什么？

Communicative Mode: Interpretative
Performance Level: Intermediate-low
Can-do Statement:

Students can identify and match items with appropriate location and position words in existential sentences.

Technology Tools: Quizlet interactive diagram

Instructions:

Step 1: The teacher creates or finds an image or photo with all the study room items for students to learn.

Step 2: The teacher uploads the image into the interactive diagram.

Step 3: The teacher clicks "Add a point" and then "Term" and "Definition" to add the language items. See the sample existential sentences with language items in Table 5.1.

Table 5.1 Study Room Terms

Term	Definition
东边的墙上有……	一幅中国画
西边的墙上有……	一幅中国书法
屋顶上有……	一盏吊灯
小桌子上有……	一台电脑
咖啡桌上有……	一套茶具
书架上有……	四本中文书
地板上有……	一盆花
书桌上有……	一个砚台

Step 4: The teacher assigns this learning activity to students through a shareable link.

Step 6: The teacher tells students to practice the study set of "书房里有什么？" with the function of Learn, Write, Spell, and Match in order to achieve the best learning outcomes, because Flashcard or Gravity could not show the interactive diagram (see Figure 5.7).

书房里面有什么?

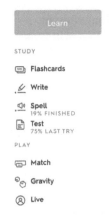

Figure 5.7 Interactive Diagram

Image Source: quizlet.com

Instructional Strategies:

1. Many teachers use Quizlet for vocabulary learning, but it can also be extended to sentential levels in meaningful and communicative contexts as illustrated in the Interactive Diagram (Figure 5.7).
2. Other strategies to push up to the sentential levels include question and answer, fill in blanks, matching lines for a dialogue, and so on.

Task 3: Rearrange Word Order 字词顺序重组

Communicative Mode: Interpretative
Performance Level: Intermediate-low
Can-do Statements: Students can identify the accurate word order of different components in 把 (*Ba*) structures.
Technology Tool: Quizlet

Instructions:

Step 1: The teacher prepares all sentences with 把 structures for students to work on.

Step 2: The teacher creates a set of *Ba* sentences in a Quizlet set. Click "Term" to add different lexical items that are not in accurate order and then click "Definition" to add complete sentences with accurate order (see Figure 5.8).

Step 3: The teacher sets the language so both term and definition are in Chinese (see Figure 5.9).

Step 4: The teacher shares the study set with students using a shareable link.

Step 5: Students can review and practice with these sentences using the Learn and Write function.

Instructional Strategies:

1. The teacher follows the following steps to create the study set:

   1) Click "Term" to add different lexical items that are not in accurate order, such as "大家 / 请 / 作业本儿 / 把 / 拿出来".

   2) Click "Definition" to add complete sentences in accurate order, such as "请大家把作业本拿出来".

   3) Click "Choose Language" to set up "Chinese (Simplified)" for both "Term" and "Definition" to make sure the study set would only show "Term" and "Definition".

2. To achieve learning goals, remind students to do the following:

   1) Review the study sets with the "Learn or Write" function in Quizlet.

   2) Choose the "Answer with definition" option to start the review activity.

Without these steps, students would have access to the complete sentences in accurate order.

Terms in this set (7)		Original ⌄
大家/请/作业本儿/把/拿出来/。	请大家把作业本儿拿出来。	★ ◄ ✎
护照/把/我/丢了/。	我把护照丢了。	★ ◄ ✎
想/我/把/美元/人民币/换成/。	我想把美元换成人民币。	★ ◄ ✎
吧/把/关上/门/。	把门关上吧。	★ ◄ ✎

Figure 5.8 Rearrange Word Order in Quizlet

Image Source: quizlet.com

Figure 5.9 Choose Language for Term and Definition

Task 4: Flipped Learning Through Interactive Videos 课前翻转学习的互动视频

Communicative Modes: Interpretative, Interpersonal
Performance Level: Intermediate-low
Can-do Statements:
    Students can comprehend the content of a short conversation with a host family.
    Students can engage in a conversation with a host family and visitors in appropriate manners.
Technology Tools: PlayPosit, Edpuzzle, or H5P

Instructions:
Step 1: The teacher records the asynchronous lecture video of "有客人" according to the teaching content.
Step 2: The teacher creates the activity starting with "Add New Bulb" from the PlayPosit.

Step 3: The teacher uploads the video resources into PlayPosit and then chooses the options of interaction type (for example, question type), to check for understanding. The following short dialogue between a hostee and his or her host family shows a set of comprehension checks created by three question types for an interactive task: fill in the blank, multiple choice, and free response.

    1) [Fill in the Blank]

        Susan 是从美国到中国的 (   ) 学生。

    2) [Multiple Choice]

        王宁是谁的同学？

        1. Susan 的同学 2. 李明的同学

    3) [Multiple Choice]

        朋友 A: 你的中文老师教你唱过中文歌吗？

        朋友 B：(   )

        1. 不教过我唱中文歌 2. 教我唱过中文歌

    4) [Multiple Choice]

        中国人喜欢去 KTV 做什么？

        1. 跳舞 2. 唱歌 3. 睡觉

    5) [Free Response]

        你去过 KTV 唱歌吗？

    6) [Multiple Choice]

        如果我唱歌唱得不好，我希望别人 (   )。

        1. 别哭我 2. 别笑我 3. 别爱我

Step 4: The teacher reviews the activity after placing the interaction type and decides on the playback options, or ways students can complete this task.

Step 5: The teacher can save and exit after one more preview and share this activity with students.

Step 6: The teacher can check the scoring report right after students complete it.

Instructional Strategies:

    1. Teachers can select any video available from a popular channel or record their own videos.

    PlayPosit accommodates the following six question types: multiple choice, free response, poll, check all, fill in the blank, and discussion. These can be used to check for comprehension in listening, reading, and writing, but not in speaking. The content of the questions can focus on learning in vocabulary, grammar, and different aspects of learning as identified by the teacher.

    2. PlayPosit allows teachers to create multiple versions of a video for differentiated instruction. With this tool, teachers can conduct formative assessments, introduce

new topics, review concepts, and increase students' engagement and accountability (see Figure 5.10).

Figure 5.10 Flipped Learning for a PlayPosit Interactive Video

Image Source: playposit.com

Task 5: My Host Family in China 我的中国家庭

Communicative Mode: Interpretive

Performance Level: Novice-high

Can-do Statement:
Students can comprehend and interpret different sources of authentic materials in a culturally appropriate way.

Technology Tools: Google Forms or Nearpod quiz

Instructions:

Step 1: The teacher creates a Google Form with question items related to "我的中国家庭".

Step 2: The teacher sends out the link to students for them to complete and submit the responses.

Step 3: The teacher clicks the "Responses" and checks automatically generated reports with grades and statistics from the Google Form.

Instructional Strategies:

1. Many language teachers have experience in creating Google Forms for students to complete a survey to check for understanding or gather feedback on the course. Google Forms can include many types of questions, such as short answers, multiple

choice, checkboxes, dropdown, linear scale, multiple choice grid, and checkbox grid. The teacher can also create a Dropbox for students to upload their projects.

2. To make the assessment fun, meaningful, and engaging, the teacher can embed multimedia resources such as images with captions, audio clips, or videos in the target language into the Google Form. Students can engage in interpretive communicative activities or upload recordings or writing assignments in the presentational communicative activities.

3. The following screenshot shows an inherently motivating game called "Escape Room" (密室逃脱) that was created with multimedia authentic materials to check for understanding about learning materials in a topic on "我的中国家庭". Students enter each Lock Room to complete a task based on a stimulus provided. When students answer correctly and see "You Escaped — Nice Work", they can continue to enter the next Lock Room to try another activity. If they answer incorrectly, then the screen will show "Sorry Still Locked", and students will return to the same Lock Room to try it again with or without seeing explanatory notes for a review. Whether students see the notes or not depends on how the teacher sets up the game (see Figure 5.11).

4. The "Escape Room" game is good for items with fixed answers, but not those with free responses. Although the task described here is targeted at the Novice-high level for a topic on Chinese host family, it is also appropriate for formative or summative assessments in all topics across all levels.

Figure 5.11 Google Form Assessment on "Escape Room"

Image Source: kodamabutts.tumblr.com

Task 6: I Am a Rock Star 我是摇滚明星

Communicative Modes: Interpretive, Interpersonal, Presentational
Performance Level: Intermediate-low
Can-do Statements:

> Students can comprehend and interpret Chinese songs.
>
> Students can sing a Chinese song.
>
> Students can interact with their peers by commenting on their recorded songs.

Technology Tool: Flipgrid

Instructions:

Step 1: Pre-Task (Teachers)

> 1) Set up a Flipgrid educator account.
>
> 2) Create a Grid for each Chinese class.
>
> 3) Create a topic with added instructions under the Grid.
>
> 4) The teacher shares the Flipgrid URL with students (e.g., flipgrid.com/FlipCode). Students then use their school email, any self-created email, student ID, or QR code to join and click the green plus sign to record a video. Students can record multiple times and upload the video that they feel most satisfied with.

Step 2: Pre-task (Students)

> Students pick a song from the list of Chinese songs provided by teachers and practice singing it with the accompaniment of music and lyrics.
>
> Scenario: 你是一位美国的交换学生，今年暑假在中国学习中文，今天你到中国朋友家做客。大家吃过晚饭后打算一起去卡拉 OK 唱歌，于是你准备了一首歌准备一展歌喉。
>
> Option 1: Choose a karaoke version of a Chinese song on YouTube and record your singing for at least 90 seconds.
>
> Option 2: Choose the melody of a favorite English song, replace the English lines with Chinese lyrics, and then record yourself singing.

Step 3: During Task

> Students start recording their singing multiple times and upload the video that they feel most satisfied with. Each student watches peers' flipgrid singing and comments on at least three of their classmates' songs with compliments in Chinese.

Instructional Strategies:

> 1. The Grid can be visualized as a classroom. Create a name for each Grid to match each class. The teacher should select two options for students to access the Grid in Grid Type. First, use students' school emails and add multiple email domains as needed, such as emails ending with @stu.school.edu, @school.edu, or @teacher.

school.edu. Second, add a student ID that is easy for students to remember, such as names in Pinyin. The best option for younger learners to access the Grid is to use their ID or their personal QR code, rather than an email account.

2. Flipgrid is a great tool that helps students develop speaking skills. Creating a Flipgrid video is fun, interesting, and engaging. Although teachers can provide written instructions for students, it is highly recommended that teachers model the task and give instructions in a Flipgrid video.

3. Teachers may record a Flipgrid video themselves, ask native speakers to record, or search for video from YouTube and other internet resources.

4. In addition to watching the instructional video, students can follow up by clicking the "Immersive Reader" button. This allows students to read the introductions in the target language (Chinese characters) and practice listening through reading aloud (see Figure 5.12). The immersive reader provides a full-screen reading experience to increase the readability of content. Students can choose to have the text read aloud, select individual words to be pronounced in Chinese, or select words to be translated into English or Chinese.

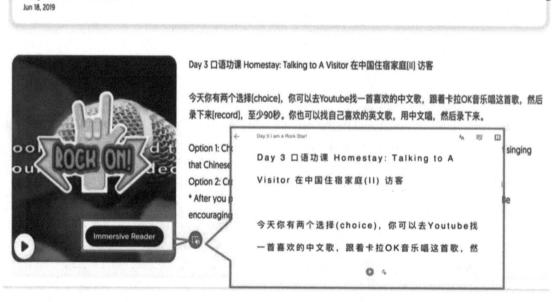

Figure 5.12 Karaoke in Flipgrid

Image Source: flipgrid.com

Task 7: My 10-day Journey in Beijing 北京十日游记

Communicative Modes: Interpretive, Interpersonal, Presentational

Performance Level: Intermediate-mid to Intermediate-high

Can-do Statements:

Students can post their logs to describe their 10-day trip to Beijing.

Students can comprehend and interpret logs posted by their peers.

Students can interact with their peers by commenting on their posted logs.

Technology Tools: Padlet or Nearpod collaborate

Instructions:

Step 1: The teacher creates a Padlet account and clicks "Make a Padlet" to create the written task of 10 days' Journey in Beijing.

Step 2: The teacher sets up the Padlet to be "Shelf Format", and uses "Modify" to turn on comments.

Step 3: The teacher posts instructions in each of the 10-day columns. The top of each column shows each individual student's name, so the logs posted by each student can be easily tracked vertically (see Figure 5.13).

Step 4: The teacher shares the Padlet link with students for them to post their writing homework.

Step 5: Students read their peers' posts and comment on at least three posts from Day 1 to Day 10.

Instructional Strategies:

There are two ways to organize students' work. The first is to organize the column with each student's name, so students can stack their writing journals and show their progress (see Figure 5.13). The other is to organize the column with different topics for students to share their writing with other students on any given topic.

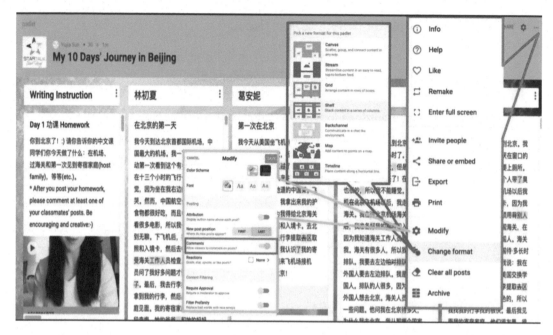

Figure 5.13 Writing Journal in Padlet Shelf

Image Source: padlet.com

Task 8: **Make Dumplings 包饺子**

Communicative Mode: Presentational
Performance Level: Intermediate-mid to Advanced-low
Can-do Statement: Students can explain the procedure of making dumplings.
Technology Tool: Adobe Spark

Instructions:

Step 1: Students watch a video of making dumplings and discuss what they should prepare before making dumplings. 怎么包饺子？ (https://spark.adobe.com/video/PljZt9OWLbti5)

Step 2: Students list the ingredients and amounts that they should prepare for making dumplings.

Step 3: Students list the steps on the Google Doc by using guided structures.

Step 4: Students collect photos and video clips, which they have recorded or found on YouTube, upload them into Adobe Spark, and add instructions in Chinese.

Step 5: Students record the cooking procedure in Chinese for each slide.

Step 6: Students click "Adobe Spark" to generate and upload the video (see Figure 5.14).

词汇与语法：

先……，再……，然后再……，然后……，最后，……

把＋something＋放在＋something里 (location word)

包饺子材料

饺子皮：水、面

饺子馅料：蔬菜（洗净、切碎，放少许盐，等10分钟）

肉馅（可选猪肉、牛肉、羊肉、鸡肉……）

调味料：糖、酱油、盐、芝麻香油、葱花、姜末、花椒粉、白胡椒粉

包饺子步骤：和面，搅拌，均匀，揉，醒面，擀饺子皮，加入，适量，对折，从右边开始，捏，捏紧，封口处，煮开水，放入，加凉水，捞出来

Figure 5.14 Video on Making Dumplings Using Adobe Spark

Task 9: **Exit Slips**"出口"通关任务

Communicative Mode: Presentational

Performance Level: All levels

Can-do Statement: Students can present and describe what they have learned to exit class.

Technology Tool: Book Creator

Instructions:

Step 1: The teacher clicks "Create a new library" from Book Creator to set up the library for students to join.

Step 2: Students join the teacher's library using the Book Creator code provided by the teacher.

Once students join the library, they can see all books created by their peers.

Step 3: Students create their own new book in the library, including a book cover with a title in Chinese and their Chinese name (see Figure 5.15).

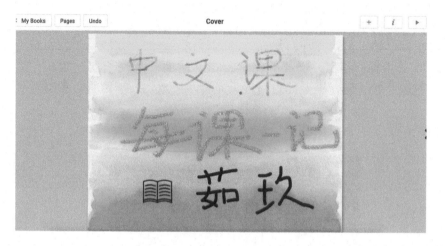

Figure 5.15 Book Cover for Exit Slips

Step 3: The teacher clearly communicates the following requirements.

1. Time: 5–10 minutes reserved at the end of class.
2. Grading: Discrete and accumulative points.
3. Required content: 1) three things they have learned, 2) two things they are interested in, 3) one question they have.

Step 4: Students design the layout, graphics, and any other artistic aspects of their own book.

Step 5: Students complete one or more than one of the following aspects of tasks, chosen by the teacher or negotiated with students: 1) typing in Chinese characters; 2) oral recording in Chinese; 3) adding images; 4) adding hyperlinks; 5) drawing; and 6) adding any other creative elements (see Figure 5.16).

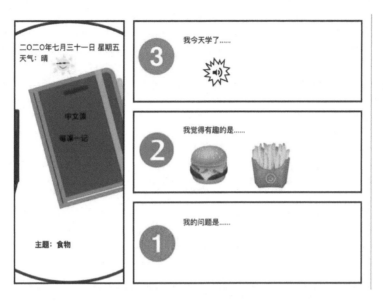

Figure 5.16 Exit Slips Using Book Creator

Instructional Strategies:

1. The teacher can assign this project at each class or as a regular task in most classes.
2. Students start working on the exit slip task at the reserved end-of-class time and continue to work on it as homework if incomplete during class time.

Task 10: **A Virtual Tour in My Hometown 我的家乡虚拟游**

Communicative Mode: Presentational (writing)
Performance Level: Intermediate-mid to Intermediate-high
Can-do Statement: Students can describe landmarks and places of interest in their hometowns.
Technology Tool: Google Tour Builder

Instructions:

Step 1: Pre-task

The teacher introduces the task as follows.

Scenario: You have a Chinese pen pal who lives in China. He or she has never visited your hometown in the United States. You plan to introduce at least four landmarks. For each landmark, you plan to collect at least three pictures or one video. You are also looking for one photo or image to appear on the cover page. The description includes the following aspects of information.

城市的位置和历史

城市的气候 / 交通 / 环境

城市的人和他们的故事

城市的名胜古迹

城市的动物园 / 公园 / 博物馆 / 娱乐中心

城市的购物中心 / 餐厅 / 酒店

其他

Step 2: Students log in to the Google Tour Builder account and create a Tour title that includes the name of the hometown.

Step 3: Students add a cover photo and descriptions of the chosen photos or videos.

Step 4: Students share the link with the teacher and their classmates after completing the editing.

词汇与语法：

位置在……

总人口约……

是……的城市之一

使这里成为……的城市

最早的

最……的

可以一边……一边……

修建于……

Figure 5.17 Virtual Tour Using Google Tour Builder

Instructional Strategies:

1. Google Tour Builder adds locations using Google Street View, which has both "Street View" and "Photo Sphere" functions (see Figure 5.17). The former allows learners to view maps with interactive panoramas from different angles at the street level, and the latter allow viewers to view 360 degree images. Both functions are available for American maps and locations, but only "Photo Sphere" is available for Chinese locations. Adding a description of the route of a tour is a viable option for Google Tour Builder.

2. The virtual tool is designed for learners to generate long essays. Encourage learners to describe each landmark as extensively as possible. It is created mainly for typing, not for speaking.

Task 11: **A Dream City in China 我梦想的中国城市**

Communicative Mode: Presentational (writing and speaking)
Performance Level: Intermediate-mid to Intermediate-high
Can-do Statements:

Students can describe a virtual trip to a Chinese city they have never been to.
Students can provide reasons why they like a city.

Technology Tool: Google Tour Creator

Instructions:

Step 1: The teacher introduces the task with the following scenario.
（城市名）是你非常向往的城市，你从来没去过。现在你打算用 Tour Creator 先去那个城市看看，准备一共要待五天。请你先介绍一下这个城市的地理位置和人口，然后选择几个地方来介绍这里的美食、住宿、交通、购物和旅游景点，并且说明你为什么选择这几个地方。

Step 2: Students log into the Tour Creator account and start to create a virtual tour by clicking "New Tour".

Step 3: Students create a name for this virtual trip with the city's name in it, for example 香港之行 or 到香港旅行, and upload an image as the cover photo.

Step 4: Students add the location and population information of the city on the cover page.

Step 5: Students introduce at least four scenes, each with three points of interest in text and audio. Students could add 3D images either from Google Map Street View or uploaded from their own computers.

Step 6: Students share the link with teachers and students once completed.

词汇与语法：
一直想去……可是……

从没去过……
位于……
人口
面积
打算
游览……旅游景点
打算吃……美食
打算住在……酒店
打算去……逛逛 / 观光
打算去……买……礼物 / 纪念品

Figure 5.18 Virtual Trip Using Tour Creator

Instructional Strategies:

Tour Creator differs from Google Tour Builder in several ways (see Figure 5.18). First, it is not suitable for long essays in typing, so short descriptions are encouraged. Second, both text and audio recording are compatible, so students should be encouraged to add both typed text and accompanying audio files for focused points of interest. This resembles real-life experiences for many 360-degree tours in real worlds. Third, the former is designed to view full scenes in 360 degrees, and the latter is to view scenes in detail such as stores, restaurants, bars, and others at identified location points.

Task 12: Weather Forecast Report 天气预报

Communicative Mode: Presentational
Performance Level: Intermediate-low to Intermediate-mid
Can-do Statement:
    Students can present a five-day weather forecast report at a simulated TV station.
Technology Tool: WeVideo

Instructions:

Step 1: The teacher introduces the task scenario as follows:

    A local TV station in Chinatown is looking for a weather forecast reporter. See job requirements below.

    1. Speak Chinese fluently.

    2. Work independently to compile weather information and create daily weather reports. (Need to bring a sample weather forecast video clip.)

    3. Present weather forecast for five days.

    4. Mail a sample weather forecast video clip to the TV station for review.

Step 2: Students start to compile weather information and draft their report for the weather forecasting video.

    See a sample weather forecast report below.

观众朋友晚上好，现在是一周天气预报时间。

X 月 X 日，星期一，多云，白天到夜间最高气温……，最低气温…… 西北方 5 ～ 6 级。

X 月 X 日，星期二，晴天，……
X 月 X 日，星期三，刮大风，……
X 月 X 日，星期四，大雨转中雨，……
X 月 X 日，星期五，暴风雨，……

今天的节目就到这里，各位观众，再见！

Step 3: Students log into WeVideo to create a new video and upload images or videos with information such as weather symbols, graphics, pictures, maps, background music, and so on.

Step 4: Students organize weather information and narrate the weather forecast report (see

Figure 5.19).

Step 5: Students play the role of the TV news producers: they determine selection criteria, watch the videos, and vote on the top candidates for the job.

Figure 5.19 Weather Forecast Using WeVideo

Task 13: **Chinese Cultural Capsules 中国文化胶囊**

Communicative Modes: Interpretive, Interpersonal, Presentational
Performance Level: Intermediate
Can-do Statements:

Students can understand and interpret Chinese culture in terms of product, practices, and perspectives.

Students can describe their experiences and thoughts about Chinese and American cultures.

Students can engage in a series of discussions about the differences in American and Chinese cultures.

Technology Tool: VoiceThread

Instructions:

Step 1: The instructor finds a cultural video, upload it to VoiceThread, and provides guided questions that link to the uploaded video.

Step 2: Students type responses or record themselves speaking to communicate with classmates about the topics and questions provided (see Figure 5.20).

Step 3: Students comment on the video itself or on their peers' opinions.

Session 1 Guided Questions

    a. 你去过美国／中国的 KTV 吗？

    Have you ever been to any KTV club in China or the United States?

    b. 美国的 KTV 和中国的有什么不一样？

    According to what you've seen from the video or your own experience, what are the differences between KTV clubs in China and in the United States?

    c. 中国的年轻人喜欢跟朋友去 KTV 玩儿，美国年轻人平常喜欢跟朋友去哪儿玩？做什么？

    Clubbing in KTV is a popular way of hanging out with friends among young people in China. How about the young people in the United States? Where and what do you usually do with friends?

    d. 要是你去中国，你会跟你的朋友去中国的KTV吗？在KTV，你想做什么？

    Would you like to go to KTV with your friends in China one day? If so, what would you like to try in China's KTV clubs?

    (Video from https://www.youtube.com/watch?v=NabWfeqzFF0)

Session 2 Guided Questions

    a. 你学过中文 "客套话" 吗？你知道哪些中国人常常说的 "客套话"？他们什么时候说这些客套话？

    Have you ever learned any polite words in Chinese? Do you know any polite words that are used by Chinese people? In what context will those words be used?

    b. 你误解过中国人的 "客套话" 吗？要是曾经有些误解，请跟同学们分享一下有趣的经验。

    Have you ever misunderstood any Chinese polite words？ If so, could you share interesting experiences about this?

    c. 美国人说不说 "客套话"？说一说美国人常常说哪些 "客套话"？什么时候会用这些客套话？

    Do Americans also use polite words in daily communication? What polite words do you often say and what contexts will you use them?

    (Video from https://www.youtube.com/watch?v=amHQdJlVO1A)

Session 3 Guided Questions

    a. 你在美国吃过哪些中国菜？美国中餐馆的中国菜怎么样？分享一下你在美国吃中国菜的经历。

    What Chinese cuisine have you tried in the United States? How was the food in Chinese restaurants in the United States? Share some experiences of eating in Chinese restaurants here.

    b. 你去过中国吗？吃过哪些中国菜？中国的中餐馆和美国的中餐馆有什么不同？

    Have you been to China? Have you eaten Chinese food in Chinese restaurants in

China? What are the differences between the Chinese restaurants in the United States and in China? Any fun experiences to share?

c. 要是你的美国朋友第一次吃中国菜，你有什么建议要告诉他／她？

What's the advice would you like to offer to your American friends who wants to try Chinese food in a Chinese restaurant for the first time?

(Video from https://www.youtube.com/watch?v=Xn_bI4z6OfI)

Session 4 Guided Questions

a. 你收到的礼物当中，最酷的礼物是什么？是谁送给你的？什么时候送给你的？

What's the coolest gift you've ever received? Who gave it to you, and under which situation?

b. 现在你最想要的礼物是什么？为什么？

What's the gift that you want most now? Why?

c. 你想从中国带什么东西回美国？

If you could bring something precious back to the United States from China, what do you want most?

(Video from https://www.youtube.com/watch?v=6IUu6IkqVS8&list=RD8RDyN I3ENsw&index=5)

Session 5 Guided Questions

a. 北京人早餐常常吃什么？你吃过这些中国的早餐吗？美国人常常吃什么早餐？中国人吃早餐的习惯和美国人有什么不同？

According to the video, what do people in Beijing eat for breakfast? Have you tried any Chinese breakfast? What do Americans usually eat for breakfast? What are the differences between American breakfast and Chinese breakfast?

b. 在电影中，这个老外在早餐店遇到了哪些中国客人？他们做什么工作？哪个客人给你的印象最深刻？为什么？

In the video, the foreigner has met many Chinese customers in the breakfast restaurant. What do they do for living? Which customer's story impresses you the most?

(Video from https://www.youtube.com/watch?v=Qfv2PRw-2fs)

Session 6 Guided Questions

a. 电影中的学校在哪儿？在这个学校里，学生们的家庭背景和生活有什么特别的事情？

Where is the school that foreigners visited? Anything special about the students' family backgrounds and their lives?

b. 电影中的中国学校生活和你的学校生活有什么不同？

Any differences about the school life that you observed in the video from school life in the United States?

c. 电影中的孩子有很多梦想，哪个梦想让你印象最深刻？你的梦想是什么？
The students in the video talked about their dreams. What impresses you the most? What's your dream in the future?
(Video from https://www.youtube.com/watch?v=8RDyNI3ENsw&list=RD8RDy NI3ENsw&start_radio=1&t=0)

Figure 5.20 VoiceThread on Cultural Discussion

Image Source: voicethread.com

Instructional Strategies:

1. A diversity of multimedia resources can be uploaded to VoiceThread as stimuli or prompts, including video, voice recordings, text, photos, images, PowerPoint slides, and so on. They can be used to create different types of activities in interpretive, interpersonal, and presentational communicative modes.

2. VoiceThread is an excellent discussion tool for language-focused and culture-related learning. It encourages self-paced learning and allows differentiated instruction to take place. Please refer to Chapter 6 to see more teaching strategies.

Task 14: Show Your Store 展示你的店铺

Communicative Mode: Interpretive, Interpersonal, Presentational

Performance Level: Intermediate-mid to Intermediate-high

Can-do Statements:

Students can introduce and describe their store, including name of the store, employees, interior design and layout of the store, items for display and sale, and other relevant information.

Students can comprehend different types of information about stores.

Students can provide reasons for choosing their favorable stores.

Technology Tool: CoSpaces

Instructions:

Step 1: The teacher shares the following scenario with students.

你要在中国城开一家有中国特色的小店。现在你要决定：

— 店铺的名字

— 工作人员

— 店铺播放的音乐、家居摆设、商品陈列的方式等

— 经营的产品种类、尺寸、价格（至少要介绍 5 个商品，每个商品都要有文字介绍）

— 市场营销：传单、橱窗摆设、店内广播宣传和广告

— 顾客意见栏

Step 2: The teacher signs up for a teacher account, and create a "Collaborative Project" called "展示你的店铺" for students to collaborate by adding all students in one group (see Figure 5.21).

Step 3: The teacher assigns each student to one space for the store using the post labeled in CoSpaces (see Figure 5.22).

Step 4: Students log into the CoSpaces account and immediately see the assignment that the teacher created before class. (Students should join the class first using the code shared by the teacher if they are not in the CoSpaces class.)

Step 5: Students start to create their own stores in Chinatown with all the required information.

Step 6: Students visit all stores created by their peers and vote for their three favorite stores by posting their comments in the customer feedback area.

Sample

各位亲爱的顾客：

上午好，欢迎光临 XXX 店，XXX 店所有员工向您表示最真诚的问候。感谢您对 XXX 店的热爱与支持，我们会继续为顾客们提供最优质的服务，让您满意。

我们的工作人员一共……位，每位员工都非常认真负责，接受过严格的培训，非常了解商品与顾客的需要。商店里干净明亮，又现代又时尚，非常适

合全家人一起购物。店里有舒适的按摩椅，可以一边听音乐，一边按摩，另外，还有一个儿童游戏区，也有服务人员帮忙照顾孩子，让您专心购物。我们经营的商品物美价廉，有……价格……

今天的促销商品是……

数量有限，欲购从速！

最后，祝您购物愉快！

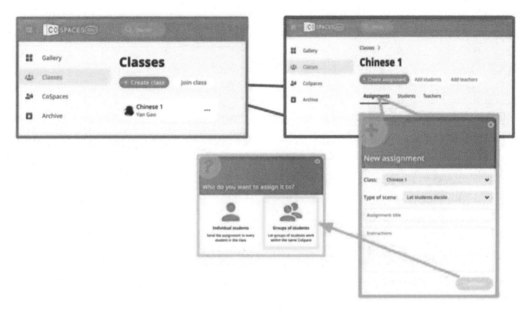

Figure 5.21 Creating Collaborative Project Using CoSpaces

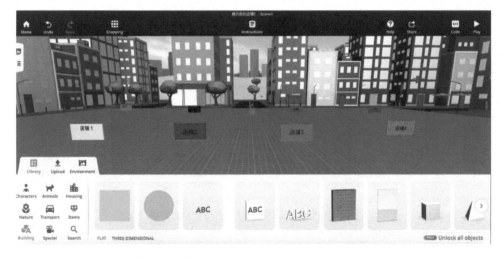

Figure 5.22 Assign Spaces from CoSpaces

Task 15: **Design a 3D Dream House** 设计一个理想的房子

Communicative Modes: Interpretive, Interpersonal, Presentational
Performance Level: Intermediate
Can-do Statements:

> Students can describe their dream house including layout, rooms, placement of furniture, and appliances.
> Students can comprehend the 3D dream house videos created by their peers.
> Students can interact with their peers as home designers by commenting on the 3D dream house videos.

Technology Tools: Loom, Padlet, and the homestyler website (https://www.homestyler.com/int/)

Instructions:

Step 1: The teacher leads the entire class to view the homestyler website (see Figure 5.23).

Step 2: The teacher records a tutorial video of the homestyler website to demonstrate how to design the dream house.

Step 3: Students log into the homestyler website and design the house with the specific information required: layout of the house, room, furniture, appliances, and comments.

Step 4: Students record and narrate the description of the dream house after they complete it.

Step 5: Students share the video link with the teacher.

Step 6: The teacher shares all students' videos uploaded into the shared Padlet.

Step 7: Students watch all 3D videos created by their classmates from the shared Padlet and comment on at least three dream house 3D videos.

词汇与语法：

> 我理想的房子……
> 正门，侧门，后门，层，间，楼上，楼下，卧室，浴室，洗手间，洗澡间，客厅，厨房，餐厅，车库，沙发，椅子，书架，相框，咖啡桌，镜子，舒适，明亮，干净，现代，时尚，时髦，漂亮，宽敞
> 不但……而且……
> 虽然……可是……
> 又……又……
> ……在……旁边 / 右边 / 左边 / 中间 / 前面 / 后面
> 房间里有……
> ……在……右边 / 左边 / 前边 / 后边 / 上边 / 下边
> 桌子上放着 / 挂着 / 摆着……

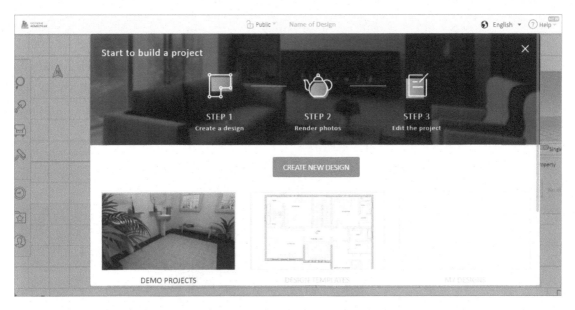

Figure 5.23 Homestyler Website for Creating Dream House

Task 16: **Facebook Communication 脸书交流**

Communicative Mode: Interpersonal
Proficiency Level: Intermediate
Can-do Statement:
   Students can exchange ideas and share comments with others in Facebook.
Technology Tools: Facebook or any social media

Instructions:
Step 1: The teacher creates a group as a community and invites students to join (see Figure 5.24).
Step 2: Students click the link provided by the teacher to join the group and start communicating with others through prompts and postings.
Step 3: The teacher assigns a topic each day for students to discuss, and each student takes turns to leading the discussion about that topic.
Step 4: Students comment on at least three of their classmates' posts for each topic.

Instructional Strategies:
   1. Provide an orientation to the students to make sure they could use the tool appropriately and purposefully to serve your course.
   2. Remind students of social media etiquette and digital citizenship to make sure they present professionally in the online community.

3. Research the accessibility and privacy policies and support site information to ensure that students can use them within the course.

4. Clearly explain grading criteria and expected participation rate with students before the social activity. Making it completely voluntary may result in a very low participation rate.

Figure 5.24 2019 UVA STARTALK Discussion Community at Facebook

Chapter 6

Technology Resources

Technology tools can support online language learning by enhancing motivation, fostering engagement, maximizing learning outcomes, and achieving productivity. They enable teachers to differentiate learning to cater to individual needs, save instructional time, and encourage cooperative behavior. But the prospect of learning how to use these tools can be daunting, especially for language educators who are grappling with such a wide array of tools and applications. Therefore, it is crucial to wisely select and use technology to empower language learning. To appropriately incorporate technology, teachers must make sure to choose tools whose functions are in close alignment with curricular goals and learning objectives. It is best to use tools that are familiar and have proven pedagogical effects. Avoid using unfamiliar technology tools that have not been tested in the language classroom. Technology can be too fancy to keep the focus on learning, so be cautious and evaluate technology with an eye to enhancing language learning rather than distracting from it.

There are tons of technology tools, but "less is more" is always a good principle, considering that most language educators are on a tight schedule that leaves little time to learn the newest tools. It is best to focus on those you are already using and to explore adding functions to satisfy your teaching needs. Many technology tools have very similar functions, so rather that spending time to learn new tools and applications, which may take away focal time on teaching and planning, stay with those that you know very well and keep checking for updates and new functions. It is better to introduce students to only one new tool at a time. Introducing too many technology tools in a language class suggests that the emphasis is on technology learning instead of on language learning, and should therefore be avoided.

This chapter is not intended as a tutorial of technology tools, but as a guide to help teachers navigate the settings and features of technology tools and make good decisions as they consider selecting them. The technology tools discussed in this chapter are grouped into categories based on how they serve language teaching and learning (see Table 6.1). Each tool is introduced individually with explanations of what it does and how you can use it in the classroom, along with a screenshot of the tool in use.

Table 6.1 Applications and Functions of Technology Tools

Technology Tools	Mode	Main Functions
Video Conferencing Platforms • Zoom • Google Meet • Blackboard Collaborate Ultra • Microsoft Teams	Interpretive Presentational Interpersonal	Synchronous online teaching Pre-recording videos Office hours/Tutorial meetings Archive of recorded synchronous sessions
Interactive Whiteboards • Google Jamboard • Microsoft Whiteboard • Whiteboard.fi	Interpretive Presentational Interpersonal	Interactive whiteboard for synchronous and asynchronous tasks Collaborative activities
Pre-recorded Content Videos • Zoom • Loom • Hippo Video • Panopto • Screencastify • Screencast-O-Matic	Presentational	Welcome video Giving announcement/instruction/feedback Student presentational task
Interactive Activities • Nearpod • Pear Deck	Interpretive Presentational Interpersonal	Interactive activity games for checking for understanding and collecting assessment results
Gaming Shows • Quizlet • Kahoot! • Gimkit	Interpretive Presentational	Gaming to check for understanding (vocabulary, grammatical structures, reading comprehension, etc.)
Polls and Surveys • Google Forms • Poll Everywhere	Interpretive	Poll or survey to check for understanding and collect assessment results Instant results
Interactive Video Platforms • Edpuzzle • PlayPosit	Presentational Interpretive	Instant feedback and scoring Interactive comprehension checks
Story Creators • Book Creator • StoryJumper	Presentational Interpersonal	Story creation to show presentational skills in writing and speaking

Technology Tools	Mode	Main Functions
Collaborative Spaces		Instructional lecture
• VoiceThread	Interpretive	Student presentation
• Flipgrid	Presentational	Role-play/debate/discussion
• Padlet	Interpersonal	Oral presentation
• WeVideo		Collaborative activities
3D or 360° Tours		
• CoSpaces Edu	Interpretive	
• Google Tour Builder	presentational	Virtual tour
• Tour Creator	and interpersonal	

Video Conferencing Platforms

Video Conferencing Platforms are like cloud classrooms in which teachers and students to teach and learn online. In recent years, some incredible video conferencing platforms have come along to make online teaching more thorough and efficient. Many teachers already use different platforms, because of school expectations, familiarity, and so on. While each meeting platform has different features, teachers can still achieve the same teaching goals in any of the platforms, with the help of auxiliary tools. Knowing the features of video conferencing platforms is essential for good online instruction.

A comparison of the features of the most popular video conferencing platforms is helpful for teachers deciding which to use for their own teaching strategies (see Table 4.1). Some practical tips for using platforms based on Zoom and Google Meet are shared here.

Zoom

Website: https: //zoom.us/
Platform: Web, iOS, Android
Communication Modes: Interpretive, Presentational, Interpersonal
Similar Tools: Google Meet, Blackboard Collaborate Ultra, Microsoft Teams

Practical Tips:

Zoom is a video conferencing meeting platform that allows teachers to host a synchronous online class of up to 40 minutes and up to 100 participants with a free account. If it' s your first time using Zoom, sign up for an account first, schedule your class in the Zoom application for the desired date and time, and copy the invitation details to send to students. Please note that students will not need to register for an account to join.

In order to teach effectively, do the following before starting an online language teaching session (see Figure 6.1):

1) Enable Personal Meeting ID (PMI), which provides students a stable online classroom. Teachers can share the PMI with a unique class passcode for each class. Before starting a class, the teacher should check the passcode to make sure it is correct for that class.

2) Enable Chat for all or host only, which allows meeting participants to send a message visible to all participants or not. This feature will allow teachers to design different interactive activities; please refer to Chapter 4 Task 2: You Act, I Guess 你比我猜 (Hobbies 爱好) and Task 3: Pictionary 猜成语 . Disabling the Private Chat is recommended for young students, who may be distracted by it.

3) Enable Nonverble feedback and Meeting reaction would allow students to be active and participate with the teacher instantly. Students in a meeting can provide nonverbal feedback and express opinions by clicking on icons in the Participants panel. Meeting reaction allows students to communicate without interrupting by reacting with an emoji that shows on their video. Reactions disappear after 10 seconds. Please refer to the activity from Chapter 4 Task 4: True or False 真真假假 .

4) Enable Share screen, Annotate, and Whiteboard, which allow the host and participants to share their screen or content during meetings. These features allow students to complete more interactive activities by using Draw or Text on the screen or whiteboard. Please refer to Chapter 4 Task 5: Class Schedule 课程表 ; Task 6: How to Write a Chinese Home Address? 中国的住址怎么写 ?;Task 10: Entry into the Customs Area 入境过海关 ; and Task 14: Traditional Chinese Festivals 中国传统节日 .

However, teachers should consider when to allow students to share and annotate according to the teaching purpose and class management concern. The teacher should disable these features when students are not using them, especially for young learners, to reduce unnecessary distractions.

5) Breakout Rooms in Zoom is a powerful function that allows the teacher to work on the group students into separate, smaller rooms. Teachers set this feature to assign participants to breakout rooms when scheduling, which is convenient for planning ahead. Various interactive activities need Breakout Rooms in Zoom. Please refer to Chapter 4 Task 8: Which House Would You Like to Pick?

你会选哪个房子？; Task 9: Which Chinese Restaurant Would You Like to Recommend? 你推荐哪家中餐馆？; Task 20: Dub a Film Clip 电影配音 .

6) Turn on the virtual background feature, which allows the teacher to display an image or video as the background during the synchronous online teaching time. Virtual backgrounds are useful in private video calls, as well as in the Zoom setting. The teacher needs to find all needed images or videos and add them into the virtual background, and then select the one to be presented (see Figure 6.2). The virtual background makes the video conferencing more engaging and creative, and allows the teacher to make it appropriate for a specific topic. For example, a Beijing photo can be a virtual background for a class on a trip to China (see Figure 6.3). Teachers should be mindful that virtual backgrounds should be for educational purposes and distraction-free. When teaching a specific topic, teachers can utilize theme-specific backgrounds — real situations that match the teaching topic. These offer students a sense of consistency and a creative reminder of the topic of the class. Other ideas for virtual backgrounds in synchronous teaching include virtual background images or videos as instructional boards.

7) The teacher can change the feature settings instantly from the Zoom meeting room, which is a convenient way to adjust the settings to fit different activity requirements (see Figure 6.4).

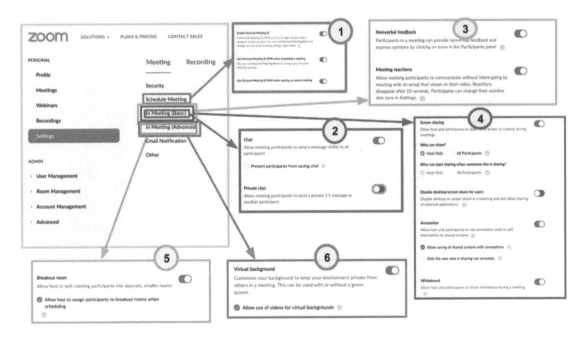

Figure 6.1 Setting Up Preferences in Advanced Settings

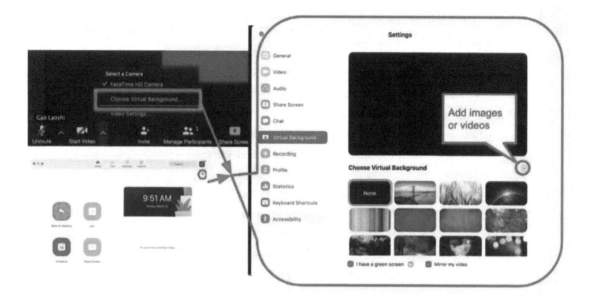

Figure 6.2 Zoom Virtual Background Setting

Figure 6.3 Virtual Background for Beijing Trip

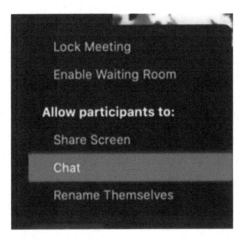

Figure 6.4 Feature Settings from Zoom Meeting Room

Google Meet

Website: https://meet.google.com/
Platform: Web, iOS, Android
Communication Modes: Interpretive, Presentational, Interpersonal
Similar Tools: Blackboard Collaborate Ultra, Microsoft Teams, Zoom

Practical Tips:

Google Meet is a simple video conferencing meeting platform. There are not a lot of settings the teacher should worry about. The teacher could follow the steps here to start an online meeting (see Figure 6.5):

1) Go to https:// meet.google.com (or open the app on iOS or Android, or start a meeting from Google Calendar).
2) Check the audio and video settings to make sure everything is working well.
3) Click "Start new meeting", or enter your meeting code.
4) Click Join or Present to start the online teaching time. If you click Join, you will be in the Google Meet room without sharing anything. If you click Present, you should decide what you would like to share now.
5) You need to decide what to share (tabs, entire screen, or application window).

The teacher can use Google Meet to:

1) Share the screen to present teaching materials.
2) Allow students to chat from the chat box to make interactive activities.

However, Google Meet lacks certain features needed for making interactive activities or grouping activities. To compensate, the following suggestions are to help the teacher to make these activities:

1) The teacher could download a separate virtual background app, such as ManyCam, Snap Camera, or CamTwist (https://www.lifesize.com/en/video-conferencing-blog/virtual-backgrounds).

2) Interactive whiteboard and annotate functions can be achieved in Google Meet through the Google Jamboard.

3) The teacher could open multiple Google Meet rooms and share the link for each one, so students can click and join, and then to be grouped in different Google Meet rooms.

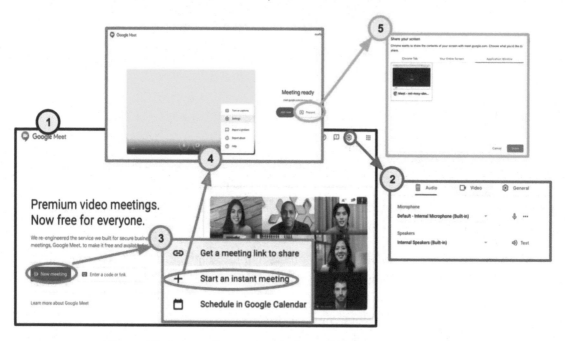

Figure 6.5 Steps to Start a Google Meet Online Teaching Session

Interactive Whiteboards

A collaborative, real-time tool, the interactive whiteboard is essential to online teaching because it allows students to interact with the learning material in ways that increase and focus their attention, collaboration, and engagement. The interactive whiteboard is needed when starting a video conferencing meeting or working on prerecorded lecture videos. Many video conferencing meeting platforms conveniently include an interactive whiteboard; among these are Zoom, Blackboard Collaborate Ultra, and Microsoft Teams. Google Meet has also announced its plans for the feature updates although it currently does not have an interactive whiteboard. However, if teachers are not satisfied with the integrated whiteboard tool, an outside interactive whiteboard tool can be used in the class along with the main platform. There are plenty of interactive whiteboard options for the teacher to choose according to their teaching purpose (see Table 6.2).

Table 6.2 Interactive Whiteboard Options

Function	Whiteboard in Zoom	Jamboard	AWW	Whiteboard.fi	Deskle	Miro
Log in	Zoom login	Google login ·	No login/ Google login	No login	Sign-up needed	Google login
Sharing via	Zoom platform	Url link	Url link/ Email/ Embedded	Url link/ Room code	Url link/ Email	Url link/ Email
Draw	Yes	Yes	Yes	Yes	Yes	Yes
Text	Yes	Yes	Yes	Yes	Yes	Yes
Image/PPT/ PDF	No	Image	Image/PPT/ PDF	Image	Image/GIF	Image/ GIF/PDF
Shape	No	No	Yes	Yes	Yes	Yes
Sticky note	No	Yes	Yes	No	Yes	Yes
Background	No	Yes	No	Yes	Yes	Yes
Export	PNG	Image/PDF	Image/PDF	PDF	Image	Image/ PDF
Chart	No	No	No	No	Yes	Yes
Comment	No	No	No	No	Yes	Yes
Create area	No	No	No	No	Yes	Yes

An interactive whiteboard can be used for a variety of online teaching activities.

1) Use the whiteboard as a traditional whiteboard to allow students to write or type sentences or stories on the board at the same time using the assigned area. This most often happens during synchronous online teaching time.

2) Students could use the whiteboard to draw while telling the story to practice their speaking skills and listening skills (refer to Chapter 4 Task 3: Pictionary 猜成语).

3) The teacher could upload an image into the interactive whiteboard and ask students to describe it in detail in the target language while circling or drawing on the image (refer to Chapter 4 Task 21: Narrate a Story 看图写故事).

4) Students can practice their listening skills by drawing or writing (typing) out according to what the teacher or other students talked about.

5) The teacher can upload a bingo game background photo for students to draw "X" and play bingo.

Pre-recorded Content Videos

Creating videos is important for both synchronous and asynchronous online teaching. Online language classes are different from subject-based classes, because development of language skills requires real communicative situations with a variety of learning styles including visual, aural, physical, or verbal.

Pre-recorded videos serve two crucial functions in online classes: equity and effective learning. In terms of equity, they meet the needs of students who can't attend class at the scheduled meeting time or who have unstable or weak internet access. They also offer multiple and flexible ways for students to engage with the course material, in accordance with the principles of Universal Design for Learning.

Videos structure and deliver content in ways that align with student attention and expectations. Even more importantly, prerecorded videos enable a flipped classroom: when students watch these videos before or after class, the in-class time can be more fully devoted to interaction, which is so important for language learning especially. Students can watch the videos before class to prepare, and after class to review; this latter function is especially important in classes that move quickly or that introduce key content via lecture. Finally, with videos that they can play and replay, students can engage at their own pace, which is necessary for those who need or want more time to process the material.

Videos can be used in a variety of ways in language teaching: please refer to the examples in Chapter 4. It is thus helpful to know how to make different types of videos for teaching purposes. A general process for pre-recorded videos follows:

Step 1: Evaluate and test existing recording software in accordance with pedagogical purposes.

Step 2: Choose a recording software with which you feel most familiar, comfortable, and competent.

Step 3: Organize different types of authentic materials and other teaching materials to create teaching slides.

Step 4: Finalize narration notes to match teaching slides.
Step 5: Start recording with a high-quality camera and microphone.
Step 6: Edit the video to make sure it is well-sequenced and presented.
Step 7: Upload it to Google Drive, YouTube, or Vimeo and share with students.

The following recommendations are helpful when creating the effective pre-recorded videos:

- Limit videos to about three to five minutes.
- Maintain an engaging and enthusiastic tone to keep learners motivated.
- Properly balance auditory and visual elements.
- Create videos based on topic or theme.
- Design follow-up interactive or responsive activities, such as a short quiz or discussion.
- Consider adding captions or subtitles to help students access and process information.

There is a range of technology tools or software to create pre-recorded videos. In terms of hardware, it is convenient to use a video camera, tablet, or smartphone. Not only is recording through these devices good for those teachers who are used to teaching in a F2F classroom, but they are also more suited for field recordings or showing multiple viewpoints in a demonstration.

Some screencasting tools can be used to create prerecorded lecture videos in addition to recording with a video camera or smartphone. These include Hippo Video, Screencast-O-Matic, Loom, Panopto, Screencastify, Zoom, and Camtasia. Videos created with these tools can be very creative, diverse, and versatile (see Table 6.3). The teacher should choose the tool most appropriate to the learning objectives.

Table 6.3 Screencasting Tools for Pre-recorded Videos

	Hippo Video	Screen-cast-O-Matic	Loom	Panopto	Screen-castify	Zoom	Camta-sia
Download Required	No	Yes	No	No.	No	No	Yes.
Chrome extension	Yes	No	Yes	No	Yes	No	No.

	Hippo Video	Screen-cast-O-Matic	Loom	Panopto	Screen-castify	Zoom	Camta-sia
"Live" screen recording	Yes	Yes	Yes	Yes	Yes	Yes	Yes
Annotate while recording	Yes	Only for paid plan	No	No	Yes	Yes	No
Video editing	Fairly robust	Fairly robust	Limited	Fairly robust	Limited	Limited	Yes
Max length	5 minutes for free plan	15 minutes for free plan	No limit	5 hours for free plan	5 minutes for basic plan	No limit	No limit
Can students use it to record?	Yes	Yes	Yes	Yes	Yes	Yes	Yes
Video sharing	Social channel/ email	Shareable link/ YouTube	Shareable link/ Facebook/ Twitter/ Email	Shareable link/ Facebook/ Twitter	Shareable link/ Email	Upload to public domain	Social channel / local download
Student engagement tools	Text comment area under video; limited video quiz (MC/TF/ Reflection point/ open-ended)	Comments and reaction	Call-to-action to create button text and web link	Limited text comment area under video; limited video quiz (not very intuitive)	Video, audio, or text comments + pen annotation; create "VT Assignments" to track viewing, require comments, etc.	No	Quizzing and Surveys

Since most pre-recorded videos are one-way, it is the teacher's responsibility to add a two-way interaction. If the video created does not have built-in interactive functions, then the teacher should add follow-up activities to ensure true learning: these might include instant feedback and scoring, or checks for understanding through interactive video platforms such as PlayPosit or Edpuzzle. Videos for flipped and asynchronous learning can be enhanced with interactive quizzes (H5P, Camtasia, Kaltura, SnagIt), so students can check their comprehension before moving on.

Interactive Activities

Both Nearpod and Pear Deck are centralized lesson repositories for teachers to create slides that increase student engagement through formative assessments, interactive activities, and teacher analytics. Both tools are able to be used for remote learning, flipping lessons, differentiating or scaffolding instruction in the classroom, giving quizzes, assigning homework, assigning a lesson to a student who missed class, or substitute teaching. Creating a lesson and presenting it "live" in class or assigning it as homework with a "student-paced session" can also be done with both of these tools. Nearpod and Pear Deck are very similar tools and play the same role in teaching, though they differ in some functions, especially in the procedure for adding slides and types of content. Teachers should use the tool they are already most familiar with or have already used with students; if both tools are new, the teacher can decide which to use according to the features of each tool (see Table 6.4).

Table 6.4 A Comparison of Nearpod and Pear Deck

	Nearpod	Pear Deck
Log in	Google Microsoft	Google Microsoft
System	iOS App Android App Windows App Browser	Browser
Create lessons	Lesson in Nearpod Lesson in Google Slides Video Quick launch	Lesson in Google Slides Direct template Create a vocab list

	Nearpod	Pear Deck
Live session (Instructor-paced)	Session kept 15 days	Session kept 30 days
Student-paced	Session kept 30 days (student-paced should be decided before starting session, cannot switch)	Session kept 30 days (student-paced could be turned on or off anytime from instructor-based)
Import slide	PPT Google Slides PDF Image files	Google Slides PPT
Options of interactive activities	Time to Climb (combination of multiple choices) Multiple choice Open-ended questions Matching pairs Flipgrid Draw It Collaborate Board Fill in the blank Memory test	Text Choice Number Draw Draggable
Content	Video (can add open and multiple choice questions) Slide (with text/audio/image/video) Web content (hyperlink) Flocabulary video Nearpod 3D Simulation Field trip (VR) Graphing calculator BBC video Sway Slideshow Audio PDF viewer	Audio Website

	Nearpod	**Pear Deck**
Quick launch (Fly-out)	Open-ended questions Draw It Timer Collaborate!	Text Multiple choice Draggable Drawing
Storage space limit	50 MB (free account)	No limit
Lesson size limit	20 MB (free account)	No limit
Immersive reader	Yes	Yes
Timer	Set up before starting activity with any 0-100 minutes	Set up anytime with only three choices: 30 seconds, 1 minute, 3 minutes Lock screen
Conversation result	None of the original animations kept after converting from Google Slides to Nearpod slides	Keep the original animation with extension of power-up
Share lessons with others	Yes	Yes
Student report	Yes	Yes
Auto grading	Yes	Yes
Immersive reader	Yes	Yes
Student notes/Takeaways	Yes	Yes

Nearpod

Website: https://nearpod.com/
Platform: Web, iOS, Android
Communication Modes: Interpretive, Presentational, Interpersonal
Similar Tool: Pear Deck

Practical Tips:
1. There are three ways to create interactive lessons using Nearpod:
   1) Slides created in Google Slides could be converted to Nearpod teaching slides

directly using adds-ons (see Figure 6.6). The teacher can either convert an existing Google Slide or create a new one. The Nearpod slides cannot be copied or pasted because copied slides lose functionality.

2) A lesson could be created in Nearpod with all types of content or activities (see Figure 6.7).

3) A "Fly-out" Nearpod slide could be immediately launched if the teacher clicks the icon "Quick Launch" in Nearpod, which is only available for Open-ended Questions, Draw It, Timer, or Collaborate! (see Figure 6.8).

2. Both "Live Participants" (synchronous) and "Student-paced" (asynchronous) options are available. For students to join Nearpod, they either type in a join code at "join.nearpod.com" or in the app, or they click the shareable link to start the learning process. The teacher should be aware that the link for Live Participants expires in 15 days, and for Student-Paced in 30 days. The teacher can resume the same link within that period.

3. Checking for understanding is one of important activities in the language learning process. Nearpod's interactive activities are very useful for this; they include Polls, Quiz, Open-ended Questions, or Fill in Blanks. Time to Climb, Nearpod's game-like learning activity, increases engagement through friendly classroom competition while enabling the teacher to assess students' learning results, like Quizlet Live or Kahoot!.

4. One of the most popular features on Nearpod is Draw It, which can be used for practicing writing Chinese characters and sentences or any activities needing annotations (refer to Chapter 4 Task 3: Pictionary 猜成语 ; Task 4: True or False 真真假假 ; Task 5: Class Schedule 课程表 ; Task 6: How to Write a Chinese Home Address? 中国的住址怎么写? ; Task 10: Entry into the Customs Area 入境过海关 ; Task 14: Traditional Chinese Festivals 中国传统节日 ; Task 16: How to Eat a Hotpot? 怎么吃火锅 ?; Task 17: Where do You Want to Go? 你想去哪里? ; Task 18: What Did the Teacher Do Last Night? 老师昨天晚上做什么了 ?)

5. Nearpod's Collaborate is an interactive brainstorming tool for teachers and students to collaborate and share text and images in real time, similar to the function as Padlet (refer to Chapter 4 Task 8: Which House would You Like to Pick? 你会选哪个房子? ; Task 9: Which Chinese Restaurant Would you Like to Recommend? 你推荐哪家中餐馆? ; Task 11: Role Play on Airport Pickup 接机角色扮演). The posts can be "liked" by students and are sortable by the teacher.

6. Nearpod has several types of multimedia activities the teacher can incorporate in language teaching lessons, including videos, audio, PDF viewer, websites/web content, live Twitter stream, virtual field trips, 3D objects, phET, and BBC videos. Nearpod VR allows students to have virtual reality experiences together. The teacher can assign students to go on a virtual field trip of the target language

country, which is good for building their cultural knowledge.

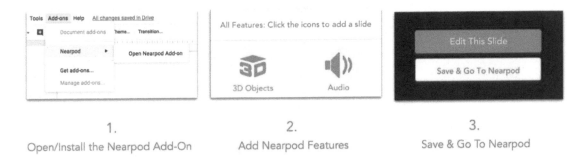

1.
Open/Install the Nearpod Add-On

2.
Add Nearpod Features

3.
Save & Go To Nearpod

Figure 6.6 Creating Nearpod Lessons from Google Slides

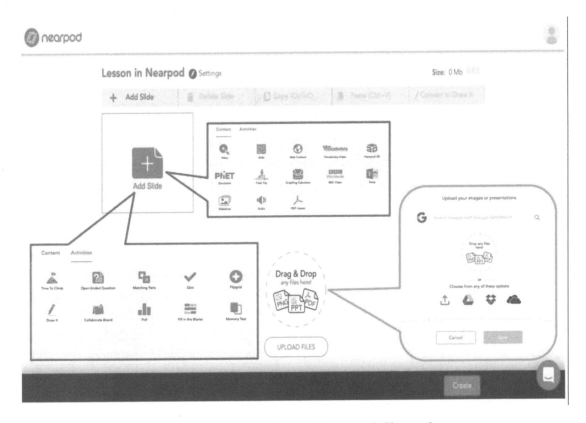

Figure 6.7 Creating Nearpod Lessons in Nearpod

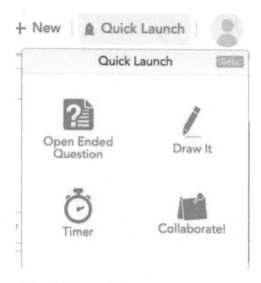

Figure 6.8 Quick Launch Nearpod Lessons in Nearpod

Pear Deck

Website: https://app.peardeck.com/
Platform: Web
Communication Modes: Interpretive, Presentational, Interpersonal
Similar Tool: Nearpod

Practical Tips:
1. Ways to create Pear Deck lessons:
   1) The teacher can make new presentations or add Pear Deck Interactive Questions to existing presentations in Google Slides or PowerPoint Online.
   2) The teacher can start the interactive activities by opening a session through choosing a prompt in Pear Deck.
   3) The teacher can have students work together to create vocabulary flashcards using Pear Deck Vocabulary: they can write example sentences and make illustrations for a list of vocabulary terms. At the end of the game, the teacher and students can review the cards and select the final set together. The final set could be exported to Gimkit.
2. The teacher could directly use templates in Pear Deck called Beginning of Class, During Class, End of Class, and Critical Thinking to pose critical thinking questions and allow students to reflect on and analyze what they have just learned (see Figure 6.9).

3. Draw in Pear Deck is similar to Annotate in Zoom or Draw It in Nearpod, and the teacher can use Draw to create the same tasks, such as Chapter 4 Task 3: Pictionary 猜成语；Task 4: True or False 真真假假；Task 5: Class Schedule 课程表；Task 6: How to Write a Chinese Home Address? 中国的住址怎么写？；Task 10: Entry into the Customs Area 入境过海关；Task 14: Traditional Chinese Festivals 中国传统节日；Task 16: How to Eat a Hotpot? 怎么吃火锅？；Task 17: Where Do You Want to Go? 你想去哪里？；Task 18: What Did the Teacher Do Last Night? 老师昨天晚上做什么了？

4. The teacher could create activities to check for understanding using Text (open-ended response questions), Choice (multiple-choice questions), Number (questions requiring numbers as answers). The teacher can use Number to create the same tasks for sequencing sentences, such as Chapter 4 Task 16: How to Eat a Hotpot? 怎么吃火锅？；Task 17: Where do You Want to Go? 你想去哪里？；Task 18: What did the Teacher Do Last Night? 老师昨天晚上做什么了？

5. Draggable enables students to drag an icon to a specific part of the screen (generally over an image or map). For example, using "thumbs up" and "thumbs down", students can place a dot indicating whether they agree with a statement; this could be used for any true or false activities, like Chapter 4 Task 4: True or False 真真假假.

6. One unique feature in Pear Deck is that teachers could lock student screens at any time so that they cannot change an answer.

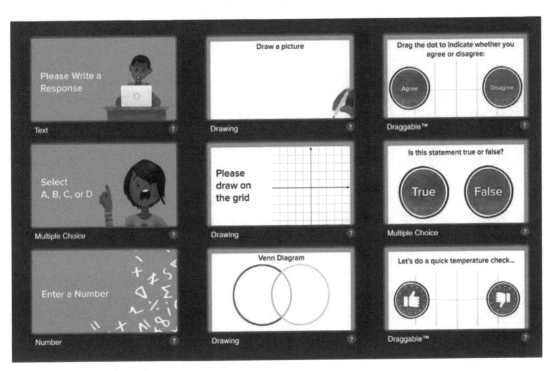

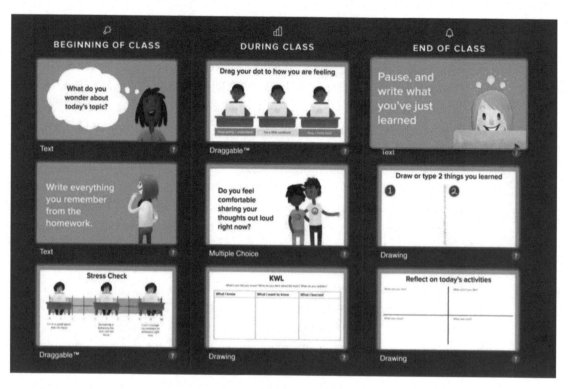

Figure 6.9 Pear Deck Template

Gaming Shows

Quizlet, Kahoot!, and Gimkit are three gaming tools; they are often the most popular activities because they are fun and engaging ways to help the student to learn vocabulary. The digital flashcard function is a very popular way for teachers and students to study new vocabularies. The tools enable teachers to create digital flashcards, and they also include more options for teachers to create fun learning activities beyond just learning vocabulary, so they are good for formative assessment and reviewing content with students. A comparison of three tools is showing in Table 6.5, along with suggestions for how to use these three tools in language teaching. Teachers may decide the tools needed to review and teach in the classroom accordingly.

Table 6.5 A Comparison of Quizlet, Kahoot!, and Gimkit

	Quizlet	Kahoot!	Gimkit
Individual or Team	Both	Both	Both

	Quizlet	Kahoot!	Gimkit
Delivery	Live and student-paced	Live and student-paced	Live and student-paced
Mobile app	Yes	Yes	No
Earning	Points	Points	Money
Question types	Flashcard Learn Spell Write Test Match Gravity Quizlet Live	Quiz True or false Type answer Puzzle Poll Slide	Multiple choice Text input
Multimedia	Image, GIF, audio (paid)	Image, GIF, YouTube video	Link, image, GIF, audio (paid)
Timed	No	Yes	No

Quizlet

Website:

https://quizlet.com/

https://quizlet.com/live (for students to join Quizlet Live)

Platform: Web, iOS, Android

Communication Mode: Interpretive

Similar Tools: Kahoot!, Gimkit

Practical Tips:

Quizlet offers various functions for vocabulary learning activities (see Figure 6.10) that teachers and students can use based on what works for them, but teachers should not be limited to vocabulary learning with these functions. Some ideas about activities extending to grammatical structure are recommended:

1) Create a Quizlet Interactive Diagram.

Interactive diagrams enable students to practice using visual material in engaging and effective ways, such as think maps, charts, and illustration. Teachers can upload an image and then click on areas of the image to mark items, creating an interactive diagram for students to practice dialogues with positional and directional words. This works really well with a scene like what you would find in an IKEA catalog or items in a room (refer to Chapter 4 Task 2: What is in the Study Room? 书房里面有什么？). Quizlet's Learn, Match, or Spell activity are fun ways to review interactive diagram sets like these.

2) Make correct grammatical structure from words and expressions.

The teacher can place a correctly written sentence in Quizlet's "Definition" section, and mix up sections of the sentence in the "Term" section. This also could be used to create practice activities for the usage of measure words. The teacher can ask students to practice these study sets with Quizlet's Write activity, which would help them practice writing correct sentences with the appropriate word order (refer to Chapter 4 Task 3: Rearrange Word Order 字词顺序重组).

3) The teacher could create a comprehension set for students to practice, since Quizlet has no limit in the number of words in a study set. For example, a Chinese idiom term would be typed in a "Term" session, and the whole story describing the Chinese idiom can be typed on the "Definition" session; this is good for checking students' reading comprehension skills.

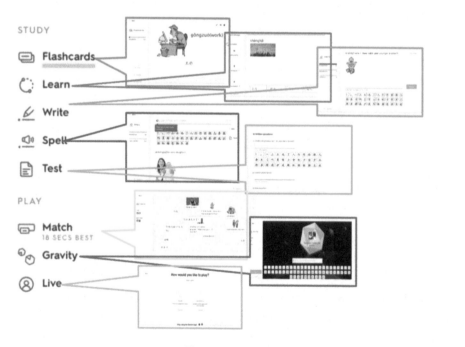

Figure 6.10 Options for Quizlet

Image Source: quizlet.com

Kahoot!

Website:

    https://create.kahoot.it/ (for teachers to create study set)

    https://kahoot.it/ (for students to join the game)

Platform: Web, iOS, Android

Communication Modes: Interpretive and Presentational

Similar Tools: Quizlet, Gimkit

Practical Tips:

Kahoot! is a game-based online platform that allows users to create interactive quizzes for invited participants to take via a personal electronic device. Using Kahoot! helps students build cultural knowledge and context, while making it fun to learn new vocabulary and structures, through features including Quiz, True or False, Type answer, Puzzle, Poll, and Slide (see Figure 6.11).

Below are some new ideas for using Kahoot! creatively (see Figure 6.12):

    1) Icebreaker at the beginning of school.

        The template of the teacher's selfie Kahoot! can be used to introduce the teacher in a fun way. The teacher can ask students to guess some personal facts about the teacher (hobbies, for example) and use that as a conversation starter. To make it even more engaging as well as changing the dynamics, the teacher can place clues for next questions throughout the Kahoot!

        The template of student's selfie Kahoot! allows students to get to know each other better. The teacher can ask students to create a short quiz about themselves, so that others in the class get to know them better. The question type could be diverse and creative.

    2) Check for understanding.

        Kahoot! is a great tool for creating interpretive tasks to check for understanding. In one example, the teacher could create a task with a short film clip with questions to check for understanding. Students will be able to understand the main ideas of the movie clips by answering the questions that pop up. This activity is designed for students to develop language skills by talking about the detailed information according to the movie clips watched. (Refer to Chapter 4 Task 22: Watch a Film and Play Kahoot! 看电影玩 Kahoot!)

    3) Storytelling Kahoot!

        Encourage students to share their stories through a game by creating a Kahoot! with their own photos. Students create questions based on their own photos and ask their classmates to guess the story behind the photo. Not only this is a fun ice-breaking activity, but it also helps to develop learners' storytelling skills.

4) Blind Kahoot

Blind kahoots are designed to support students to be motivated throughout the game. In a game, the teacher can stimulate students' curiosity about a new topic, laying the foundations for understanding increasingly complex concepts, and giving students the opportunity to immediately and successfully apply their knowledge (the specific procedure is at: https://files.getkahoot.com/academy/ Kahoot_Academy_Guide_1st_Ed_-_March_2016_-_WOA.pdf).

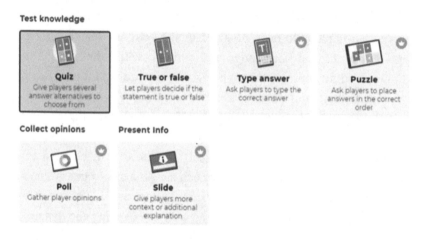

Figure 6.11 Kahoot Question Types

Figure 6.12 Kahoot New Activity Templates

Gimkit

Website: https://www.gimkit.com/
Platform: Web
Communication Modes: Interpretive and Presentational
Similar Tools: Quizlet, Kahoot!

Practical Tips:

Gimkit combines features of Quizlet and Kahoot!, including a flash card function. The teacher could import Quizlet sets (text only) into Gimkit. Using either the Quizlet import feature or the collaborative quiz-building KitCollab mode, the teacher can create a Gimkit game easily. Most learning activities created from Quilzet or Kahoot! can also be created in Gimkit. Teachers can also use the assignments feature to give homework: the teacher sets a due date, and students work through the kit at their own pace, answering questions until they reach a set goal.

One incredible feature in Gimkit is that it allows students to create questions in real time from KitCollab (see Figure 6.13). After students enter the game code, they are asked to create their own question. Once they submit the question, the teacher can accept or reject, and then, once the teacher starts the game, students can play Gimkit with the questions they have just created. Students can even attach photos to their questions using Take Photo. Thus, for example, students could take a selfie and then decide what kind of question they want to ask, such as what they are wearing, what they are doing, what they are holding, and so on.

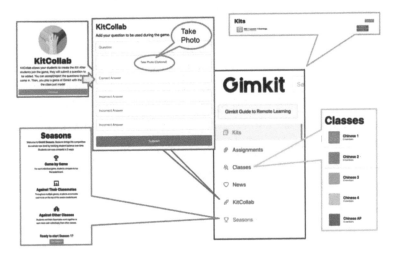

Figure 6.13 Options in Gimkit

Polling or surveying is a quick method to track how students are faring in the class. It is an easy way to conduct formative assessments during class teaching time. Along with the poll functions in Zoom and Nearpod, Google Forms and Poll Everywhere are most used in the language classes for this.

Google Forms

Website: https://www.google.com/forms/about/
Platform: Web
Communication Mode: Interpretive
Similar Tools: Poll Everywhere, Survey Monkey, Mentimeter

Practical Tips:

Google Forms allows teachers to easily create polls and surveys using a wide variety of forms and question types. It can support multimedia materials such as images and videos. Its collaborative features enable teachers to build a survey or poll together. Responses to surveys are neatly and automatically collected in Forms, with real-time response info and charts. The data can be further analyzed in Google Sheets (see Figure 6.14).

Some practical tips will help teachers assess students' learning or check for understanding.

1) Google Forms is usually good for teachers to check for understanding with opinion surveys or quick polls. The teacher may include names with answers or make them anonymous. Closed-ended questions can be displayed as graphs immediately using the "Responses" tab in the form.

2) Google Forms can be used as autograded quizzes to save more time for teachers. If the teacher creates a quiz or other assessment with closed-ended questions, Google Forms can autograde it. To do this: (1) Create a quiz and click the gear (settings) button. (2) Choose the "Quizzes" tab and turn on "Make this a quiz" . (3) Go through the questions and select the correct answer with certain points (see Figure 6.15).

3) Google Sheets, a detailed grading summary, can be created from Google Forms with student results from an assessment. When students complete a quiz/assessment in Google Forms, click the "Responses" tab and then the little green Sheets button. This Google Sheet will be created as a spreadsheet of results from the quiz/assessment. Flubaroo, an add-on to Google Sheets, can be used to

autograde assessments and create a summary that shows average student grade and individual student grade (plus which questions each student got right or wrong). This would help teachers identify the questions students struggled with and more.

4) Google Forms can be used for the flipped classroom. For example, teachers can have students watch a video and then answer comprehension questions. This is easily done in Google Forms by creating a form with a YouTube video (created by the teacher or found on YouTube) and questions.

5) Engage students with digital escape room locks. The teacher could use data validation to create a set of "locks" in a Google Form, simulating the Escape Room game. This format has built-in assessments because students must type in the correct answer in order to submit the form and "escape" (refer to Chapter 5 Task 5: Homestay: My Host Family in China 我的中国家庭).

Figure 6.14 Google Form Settings

Figure 6.15 Create Google Form as a Quiz

Poll Everywhere

Website: https://www.polleverywhere.com/
Platform: Web
Communication Mode: Interpretive
Similar Tools: Google Forms, Survey Monkey, Mentimeter

Practical Tips:

Poll Everywhere is designed for real-time responses to engage participants. The teacher can use interactive questions to check for understanding and adjust the teaching process based on student feedback. Since students' responses and feedback are anonymous, everyone can focus on what is said rather than who said it. All students have an equal opportunity to be heard, which provides a smooth transition to discussion and the upcoming lesson. Poll Everywhere can serve to measure students' learning progress or to provide a point of reflection. It can also help resolve more practical matters in a timely fashion: the teacher can get instant results from the whole class and provide immediate feedback to students or revise their instruction.

There are many creative ideas teachers could try using Poll Everywhere (see Figure 6.16):

1) Word cloud at Poll Everywhere could show dynamic pictures with information to capture students' ideas and emotions. Word cloud can engage students through icebreaker questions, flashbacks to what they learned, broad questions meant to reach a consensus as a group, summary of understanding, and brainstorming ideas for an essay or speech. After sharing something personal in the anonymity of the word cloud, students often feel empowered to discuss personal topics out loud.

2) Poll Everywhere can be used to check for understanding or to stimulate interest by relating the lesson content to the opinions and real-world knowledge of students. The teacher could ask a question and let students choose from a list of answers with Multiple choice, Competitions, Survey, Donut charts, or Open-ended.

3) Clickable image is good for collecting information from an uploaded photo, such as using warm up questions 你今天的心情怎么样? to start a class. The teacher can also upload a map to ask 你想去哪里旅行? Students could start the discussion after clicking anywhere on the image to respond.

4) Q&A is great for gathering consensus through students' responses to a question, and then having them upvote and downvote other answers.

5) Ranking in Poll Everywhere can be used to indicate the order of actions, which is good for creating activities with sequencing words (refer to Chapter 4 Task 18: What Did the Teacher Do Last Night? 老师昨天晚上做什么 ?).

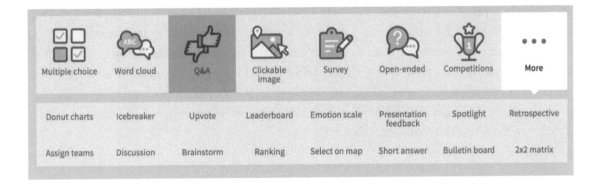

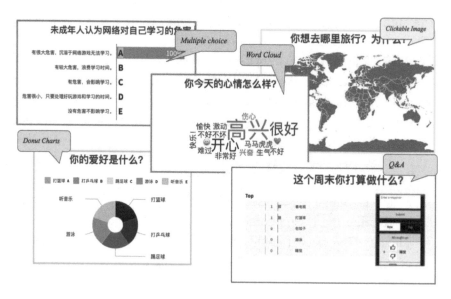

Figure 6.16 Poll Options

Image Source: http://www.polleverywhere.com

Interactive Video Platforms

Both Edpuzzle (see Figure 6.17) and PlayPosit (see Figure 6.18) are excellent ways to provide differentiated instruction, because students will pick up on whatever they are able to based on their current level of language ability.

They are both good for interpretive activities, which allow students to interactively engage with videos through questioning and audio notes. They both auto grade, allow the teacher to crop videos and upload their own videos, and connect to Google Classroom. However there are some differences. PlayPosit offers more options in the types of the question choices, such as Discussion, Poll, and Fill in the Blank, whereas Edpuzzle doesn't; while Edpuzzle allows Voiceover, PlayPosit does not (see Table 6.6).

Table 6.6 A Comparison of Edpuzzle and PlayPosit

	Edpuzzle	PlayPosit
Multiple choice	Yes	Yes
Free response	Yes	Yes

	Edpuzzle	PlayPosit
Audio notes	Yes	Yes
Check all	Yes	Yes
Voiceover	Yes	No
Reflective pause	Yes	Yes
Discussion	No	Yes
Poll	No	Yes
Fill in the blank	No	Yes
Web link	Yes	Yes
Grading	Yes	Yes
Trim video	Yes	Yes

Edpuzzle and PlayPosit

Website:
> Edpuzzle: https://edpuzzle.com/
> PlayPosit: playposit.com/

Platform: Web, iOS, Android

Communication Modes: Interpretive, Presentational

Practical Tips:
> Teachers need to use the web-based Edpuzzle and PlayPosit to create the tasks. To work on the tasks, students can use web-based PlayPosit, or either web-based or mobile Edpuzzle.
>
> Both tools allow teachers to insert questions to linked or uploaded videos. They allow teachers to take videos from sites like YouTube, add questions and comments, and then easily share the activities with students. It's efficient, engaging, flexible, and free. Here are some ways to use Edpuzzle or PlayPosit in language class:
>
> 1) Teachers could create interpretive tasks for students watch video and answer questions, which is good for conducting a formative assessment, introducing a new topic, or reviewing concepts (refer to Chapter 4 Task 4: Flipped Learning

Through Interactive Videos 课前翻转学习的互动视频).

2) Teachers could create a presentational task in which students watch a silent film clip, which does not have any words, just some fun sound effects. Students talk about what is happening in the film clips using vocabularies or sentence patterns they have just learned. This is good for a variety of topics, including prepositions and *Ba* structure.

3) Teachers could use the "Voiceover" function, which is only in Edpuzzle, to introduce a topic to students by talking over any video. For example, if the teacher finds a video that will be useful to students but is not in the target language, the teacher could use the voice over function to record commentary in target language. The teacher can also have students use "Voiceover" to dub a provided film clip to show their presentation skills.

4) The teacher can start a debate with these tools by sharing an interesting topic from a YouTube video or uploaded video with embedded open-ended questions asking for point of view and using those responses to start a debate in class.

5) Use 360 degree videos from YouTube or upload one for virtual field trips. For example, the teacher can take students to China virtually, allowing them to explore the culture and listen to native speakers (refer to Chapter 5 Task 10: A Virtual Tour in My Hometown 我的家乡虚拟游 ; Task 11: A Dream City in China 我梦想的中国城市).

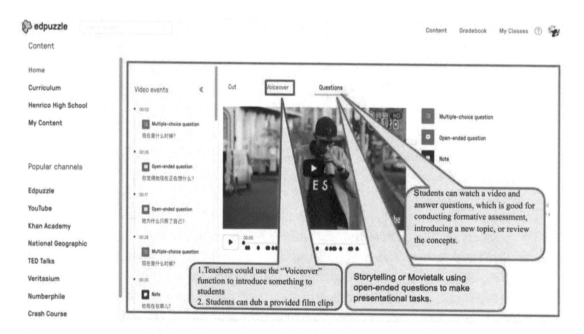

Figure 6.17 Edpuzzle Activity

Figure 6.18 PlayPosit Activity

Recommendations:

1) The teacher should make sure every minute of video is appropriate for students' learning purposes, and help students to remain focused on what matters by cropping the video to exclude all irrelevant content.

2) The teacher should wisely use different question types to address diversity by targeting a range of skill levels, providing a more realistic picture of the students' progress. For example, a free-response writing task can more appropriately be used to tap into an advanced student's writing skill, while a multiple-choice item may be used for lower-proficiency levels.

3) The teacher should demonstrate how to use different functions of Edpuzzle or PlayPosit first, and then have students practice a few times with the video to understand what is expected of them. The teacher may assign one or two videos per week for students to watch at home. Measure the number of assignments completed and get feedback from the students on the length of the video, the difficulty of the questions, and the content of the lesson.

4) Through the gradebook capability, Edpuzzle and PlayPosit allow teachers to obtain meaningful data about their students either while they watch the video lesson or after they have completed it as homework. The gradebook shows progress calculation, total score, total time spent in the assignment, assignments turned in late, students' individual reports, and range of dates.

Story Creators

Digital storytelling as a pedagogical strategy with multimedia approach (combining video, photography, sound, text, and music) creates a powerful exchange of information that allows students to develop their language skills by effectively communicating stories through digital media.

Book Creator (see Figure 6.19) and Storyjumper (see Figure 6.20) are both engaging story creator tools that allow students to express meaning while practicing the cognitive processes of bridging language skills. As they are very similar, teachers may choose either as the class digital story tool based on the comparisons of features below (see Table 6.7).

Table 6.7 A Comparison of Book Creator and Storyjumper

	Book Creator	Storyjumper
Sign in with Google	Yes	Yes
Co-teacher	Yes	Yes
Shared folder (Class or Library)	Yes	Yes
Review students' work while the writing project is in progress	Yes	Yes
Text	Yes	Yes
Drawing	Yes	No
Image	Yes	Yes
Shape	Yes	Search from image
Audio	Voice record (about 5 minutes)	Voice record (more than one hour) Music Sound effect
Upload file from computer	Yes	Only photos
Map	Yes	No
Upload file from Google Drive	Yes	No
Embedded content	Yes	No
Design characters	No	Yes

Book Creator and Storyjumper

Website:
    Book Creator: https://bookcreator.com/
    Storyjumper: https://www.storyjumper.com/
Platform: Web
Communication Modes: Presentational, Interpersonal

Practical Tips:

Both Book Creator and Storyjumper users have the option of registering as a student or teacher. The student accounts allow students to read, write, and publish books. The teacher accounts allow the teacher to create a library (in the form of a class set-up) to be shared with students to access resources. Both are simple tools for creating awesome digital books. Teachers and students can combine text, images, audio, and video to create the following:

1) Conversational comic books by paired students to collaborate together.

2) New versions of legends for traditional Chinese festivals, such as 除夕的传说，后羿射日，嫦娥奔月，端午节的传说，七夕, etc.

3) A tutorial or instruction manual project, such as "how to make Chinese knotting" or "how to make dumplings".

4) A collection of work over a unit, which helps students reflect on their learning

5) An exit ticket for each class, in which students can summarize what they learned and share their questions for the class (refer to Chapter 5 Task 9: Exit Slips "出口" 通关任务)

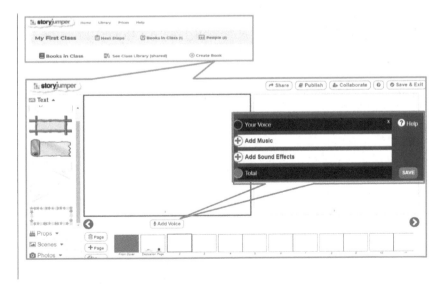

Figure 6.19 Create a Story Book with Book Creator

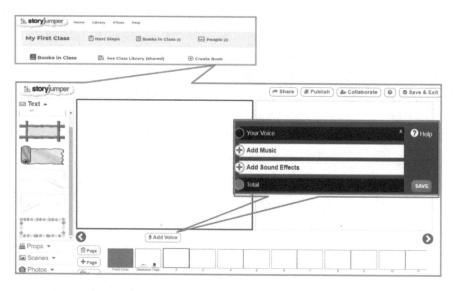

Figure 6.20 Create a Story Book with Storyjumper

Collaborative Spaces

Language learning takes place throughout daily life, as communication happens in all fields and all the time. In the language teaching process, various collaborative activities, such as pair work, group work, cooperative learning, and collaborative learning make the language learning more meaningful and interesting.

Teachers should use technology tools to provide collaborative spaces for students to work and learn together in a language class.

This section gives an introduction to collaborative learning using different technology tools and explains best practices for collaborative learning with some technology tools.

VoiceThread

Website: https://voicethread.com/
Platform: Web, iOS, Android
Communication Modes: Interpretive, Presentational, Interpersonal

Practical Tips:

VoiceThread is one of the powerful collaborative tools for teachers to use for both synchronous and asynchronous teaching. VoiceThread can transform media (images, documents, and videos) into a collaborative space for video, voice, and text commenting, which is efficient and adaptable for allowing students to practice their language skills, especially their speaking and listening skills. Following are some ideas for teachers (see Figure 6.21):

1) **Debates.** Project-based debate is a powerful tool for students to practice language skills like persuasion, argumentation, speaking and listening, and use of evidence. Teachers may record a debate topic with related video or images and upload it into VoiceThread. Students could record their own thoughts or opinions for the topics. The pre-recorded content means all students have enough time to scaffold to become good debaters. Students would be able to understand what others are saying since they can listen again and again, and they could record their comments several times until they are satisfied with their recording.

2) **Global collaboration.** Teachers also could provide one topic for students from different countries to discuss together by recording their conversation at VoiceThread. This global collaboration allows students to communicate with native speakers. For example, the teacher could ask students from different countries to share their daily schedule and comment on each others' schedules to have a further understanding. These simulated conversations allow students not only to practice language skills but also to share their thoughts in different cultural environments.

3) **Storytelling or dubbing.** VoiceThread is a good tool for students to practice storytelling or dubbing. It is a great source to provide verbal feedback. It provides students the opportunity to move past grammar toward narrative communication. The teacher can upload images or videos for students to talk about. This is similar to voiceover from Edpuzzle, but it is more flexible as it allows instructors to provide specific feedback for every moment. Students also could see their peers' comments, which improves engagement and accountability and makes the task more productive.

4) **Cultural discussion.** The instructor may share a culture video with students, and ask students to have a discussion based on guided questions provided. Students could either type messages or speak to communicate with classmates about the topic and questions provided (refer to Chapter 5 Task 13: Chinese Cultural Capsules 中国文化胶囊).

5) **Flipped class.** The teacher can use VoiceThread to design an engaging, student-centered, flipped class by recording the teaching content with a drawing pen that encourages students to think.

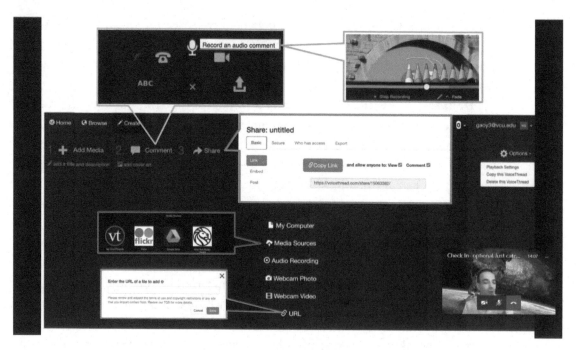

Figure 6.21 Creating Tasks in VoiceThread

Flipgrid

Website: https://info.flipgrid.com/
Platform: Web, iOS, Android
Communication Modes: Interpretive, Presentational, Interpersonal

Practical Tips:

Flipgrid is another excellent collaboration tool. It helps students develop speaking skills in order to communicate verbally what they have learned (see Figure 6.22).

1) A simple way to use Flipgrid is for teachers to ask students to record a video about a topic assigned based on the content they learned. For example, Flipgrid can be used for Karaoke, in which each student would be able to show and share their own favorite Chinese song with others (refer to Chapter 5 Task 6: I Am a Rock Star 我是摇滚明星).

2) Flipgrid allows teachers to pose a question to a group of students, and have students respond to that question by recording a short video of themselves talking. This tool allows both teachers and students to record themselves responding to a prompt through video and allows viewers to make video comments.

3) Using the "student-to-student replies" option, everyone in the class can view and respond to each other's videos. For example, a student can post a video to share a project they have completed, then their peers can compose video responses, providing positive feedback on the work completed. In general, teachers may require students to comment on two or three classmates' projects.

4) Teachers can begin a story, and ask each of the students to reply with video to continue telling the story until the last students to provide the ending. Also, instructors could have students collaborate in telling a story in the target language by using distinct voices to separate the perspectives of different characters.

Figure 6.22 Flipgrid Functions

Padlet

Website: https://padlet.com/
Platform: Web, iOS, Android
Communication Modes: Interpretive, Presentational, Interpersonal

Practical Tips:

Padlet is an online collaborative "Wall" , where the teacher can upload videos, photos, or documents and students can post comments or answer questions for the entire class to see and respond to. The possibilities of collaboration are endless since anyone could be invited to collaborate with a sharable link. Padlet can be used by teachers and students for different class activities or tasks with different formats including the Wall, Canvas, Stream, Grid, Shelf, Backchannel, and Map. Teachers could assign either synchronous or asynchronous tasks in Padlet. Padlet functions include type text, draw, voice recording, add a hyperlink, add a photo or video, add a place, Google search, and add a document (see Figure 6.23).

Teachers can also set up Comments (allow viewers to comment on posts) and Reactions (grade, star, upvote, or like posts) to allow students to respond to each other' s posts as well.

Here are some ideas for creating tasks in Padlet:

1) Instructors may use Padlet' s Backchannel feature to allow students to brainstorm or discuss topics, like Collaborate in Nearpod. Instructors can ask students to share their creative ideas in Padlet in real time during classroom discussion. Students benefit from interacting directly with their classmates on a given topic or imitating dialogue in real situations. (refer to Chapter 4 Task 11: Role Play on Airport Pickup 接机角色扮演).

2) Shelf format in Padlet makes it possible to stack content in columns. Teachers could use this to organize the content for a different writing purpose. For example, the teacher may organize columns by students' names for them to stack their writing journals, which would show each student' s progress (refer to Chapter 4 Task 9: Which Chinese Restaurant Would You Like to Recommend? 你推荐哪家中餐馆? ; Chapter 5 Task 7: My 10-day Journey in Beijing 北京 十 日 游 记). Teachers also could organize the column by different topics for students to share their writing with other students for given topics.

3) Wall format at Padlet packs content in a brick-like layout. It is ideal for visual information sharing. Icebreaker on the Padlet Wall is a great first feature for teachers to use at the beginning of the school year. Icebreaker questions help group members introduce themselves to each other and find common ground. It' s much easier for new people to speak up from the safety of their mobile devices. Students could also share their pictures and record their introduction at the same time as the icebreaker.

4) Map format is a layout that allows students to pin locations on an interactive map. Teachers could ask students to talk about the place they live through Map format if students are from different locations. Once a place is pinned, students

can opt to add files to it, including text, web links, photos, audio clips, videos, and more.

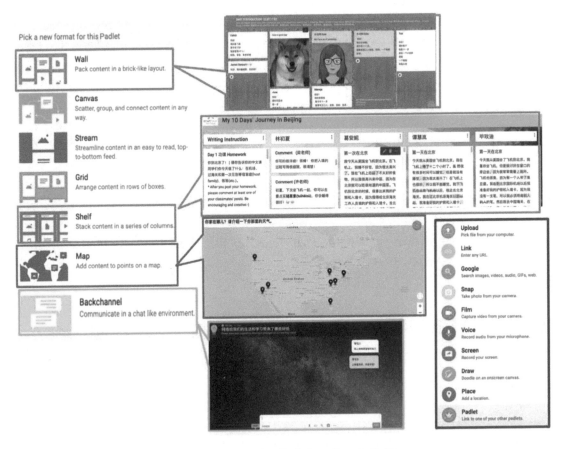

Figure 6.23 Padlet for Collaborative Activities

Image Source: padlet.com

WeVideo

Website: https://www.wevideo.com/
Platform: Web, iOS, Android
Communication Modes: Interpretive, Presentational, Interpersonal

Practical Tips:
WeVideo is an online video editing platform that allows teachers and students to create video stories and provides students flexibility and collaboration opportunities. The

teachers could create a group so a whole class can work on one video, or ask students to share their individual videos for collaboration with a few team members. Here are some ideas to engage students with video collaboration:

1) Narrator or Voice actor. The teacher provides students with pre-selected video clips and lets them be the narrator or the voice actor. The teacher could assign the same images or video clips to different groups. The teacher could choose Collaborative when creating a project for students (see Figure 6.24). Students can create sound effects, character voices, and other audio elements to add more to the story. Students can read from a book or script, or they can create a new script based on the images or clips the teacher provides. The teacher could demonstrate first.

2) Video story. The teacher could assign students a topic for them to generate a video story by recording their own real life. Topics could include My Hobbies 我的爱好, or My Favorite Books 我最喜欢的书, etc. Each student will upload their photos or videos to share their hobbies, books, or any interesting topics they would like to share.

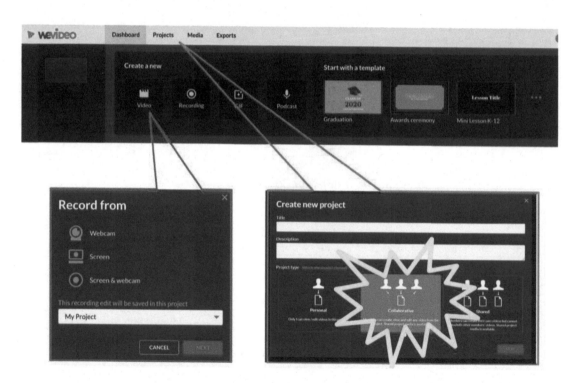

Figure 6.24 Collaborative Project with WeVideo

CoSpaces Edu

Website: https://cospaces.io/edu/
Platform: Web, iOS, Android
Communication Modes: Interpretive, Presentational, Interpersonal

Practical Tips:

CoSpaces is a mixed reality web-based application that allows teachers and students to create interactive media content. It works on any device and is relatively easy to use. Students can collaborate together in a space teacher created. There are many ready-to-use resources for teachers. Here are some steps for teachers to start using CoSpaces Edu in the language class (see Figure 6.25):

1) Register on cospaces.io/edu.

2) Create your classes.

3) Invite students to the class. Each class has a specific class code that you can find in the class you've created. Share the class code with your students to let them join your class in CoSpaces.

4) Create assignments. Inside your class, go to Assignments and click Create assignment to set up an assignment for students. You can also use an existing CoSpace as a template for your assignment. Go directly to CoSpaces, or in the Gallery, choose a CoSpace and click Use as an assignment.

Following are some CoSpaces project ideas for language class:

1) Guided virtual tour in CoSpaces: CoSpaces can simulate real-world activities and engagements, so students could create virtual tours in CoSpaces Edu. They can pretend to be a tour guide to introduce the place they have built. The topic could be a city, a museum, a zoo, a house, and so on. Students could present to others during class time, or record the narration to show their classmates.

2) Storytelling with CoSpaces: To develop comprehension, students listen to or read a story provided by a teacher or other students, and then create a visual representation of it or illustrations for it based on their understanding.

To gain speaking practice, students and teachers can create scenes in CoSpaces and discuss what they've experienced and how they built the scenes (refer to Chapter 4 Task 14: Show Your Store 展示你的店铺).

3) Gaming with CoSpaces: Students can create their own games and play them with their classmates. These games would be good for interpretive tasks. CoSpaces is

conducive to making many types of games. Students can create adventure games, in which the player experiences a story and has to go through a series of actions to win; parkours or 3D platform games, in which the player has to move to get from a start position to a finish line or goal; virtual scavenger hunts in which the players have to find hidden objects inside a virtual world; quiz games on topics from class; virtual mazes, in which the player has to answer a series of questions or solve puzzles in order to exit the maze; or even virtual escape rooms.

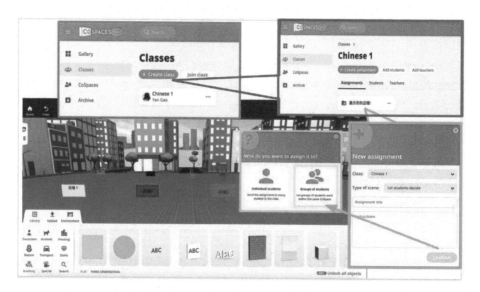

Figure 6.25 CoSpaces Settings

Google Tour Builder and Tour Creator

Website:

> Google Tour Builder: https://tourbuilder.withgoogle.com/
> Tour Creator: https://arvr.google.com/tourcreator/

Platform: Web

Communication Modes: Interpretive, Presentational

Practical Tips:

> Both Google Tour Builder and Tour Creator are web-based storytelling tools that allow teachers and students to create virtual tours using Google Maps and Google Earth, and adding multimedia content (images, 360° images, videos, audio, and hyperlinks). Although Google Tour Builder and Tour Creator are very similar, they do differ in some features. Google Tour Builder (see Figure 6.26) is more like a tour journal in which one can record the sequencing of each location with the dates

along with the map, while Tour Creator (see Figure 6.27) focuses on highlights of each location. Some suggested uses of Google Tour Builder or Tour Creator are as follows:

1) The teacher can use Tour Builder for interpretive tasks to give the students a better sense of cities in China, using multimedia resources (images/360° images/ videos/audio) at each point on the tour to add context to the locations on the map. The teacher can show pictures or videos and then ask students questions in the target language in the description area.

2) The teacher could assign presentational tasks in which students create their own reports showcasing a variety of things, such as sharing a personal experience like a summer road trip or a tour of the community (refer to Chapter 5 Task 10: A Virtual Tour in My Hometown 我的家乡虚拟游), or planning a virtual tour to a city they have never been to (refer to Chapter 5 Task 11: A Dream City in China 我梦想的中国城市).

3) The teacher can also ask students to create a virtual tour for studying places, locations of key events, settings in books, real-world issues, and more. This is a great way to get students engaged with the material and constructing their own ways to showcase their learning, such as the life of a Chinese poet (Li Bai or Du Fu), a location from a book (*Romance of the Three Kingdoms*), or locations in a Chinese historical event.

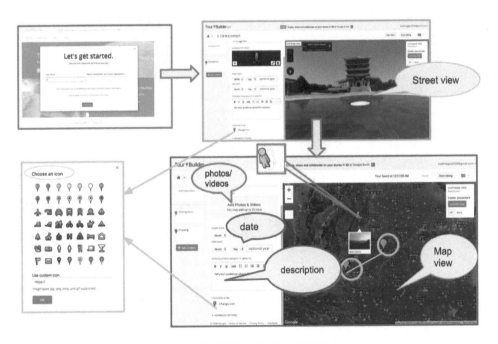

Figure 6.26 Google Tour Builder

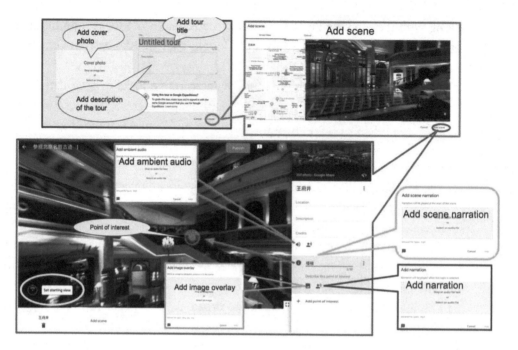

Figure 6.27 Tour Creator

The technology tools introduced in this chapter range from the essential — video conference platforms — to the specific — 3D tours. As you become more comfortable with online teaching, you can diversify the tools in your toolbox, but you should limit the number and variety of technology tools you insert in any one semester to avoid students' confusion and overload. You should add new tasks that fit your pedagogical objectives. K-12 Teachers should work with the local school or county IT to make sure what the limits are, considering some K-12 schools don't allow outside apps or their firewalls, which makes it difficult to use them. When used wisely, as in the tasks introduced in Chapters 4 and 5, these tools will help you create and foster a vibrant, inclusive, and creative online environment with and for your students.

Chapter 7
Ten Must-do Things for Creating a Successful Online Course

A transition from F2F teaching in a four-walled classroom to online teaching shifts the paradigm of course organization and planning. The online classroom has great potential to empower learners with new practices and bonding in an online community. It increases opportunities for language professionals to leverage technologies and enhances and refreshes meaningful experience. Instead of being discouraged by the shift, instructors must strive to rethink and redevise curriculum and instruction by developing a growth mindset. This chapter recommends ten must-do things to highlight the most effective strategies and offer practical tips for achieving a successful online course. It further corroborates and corresponds to the conceptual understanding and illustrated examples in the previous chapters and pinpoints "know-how' s" in realizing teaching-in-actions for an ideal online course.

Determine Delivery Mode for Online Teaching

Before backward designing a course, it is important to first determine delivery mode. Think more deeply on the following list of delivery modes and choose one that is most suited to your local classroom and learners. Be kindly reminded that delivery modes differ along several dimensions: three ways of interaction and key elements that contribute to frequent quality interaction. Whenever possible, choose the modes that are likely to bring about the best learning outcomes.

1) F2F in-person
2) Blended (F2F + synchronous online)
3) Blended (F2F + asynchronous online)
4) Online (asynchronous)
5) Online (asynchronous + synchronous)
6) Online F2F (synchronous)

After determining the delivery mode, consider instructional days in a weekly or biweekly cycle, and allot time for each day. Ponder the following questions as you structure the course.

1) How many times per week? What days of the week? How many minutes each time?
2) Is it purely synchronous or asynchronous? If combined, how many hours per week for synchronous and asynchronous learning?
3) Is it possible to divide one regular class into synchronous teaching and asynchronous interactive work?
4) Is it necessary to keep the amount of time for synchronous learning the same each class? Are there alternatives that might achieve better learning outcomes?
5) Is it possible to divide a large class into two to three groups on a certain day and engage learners in small-group synchronous discussion, led by an instructor or assistant?

Plan strategically to optimize instructional effect and diversity. Reconsider some follow-up questions to revisit the course structure.

1) Is it possible to include pre-class flipped learning as a preview activity? If so, what kind? How long?
2) How to foster interaction and engage learners in asynchronous learning?
3) How to increase incentives to take advantage of your office hours?
4) What incentives can you create for learners to actively participate in offline discussion? Is it possible to involve native speakers or assistants to offer tutorial sessions?

The following is one example showing the restructuring of a language course transitioning from F2F in-person to online teaching.

Day 1 Monday Online	Day 2 Wednesday Online	Day 3 Friday Online
11–11:50 a.m. (regular) Entire-class synchronous	11–11:50 a.m. (regular) Entire-class synchronous	Option 1: 11–11:50 a.m. (regular) Three small-group synchronous discussions, facilitated by tutors or teaching assistants & supervised by the instructor Option 2: Two 40-minute time slots Two small-group discussions led by the instructor Option 3: Three 30-minute time slots Three small-group discussions led by the instructor

Day 4 Monday Online	Day 5 Wednesday Online	Day 6 Friday Online
11–11:50 a.m. (regular) Entire-class synchronous	11–11:50 a.m. (regular) Entire-class weekly quiz (to complete individually, in pairs/groups, or entire class)	Community-based experiential learning: Five small groups for summative authentic tasks by interviewing native speakers (Time to be flexibly adjusted according to the availability of NSs and learners)

Plan for Transitioning to Online Teaching

The very first attempt to plan an online course is never an easy process. If possible, give yourself at least six months to allow sufficient time for preparation, deliberation, and planning. As horizontal and vertical coordination within the program is required, you'll need to work with a group. If you single-handedly run the program, then go out of your comfort zone to work with colleagues in other language programs to expand your horizons. Reaching out to colleagues outside your school in the same field is also highly recommended. This can help you avoid the feeling of working in isolation. Moreover, teaching online needs guidance from instructional designers who can help with pedagogical decisions on technology, so it is necessary to seek professional advice from them in additional to gathering input from learners. Figure 7.1 outlines the three aspects of influence that have impact on online course design: language instructors, instructional designers, and learners. Each element influences the others: they should not be considered as sequential, but as interconnected in a fluid and mutually reinforcing way.

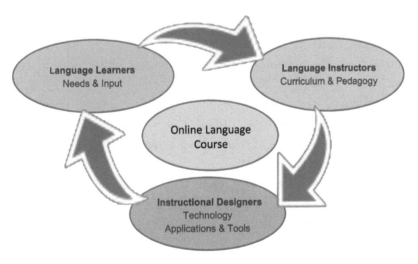

Figure 7.1 Flow for Creating an Online Language Course

When beginning to design an online class, use the following checklist to help guide your planning process. Keep in mind that these items are not organized by importance or priority, and many interconnect and overlap with each other.

1. Work with Colleagues to Ensure Horizontal and Vertical Coherence

- Collaboratively brainstorm how to restructure a F2F class as an online class and coherently streamline the course horizontally (sessions within the same level) and vertically (sessions across different levels)
- Revisit course objectives, themes and topics, and assignments, and decide either to keep them the same as in the F2F syllabus, or to modify them to make coverage less condensed
- Redesign preview and post-class work
- Rethink the design of three-communicative modes during class and modify accordingly
- Deliberate the balanced proportion of character handwriting and typing to retain long-term effects
- Revise the F2F course syllabus for an online course
- Modify assessment tasks
- Adjust scoring percentages and rubrics
- Draft and write up the syllabus
- Revise the PowerPoint slides used for F2F teaching

2. Consult Instructional Designers to Seek Advice on Technology Tools

- Explore the LMS and video-conferencing tools as candidates for an online platform for instructional delivery
- Identify needs for technology use in accordance with curricular and pedagogical objectives
- Pursue training in technology workshops to get familiar with a handful of appropriate technology tools
- Evaluate the pros and cons of selected technology tools in accordance with curricular and pedagogical objectives
- Finalize the list of technology tools to fulfill your curricular and pedagogical objectives
- Re-evaluate and confirm the list with colleagues, instructional designers, and experienced online language instructors
- Start creating technology-enhanced preview tasks, during-class tasks, and after-class

review work

- Experiment with the technology-enhanced tasks and gather feedback from your colleagues, instructional designers, and experienced online language instructors

3. Seek Students' Feedback for Modification and Improvement

- Invite students to participate in the pilot test
- Gather students' feedback and constructive suggestions
- Continue to adjust according to learners' input and comments

Outline an Online Class

Online class time varies in length, ranging from the length of a regular class to a block schedule. Regardless of delivery mode, a typical class is normally divided into three parts: beginning warm-ups, core teaching, and closure. The following table gives a glimpse of the structural layout of an online class in terms of time and content. Keep in mind that this is equally valid for in-person and online classes.

The layout of a 50-minute class

Beginning Estimated time: 5 mins.	1. Warm-ups and informal review Welcome and greetings; informal chats on learned materials with individual students 2. An overview of learning objectives (Can-do statements) Introducing the lesson of the day and informing students what they expect to learn and know

Middle
 Estimated time: 40 mins.
	Teacher-led communicative discussion precedes and builds foundation for student-centered activities.
	
	 1. Communicative modes
	   • Interpersonal tasks
	   • Interpretive tasks
	   • Presentational tasks

	2. Procedure (2 cycles required; 3rd cycle optional)
	Teacher/entire class → Between/among students task (1st cycle)
	Teacher/entire class → Between/among students task (2nd cycle)
	Teacher/entire class → Between/among students task (3rd cycle)
	I do → We do → You do
	PPP = Present → Practice → Produce
	Comprehensible input → Check for understanding → Guided practice
	3. Frequent interaction between input and output
	Teacher frequently provides comprehensible input
	Students frequently produce expected comprehensible output
	4. Integrative task
	Students demonstrate their learning in an integrative task to reach the end goal at the end of class.
Closure Estimated time: 5 mins.	Wrap-ups 1. Questions 2. Homework or assignment

The middle part is the core of teaching and takes the greatest amount of time and effort for planning and delivery. It is composed of teacher-led discussion and student-centered learning, which, together, alternate and strengthen each other across three communicative modes. The PPP sequence (present-practice-produce) complies with the three steps of teaching: I do (teacher), we do (teacher and students), and you do (students). Another way of looking at the learning process is to analyze how learners interpret and react to different types of input that lead to the production of language output, whether satisfactory or dissatisfactory.

Both young and adult learners need breaks and cognitive relief after long exposure to information presented on the computer screen. To prevent fatigue and sluggishness, it is necessary to divide instructional activities into small 5–10 minute segments to retain focal attention. This is especially needed for courses on a block schedule that may last up to 90 minutes. For a block schedule, it is wise to expand an integral task at the end of a class that synthesizes all key learning points to summarize learning experience.

It has long been advocated that language learning is most effective when learners connect with real-life experiences. Authenticity can be embodied in four aspects of teaching: contexts or settings, materials, tasks, and the process of negotiation of meaning (Mishan, 2005): see Figure 7.2.

AUTHENTICITY

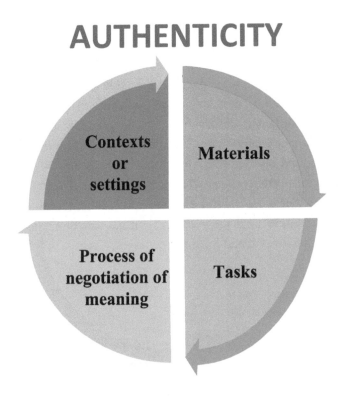

Figure 7.2 Authenticity Embodied in Four Aspects of Teaching

Here, online classes have an advantage: an instructor can easily and quickly change the virtual background to an authentic scene that matches or illustrates a particular task or cultural setting. Teachers can save photos and images on the desktop and upload them to change teaching background within Zoom or other online platforms, easily altering this virtual background during class to perfectly fit different teaching scenarios and situational learning from one scene to another. This feature conveniently embodies the notion of authenticity in virtual settings. Additionally, selecting ready-to-use 3D photo and video collections to create virtual reality effects has become highly feasible for creating online real-life settings as well. Although learners can only experience low immersion effects in front of a computer, it is more convenient and affordable than wearing an expensive goggle in a studio that many schools have not established yet due to budget constraints.

In addition to creating authentic virtual settings, an incredibly wide array of authentic materials confers another layer of authenticity for online teaching. Regardless of what printed materials or textbooks are adopted, abundant collections of authentic materials are easily searchable and compiled. Although realia and concrete objects cannot be as easily or fully displayed in front of the webcam as they might be in a physical classroom, they can still be shown sequentially and seen clearly on the screen if carefully planned.

Authentic tasks that resemble what native speakers do and say in real-life settings are mostly transferrable to online learning. Many good examples of pedagogical and authentic tasks can be found in Willis and Willis (2007) and Tseng (2014, 2018, 2020). The former includes generic tasks that apply to world languages, and the latter are Chinese-specific, though with applicability and practicability to other languages. Authentic tasks feature simulated and real-life negotiation of meaning that is observable in communication between and among native speakers. For example, a mock interview is an authentic task that mimics an interview activity between the interviewer and interviewee. The process of meaning negotiation and alternation of responses and questions characterizes what native speakers act, say, interpret, and express in real-life settings, whether a TV studio, a radio station, a sports tournament, and so on. As authenticity continues to guide language pedagogy, virtual teaching is a new realm that allows creativity and innovation to evolve and redefine.

Prepare for the First Class

The first class sets the tone for an online course, and the importance of its success cannot be underscored. Following are very practical and easy-to-follow checklists to help teachers best prepare for the first class and conduct it smoothly.

Checklist in Preparation for the First Class

1. Finalize and upload syllabus and learning materials to the LMS.
2. Update the online platform software.
3. Enable the functions you plan to use in the online setting.
   Make sure you know how to use: the webcam, host, waiting room, mute/unmute, video (stop or unstop), share screen, show PowerPoint, play video, virtual background, breakout rooms, and annotation. Upload a photo of yourself to the Zoom account.
4. Prepare Day 1's agenda and reminder notes.
5. Create a greeting and welcoming video and upload it to the LMS.
6. Send a welcome and greeting message to learners via email, inviting them to watch the welcoming video and a tutorial video on accessing the online video-conferencing tool.

Remember to follow up with reminders.

7. Encourage students to sign up for an online pre-class social hour and individual meetings. This creates a headstart for students to get connected with you before Day 1, to help you get a sense of their personality and language proficiency, and to test equipment to get familiar with the online platform system in a pressure-free setting.
8. Check possible backup devices in lieu of your major computer for online delivery (iPad, iPhone, 2nd laptop or computer).
9. Select purposeful photos for virtual backgrounds.
10. Practice projecting the best professional image in front of a webcam.

It is worth noting that facial expressions become enormously crucial and observable when teaching in front of a webcam. Consider the light in your space (at the time you'll be teaching) and the angle of the webcam, which can also make a difference in creating a professional look and visual effects in virtual settings. It will not waste your time at all to practice smiling and changing facial expressions in front of the camera, to capture the best teacher persona you can project. Before every class, remember to check and adjusting the webcam angle and lighting. Most of us are not studio recording pros, so we all need to practice before class. Be gently reminded to match the colors of your clothes with the background colors you choose. If you have time, watch recordings of your own teaching videos to revisit your facial expressions and learn "Do's and Don'ts" to constantly remind yourself. Seeing yourself in the recorded video will help you to notice things that you would otherwise not be able to see. If you plan to use body language to fulfill a certain teaching purpose, adjust the distance between your computer and where you sit before class to make sure your body language is seeable and appropriate.

Checklist for Conducting the First Class

1. Fully charge your computer and shut it down and restart if necessary.
2. Log in to an online platform via the icon course site as a host 10–15 minutes before the class start time.
3. Test microphone, video, screen share, and other built-in functions in the online platform.
4. Navigate daily learning materials and make sure PowerPoint files, videos, web links, and so on, are well-organized and easily accessible on your desktop.
5. Clean up your desktop computer and organize documents and videos to share.
6. Rehearse offline for Day 1's class.
7. Post daily agenda and to-do list in a convenient place as a reminder.
8. Play soft background music if you like.
9. Smile, welcome students, and chat with learners until class officially starts.
10. Use an iPad, iPhone, or 2nd computer as a backup device (optional).

During the Class

1. Greet and welcome students.
2. Explain classroom protocol, behavior, and etiquette and invite learners to vote and determine it together. The following offers a preliminary list of best practices for students that can be adjusted to meet local needs.

   1) Fully charge your computer or laptop before class.
   2) Make sure you have a stable internet connection.
   3) Choose a quiet place to avoid interruption, mute cell phones, lock the door during class time, or post a "No Interruption" sign on the door.
   4) Be on time and dress appropriately.
   5) Mute your microphone and turn on the webcam.
   6) Unmute to ask a question, or use "Chats" and "Raise Hand" functions to do the same.
   7) Eating is not permitted; drinking water is acceptable.
   8) Make efforts to speak Chinese almost all the time.
   9) Full presence and active participation required from the start till the end of class. See a sample rubric for daily performance and participation (Tseng, 2018) below.

	Exceeds standard	Meets standard	Approaching standard	In progress
Preparation	Strong indication of excellent preparation	Indication of sufficient preparation	Indication of mediocre preparation	Indication of inadequate or insufficient preparation
Participation	Actively & cooperatively participates with superior effort; stays attentive the entire time	Participates with satisfactory effort; stays attentive most of the time	Participates with average effort; occasionally inattentive	Participates with little effort; inattentive most of the time
Behavior	Well-disciplined, undisruptive, with excellent manners while raising questions and listening	Disciplined, undisruptive, with good manners while raising questions and listening	Occasionally undisciplined and disruptive; unsatisfactory manners while raising questions and listening	Undisciplined and disruptive most of the time; unsatisfactory manners while raising questions and listening

3. Go over the syllabus, including course objectives, schedule, requirements, homework, and grading.

4. Ask students to type their Chinese name in an online class.

5. Engage students in an ice-breaker activity: have them take turns unmuting their microphone and introducing themselves, including details such as their major, favorite sport, or similar. Stop sharing screen to see learners' faces and actions.

Example: Ice-breaker activity "我也是"
Prompts for the ice-breaker activity:

我住在弗吉尼亚州
我住在校外 / 校内
我喜欢宠物
我喜欢游泳 / 打篮球 / 打网球……
我喜欢用社交软件跟朋友说话
我喜欢网购（上网买东西）
我喜欢看中国电影
我喜欢唱卡拉 OK

Procedure:

1) The teacher generates questions for the ice-breaker game before class.

2) Before the game, the teacher explains the game rules.

3) The teacher starts to say the first statement, and students unmute their mic to say 我也是 . Those who do not share the commonality continue to mute their mics.

4) Invite those who say 我也是 to talk about themselves a bit further.

5) The teacher continues to ask several questions and repeat Step 4.

6) Invite an individual student to say a sentence and have other students engage in the game, saying 我也是 .

7) Other students continue to do the same until all have taken turns to do so.

8) Show the typed statements identical to those said in the activity, and ask for further elaboration to describe what we have found out about the entire class to build rapport and bonding for the online community.

6. Mention next class's agenda and what students need to prepare for the second class.

7. Encourage students to send you any inquiries via email and discussion board, and let them know the best ways to contact you and a reasonable time frame within which to expect your response.

8. Ask students to 1) create a flipgrid video to introduce themselves in Chinese, and 2) watch at least three peers' videos and upload a follow-up flipped video to summarize commonalities

and differences they find in comparing themselves with peers as a follow-up activity later.

9. Establish a social chat group via Facebook, WeChat, GroupMe, and/or any other means voted on by the entire class.

10. End the first day with congratulatory remarks and cheers.

After Class

1. Send a thank-you message to students for making the first class a great start.
2. Remind students of preparatory work for the second online class.
3. Ask them to complete a survey on background information and needs analysis.
4. Encourage them to send you any questions and suggestions and remind them to fully use your office hours.

Devise Teaching Slides

Online teaching places screen-to-screen presentation as the core. Whatever is presented on the computer screen will be the focus of learners' attention. In general, teaching slides for synchronous teaching should be created according to the same guidelines as for F2F in-person teaching, but for online teaching, they do need to be more detail-oriented. Teachers can choose from a wide array of presentation tools, such as PowerPoint slides, Google Slides, Prezi, Nearpod interactive slides, VoiceThread, Pear Deck, etc. Choose the one that you feel most familiar and convenient and stick to it. The following are general principles to consider regardless what kind of classroom presentation tool you use.

1. Learning Objectives Are Top Priority

Learning objectives can be best presented by can-do statements. Let these statements guide you to create, organize, and sequence teaching slides. It is a common practice to put can-do statements on the first slide, so learners know what to expect and accomplish at the onset of a class. Do not worry about layout or artistic design of the slides. Put learning objectives as top priority. PowerPoint has carved out its place as the go-to presentation software for its ease of use. This saves you time on normal days or at your busiest time when you need to scramble to put all your materials together in a short time.

2. Sequence Teaching Slides with Logics and Coherence

Class time is limited. How to arrange and sequence learning materials can be challenging. A golden rule is: organize and sequence teaching slides to make sure the content is clear, relevant, and well-connected. A general principle is to move teachable points from small to big, easy to difficult, learned to unlearned, and rudimentary to something beyond basics, and the like. Do not jam word-level vocabulary into a slide. Remember to extend it to the sentential level in meaningful and communicative contexts and spiral up, aiming at the production of a string of simple sentences even at the elementary level. When planning for instructional flow, determine which functions need to be learned first and connect them with the remaining components logically and coherently. This enables a direct route to the end rather than a wandering path toward progressive learning.

3. Maximize Visual and Audio Effects

A multimodal approach helps learners retain information and apply their new knowledge to complete assigned tasks. Presenting auditory and visual input simultaneously is beneficial for minimizing cognitive load. Using only a single source of input can be less effective. A combination of visual information such as pictures, graphics, tables, and live narration or audio files helps learners more easily process and understand information. If you have a complex graphic, break it apart into "chunks" and only present it in chunks in PowerPoint. Animations, if appropriately selected, can help you time and sequence elements.

4. Limit Bullet Points and Text

Keep text to a minimum. Asking students to read bullet point after bullet point could be boring and meaningless. It is even harder for students to read a slide packed with bullet points from the small screen of your computer. Nothing in your slide should be superfluous. Feel free to leave white space. Any words or images on your slides should be purposeful, useful, and functional. The less clutter you have on your slide, the more effective your teaching will be. Discard or simplify slides that are unnecessarily complicated or busy. To emphasize some key points, use bold, add color, or change font and size to attract learners' attention.

5. Minimize Transitions and Animation

Animation effects are visually interesting but may distract from the focus of learning. They can enhance learning only when used carefully with purpose. Choose ones that are professionally designed and cued with nuances and subtleties, including cultural elements that can't be replaced by unanimated photos or images. Admittedly, showing GIF images or using built-in animation functions in PowerPoint can diversify the design of teaching slides. However, they can mislead learners to focus on the visual effects themselves rather than the learning objective.

Overpacking animated images on slides may also raise technology-related issues while transitioning from one slide to another. This can be worse when the uploaded teaching file is very large and/or the Internet connection is unstable.

6. Use Authentic Materials But not Icons

Authentic materials are linguistically and culturally rich and are a great source of learning materials. While icons are cute, interesting, and eye-catching, they may not have the linguistic and cultural essence needed for learning. For a unit on family, showing the teacher's family photo is more effective than using icons or any type of drawing. Similarly, to help students understand how Chinese people play 乒乓球 (Pingpong) in a game, playing a short video clip selected from a tournament is more real and useful than icons or drawings. Use icons only when you cannot get real photos to capture authenticity or when revealing Chinese cultural elements become less essential.

7. Choose Appropriate Colors

Color evokes feelings and emotions. Teachers should pick appropriate colors in the planning process and help learners develop cultural awareness. Right usage of color on teaching slides is appealing and contributes to learning comprehension and retention. Following are four suggestions for the choice of colors.

1) Avoid using black and white together, as its culturally symbolic meaning is associated with death and mourning.
2) Create high contrast in chosen colors so students can easily see the difference. Darker backgrounds should go with light text and graphics in bright colors, and vice versa.
3) Steer away from colors that are too passive or aggressive. Black, orange, gray, red, and brown are in this category.
4) Avoid mixing two colors such as red and green, orange and blue, and red and blue. They are too hard to read, could cause a disturbing effect, or lack sharp contrast.

For more advice on background and text colors for slides, see Dave Paradi, "Choosing Colors for Your Presentation Slides," thinkoutsidetheslide.com (https://www.thinkoutsidetheslide.com/choosing-colors-for-your-presentation-slides/).

8. Select Appropriate Font for Characters

A character presented in different fonts is identifiable as the same by native speakers but could be very confusing for learners with limited knowledge of character writing. While this is not a concern for instructors of intermediate and advanced levels, it should be top of mind for elementary Chinese instructors. The following six characters illuminate this point. The three characters on the left are the same as the three on the right. But elementary language learners may not be able to recognize that the subtle differences (indicated in different strokes highlighted in red and blue) are stylistic rather than meaningful. Some fonts may automatically alter when teaching slides switch to a different presentation mode. Instructors should double-check the font and test it online before teaching. Most instructors choose fonts such as MS Mincho, Meiryo, Kaiti, or Arial Unicode MS. Arial Unicode MS and Meiryo are typical sans-serif fonts and very clear and bold. MS Mincho is closest to calligraphic writing. It shows strokes as if they were written with a brush, directing the emphasis of where the "brush" is heavier and lighter.

Image Source: *Hacking Chinese: A Better Way of Learning Mandarin* (https://www.hackingchinese.com/chinese-character-variants-and-fonts-for-language-learners/)

Relieve Anxiety for Learners

Always keep in mind learners' emotional condition. Learning a new language creates anxiety, and learning remotely adds to that anxiety. Language instructors recognize this issue and strive to lower learners' affective filter by creating a pressure-free and fear-free online learning setting. Whatever an instructor says, does, and asks students to do should closely relate to learners' affective reaction. following are five tips for removing or minimizing learner's anxiety in order to facilitate online learning.

1. Provide Timely and Constant Assistance to Less-prepared Students

Online learners may feel like they are wandering on a "lonely island" when embarking on digital learning. Those who are left behind may have a higher level of anxiety, due to feelings of social isolation associated more with online learning than F2F in-person learning. From students' perspectives, teacher's ignorance of such a group of learners is a signal of indifference and lack of interest in their progress. It is therefore even more necessary than in a regular F2F class for online teachers to write emails and encourage students to meet during office hours, or to make additional appointments to practice language with you individually. One-on-one advising meetings and tutorial sessions would help far-behind learners to catch up and feel more connected with course content and their peer learners. Offering informal online social hours and review sessions on a regular basis is also highly recommended.

2. Establish Rapport Through Interactive Discussion Boards and Social Media

Learners feel pressure not only from teachers but also from their peers. Connecting with peers through an interactive forum and social media helps to release tension and nurture peer facilitatory and cooperative learning. Students feel more relaxed when they can mingle with their peers without the teacher's presence. With the aid of an informal online social venue, learners have an added channel to talk about course work, see reminders, share information and feelings, catch up with any missing information, and ask for clarification.

3. Present Materials Clearly and Logically

Teaching too many things at once can be confusing and overwhelming, and can end up scaring students away. Clear, logical presentation is a good principle that applies to what a teacher says as well as to what a PowerPoint slide presents. Presenting a new concept or a new grammatical structure clearly and logically saves class time and helps learners digest information without the need for remedial instruction. Teachers should avoid assigning busy work and take into account the cognitive load imposed upon learners, so learners can process an appropriate amount of information each time and get to where they need to be.

4. Reserve Time for Pause to Check for Understanding

It is observable that the pace in a F2F in-person class may be faster than in a virtual class.

This can be partially caused by delayed reception of information and lagged response time associated with technology. Therefore, in an online class, speak the target language a bit more slowly, elicit responses with reasonable pause and patience, and repeat with grace and purpose. Students will appreciate your efforts to keep their level in mind and make your teaching pace flexible and adjustable as needed.

5. Satisfy Individual Needs

Learners differ greatly in personality and learning needs and styles. When converting to online learning, individual differences become even more salient and adaptability of instruction is even more critically needed. Some students are more visual-reliant, others are audio-oriented. As young learners are building their identities, some may be very sensitive about their self-image and how they look projected online. To satisfy these diverse needs, it may be time-effective to offer visual and audio prompts and stimuli at the same time as giving instructions. This also helps to minimize their cognitive load. When introducing a weekly schedule, use a calendar in colors with arrows in red to point to specific activities for a specific day. This is more effective than simply presenting typed characters and numbers to indicate dates. While students are viewing such information on the screen, an instructor can also use a cursor pointer to point to what is being discussed, to attract learners' eyes and make it easy to follow, while at the same time, orally introducing it to complement the visual cues. Diverse learner needs should also be considered in assessments. Try to evaluate language performance through different types of assessment and grant learners the freedom to choose from several options. For example, for a task that asks learners to introduce themselves, allow them to create a book, printed or electronic, a video, or a PowerPoint presentation. Relatedly, rubrics should be tailored to different types of assessments and adjusted to align with what is being assessed.

Foster Mindfulness for Online Learning

Mindfulness has recently emerged as an effective complement to language teaching. It helps improve physical and mental health by relieving stress, improving sleep, enhancing concentration, and reducing chronic pain. Being mindful of what we do, think, and feel empowers us to be more conscious about how we react to what surrounds us. Being more reflective about our emotions, thoughts, and state of mind betters our well-being and helps us minimize negative energy and recharge with positive energy. To help learners cope with online anxiety and tension, it is worthwhile to invite them to experiment with some mindful practices and techniques during online class. Start with something small and short and see how learners respond before doing something bigger and longer.

1. Play Meditation Music

Meditation music is soothing and helps us calm down and have some relieve from pressure. Consider showing a meditation video on the screen with music playing while waiting for students before class begins and during office hours. After you and students start talking, turn down the volume of the background music and play it very softly. With students' permission, incorporate this into your class routine and add it to your regular class time. Invite students to join you in closing their eyes and immersing themselves in the music for a minute or so. Then invite them to open their eyes and seek volunteers to talk about what their day is like, what they feel at that moment, what they feel most grateful for, and similar questions to foster a positive mindset. Class time is limited, so keep it as short as five minutes on the first day of a week, or a similar cycle that is agreeable to students. As it becomes a welcome practice, add it to more days of the week so it transitions to a steady routine. Some other mindfulness techniques — such as live in the present, focus on breathing, and body scanning — are commonly used in in-person language classes and are worth of exploration in virtual settings.

2. Express Fears and Concerns

Invite learners to talk about their fears and share concerns about online learning in or outside class, especially during the first several classes of a semester. Encourage learners to post written notes or recorded videos in the target language in the interactive discussion board or through whatever technology tools you have selected for this purpose. Allowing learners to share a photo or image to express their feelings as another viable option. A follow-up instructional activity, which is more important than the expressions of fears and concerns, is to go through shared fears and concerns and provide resolutions to reassure students that the learning setting will low-fear and low-pressure.

3. Use Animated Emojis in Lieu of Words

Emojis are not popular only with young learners; they are most welcome by adult learners as well. When wisely used, they can connect learners' emotions with predetermined pedagogical purposes. The figure shows 12 emojis from this site with animated facial expressions that can be shown on the screen to conduct a warm-up activity at the beginning of a class on the first day of class during a week.

Image Source: https://blog.prototypr.io/design-tools-get-200-free-animated-icons-to-delight-your-users-eec2df4a49c6

Step 1: Ask learners to choose a color and circle an emoji to best reflects their feelings after a long weekend, orally describe their weekend activities, and explain why they chose it.

Step 2: Lead the entire class to tally the number of emojis that are chosen by all students in the class and point out the emojis that are most frequently chosen.

Step 3: Guide learners to more precisely use verbal expressions to describe their feelings or emotions such as 高兴 (happy)，快乐 (happy)，开心 (happy)，兴奋 (excited)，难过 (sad)，伤心 (sad)，有心事 (bothered by something)，闷闷不乐 (unhappy)，笑脸迎人 (wearing a smile to welcome people)，笑容满面 (the smile is all over the face)，满面春风 (the smile is all over the face)，愁眉苦脸 (frown). Type the word expressions for chosen emojis on the main screen or the Chat box and recycle these expressions.

4. Use Drawings and Photos to Express Feelings and Emotions

Once in a while invite students to express their feelings by drawing on the screen of the computer simultaneously during class. Give them freedom and autonomy to choose whatever color they like and draw anything that best represent their feelings and emotions. Then ask volunteers to describe what they have drawn and explain why. If the computer screen has limited space for a very big class, then ask students to upload their drawings before class and have them take turns to introduce them. Some students may not be good at drawing and prefer not to do so; a good alternative that accomplished the same purpose is to ask them to upload a photo or image to Padlet or other accessible tool.

5. Reflective Practice

Reflective practice is getting more common in language learning. Taking care of well-being has proven value, but can be easily ignored when pursuing knowledge is overemphasized. In our fast-paced daily routines, competition exists everywhere and adds more complications to student life. Reading and commenting on learners' reflections is a kind gesture that encourages everyone to be thoughtful and compassionate. Reflecting on experience is not just looking back on the learning process or outcome; it is also taking a more conscious look at and more deeply analyzing affective, emotional, and psychological domains that learners would otherwise rarely have the chance to consider. Reflections give another channel for teachers to gather unnoticed clues and connect with students to cater to individual needs better. Students' reflections, guided with or without prompts, can be incorporated into the grading system, but since they are difficult if not impossible to evaluate, giving a simple completion grade is deemed most appropriate.

Engage Learners to Create a Thriving Learning Community

Creating a thriving online learning community involves synchronous and asynchronous learning. It includes student interactions with an instructor and with their peer learners both in and out of class. To promote interaction in class, instructors can create student activities in breakout rooms, encourage students to engage in the Chat box for questions and answers, frequently invite learners to respond and ask questions, and create interactive meaning-based games to achieve communicative goals, just to offer a few examples. Engaging learners to actively participate in asynchronous learning, whether individually or in groups, requires synergized collective effort from both instructor and learners. The strategies provided below shed light on ways to promote asynchronous interactive learning. It is ideal to apply as many best practices as possible, but if you cannot, start experimenting with the core strategies that are most relevant to your course.

1. Establish Group Norms Through a Co-create Process

Determine class norms and expectations collectively with students. In a co-create process, an instructor partners with students and cordially invites them to have a voice and a stake in a certain aspects of curriculum development. This inclusive approach grants authorship to students and holds them accountable, so the role of instructor becomes less authoritative and prescriptive. Working together to build a social contract and pledge is much more effective than having the teacher create it alone. It is important to set the stage from the outset of the course and model engagement expectations from the beginning, with constant reminders to reinforce learners' behavior.

2. Create Individual Virtual Portraits

During the first week of course, ask students to create their own personal portrait, starting with a self-introduction in writing, speaking, or a combination of the two. Then invite learners to take part in a "same or different" follow-up task to get to know one another better by identifying commonalities and discrepancies among them. Seek learners' input to see if they want to extend from the starting point to an end-of-semester product such as a website or a blog. Let them take the lead to come up with a feasible plan to balance instructional needs and workload.

3. Foster Collaboration Outside Class

To enhance interaction among learners, it is necessary to alternate individual work with work involving two or more learners, such as pair work, group projects, and interactive tasks outside class. Plan beforehand to alternate scheduling these two types of assignments to avoid frequent meetings for pair and group work during the busiest time of the semester for learners. Also think creatively to enhance student-to-student interaction by asking learners to learn from their peers and to comment on their peers' work. It is important to give clear instructions and diversify target tasks by covering different cognitive aspects such as analyzing, predicting, inferring, hypothesizing, problem-solving, higher-order thinking ability, etc. This goes beyond vague instructions like simply asking learners to read a typed passage or watch a peer's video and comment on posted work. Specific examples include, but are not limited to, asking learners to view apartment photos and video that their peers create and vote for the top choice, respond to a segment of a documentary film on environmental protection by offering three solutions to existing problems and critique with pros and cons, and recommending the most ideal job for someone with an identified personal profile based on job ads posted on a website. It is worth devising different types of tasks to bring about as much interaction as possible and to trigger ongoing threaded discussions to build a strong learning community.

4. Set up a Social Media Space

Social media provides a place for students to communicate outside class and builds the online learning community. Learners of younger generations already spend a growing amount of time on social media to connect with their peers. This is one of the best ways to bring language learning to life and make it more exciting, energetic, and enjoyable. Here are some suggestions for using social media in an online teaching class:

1) Conduct a needs-analysis survey before deciding on using a certain social media as a class community tool.
2) Seek students' input to determine their preference of social media tools such as Facebook, Twitter, WeChat, Instagram, WhatsApp, and so on, and brainstorm how they want to participate and manage the account or group.
3) Send a permission form or parent consent form to guardians and parents in compliance with K-12 school policies. This can be skipped at the college level.
4) Invite students to outline rules or policies and to reach a consensus on using the chosen social media.
5) Determine formal and informal topics for discussions and assignments. Thematic written or oral discussion assignments could be posted using social media as formal assignments. Announcements or Q&As could be posted as informal assignments when needed.
6) Create rubrics for formal written or oral assignments and make them transparent.

More relevant information is provided in the discussion about the discussion forum.

5. Maximize Interaction in the Discussion Board

Once built and launched, the discussion board or forum needs to be constantly and systematically monitored to make it interactive and sustainable. Its pedagogical purposes may overlap with those of social media to some extent. It is up to the instructor to choose the type of discussion board that will best serve the interests of the course and learners. The following list of tips will help you create a well-functioning and powerful discussion platform with purpose and fortitude.

1) Question initiators

The instructor must not be the only person to post questions in the discussion board or forum. Let students take the lead in initiating discussions. Student-led discussion provides a more relaxing atmosphere to free up interesting ideas and thoughts. Rotate among students to play different roles to moderate questions such as questioner and facilitator. Give ownership to students to decide how to rotate different roles.

2) Content

Relevance and interest are key to determining the content being discussed. Students are keenly interested in topics relevant to their immediate life, school settings, current issues, and future plans. Connect discussion questions with high relevancy and coverage of the themes in the curriculum.

3) Question type

Avoid posting yes-no questions, and choose open-ended questions that potentially trigger a variety of perspectives and opinions. Questions that ask for likes vs. dislikes, agree or disagree, problem vs. solution, present vs. future, and so on, foster critical and creative thinking and reinforce threaded and procedural discussions. Once students have posted their first-round responses or answers, begin to raise some follow-up questions to sustain and extend the discussion. WH-word questions could be used as effective strategies to serve this purpose.

4) Length and format

Too much text on the discussion board may be a barrier. Keep the questions succinct, to-the-point, and interesting. Bullet points and short descriptions are more effective than long posts. Use colors, different fonts, and bold and other text enhancement techniques to emphasize the foci of key points.

5) Constant monitoring

Never set the discussion board aside or let it go unmanaged. Make sure you actively answer emails, monitor discussions, and post reminders to get a good sense of student involvement and to give instant feedback as needed.

6) Grading

Complete reliance on learners' voluntary participation is not likely to generate productive discussion. Let students know that participation in the discussion board is key to the shared goal of the course. Make your expectations and guidelines clear at the onset and let learners know beforehand what questions are graded, ungraded, and optional. If graded, make grading criteria crystal clear, so students know what to do to meet your expectation and standards.

6. Office Hours and Tutorial Sessions

Individual meetings and tutorials are invaluable for students. They can provide support that they need to excel as opposed to just scrape through. While attending office hours and tutorial sessions should be optional, do encourage or require those who need extra help to take advantage of these opportunities. Students may not be aware of what they need or where they are in making progress, and they may need you to take the initiative and provide timely advice. This is even more pivotal for courses that are taught remotely, as students may need to ask for your clarification and clear instructions more often in and out of class. Getting well connected with students in class builds professional links and good relationships. Being interested in and curious about their school life and how they adjust around it shows your compassion and humanity. Students will deeply appreciate your efforts to reach out to them and explain your genuine intentions to help.

7. Ask for Feedback and Suggestions

Gathering learners' input through different means is an important process for co-creating a course with their partnership. Solicit and accept suggestions from students sometime in the first several weeks of instruction to resolve issues as early as possible. Reserve a couple of minutes at the end of class on a day early in the course to chat with students and let them know that you sincerely count on their direct and candid comments in front of the entire class. Supplement such in-class open discussion with informal early feedback forms, individual and small group discussions, email responses, and reflection journals with guided prompts on possible improvement and constructive suggestions for you.

8. Give Opportunities for Extra Credit

Extra credit is an incentive for students to improve their performance. What exactly students do is negotiable between the instructor and students. To be fair, state this opportunity in the syllabus and announce it in class to encourage interested students to seize the opportunity. Give several options that are directly linked to learned materials for students to consider and then reach a consensus on what and when to complete the extra credit project. A 30-day challenge for language learning is a welcome example for online independent learning (for a good example, see the "30 Day Challenge" offered by the Center for Applied Second Language Studies at the University of Oregon: https://casls.uoregon.edu/30-day-challenge/).

Assess Language Performance

Guidelines for language assessment in virtual, blended, and F2F learning are consistent, but online assessment requires a deeper understanding of what technology tools can offer in terms of assessment.

General Guidelines

As teachers' evaluations remain the central way for assessing learners' language performance, peer evaluation and self-assessment have been widely adopted to elevate the authoritative role of an instructor. These two assessment measures motivate learners to fully engage in the learning and evaluative process. Just as in F2F in-person teaching, a combination of formative and summative assessment is needed on a daily or weekly basis and at the end of a thematic unit. As a common practice, share checklists, rubrics, and scoring criteria with learners prior to assessments. Over 100 task-specific checklists and rubrics targeted at the novice and intermediate levels and AP Chinese can be found in the three volumes of *The Handbook of Tasks and Rubrics for Teaching Mandarin Chinese* (Tseng, 2014, 2018, 2020).

Integrated Performance Assessment

The Integrated Performance Assessment (IPA) can be implemented to conclude a unit in a F2F four-walled classroom, and it also perfectly fits in an online course. Perhaps one recommendation best suited for online assessment is to have students do a presentational task first and an interpersonal task later, after receiving input in reading, listening, or viewing to complete an interpretive task. The interpretive-presentational-interpersonal sequence gives learners time to practice and internalize learned materials and be well-prepared for interpersonal exchanges that involve unrehearsed negotiation. The main purpose of this sequence is to minimize the chance of a communication breakdown, and ultimately to lower the learners' anxiety levels and improve their language performance. This recommendation makes more sense when students are working together to discuss assigned topics in online breakout rooms without the teacher. A slightly adjusted sequence is welcome when teachers are confident of learners' ability to converse spontaneously. Under such circumstances, taking part in an interpersonal task first and then moving to a presentational task does not impede online performance or create any communication barrier.

Online Tests Completed in the LMS

Any LMS has built-in functions to provide instant scoring and feedback for true-false and multiple-choice questions. Students can receive automatically generated messages via email to get notification of successful submission of assignments and release of a grade. Although compositions and essays need to be graded and commented on by instructors, automatically generated email notification saves some time for instructors and reassures students. It also streamlines the grading process, saving instructors a lot of grading time and effort. As instructors try to fully utilize the built-in grading and testing functions within the LMS, they may also realize that the LMS might not have needed technology tools to satisfy some pedagogical goals. If so, resort to outside technology resources that can link to the LMS and systematically record scoring in the online gradebook.

Digital Learning Profile

The LMS allows instructors to create subfolders for each individual learners. It is worth making good use of this function to create a digital learning profile for each learner, so instructors can keep track of all assessment files and closely monitor learners' progress. This also allows instructors to get a holistic picture of how well learners can do from the beginning to the end of the course and offers timely assistance to help learners improve and meet expectations. The learning profile also serves purposes such as program assessments and outside review. This is one of the best practices for the collection of data-driven learning outcomes.

Handwriting and Typing for Characters

From learners' perspectives, character typing is much easier and faster than handwriting, and so perhaps it is more welcomed by learners in the digital era. This, however, does not necessarily comply with the principles for character learning and assessment. Assessing character production cannot solely rely on typing. Handwriting is a skill that needs to be progressively and proportionally incorporated in the curriculum across levels. Character writing by hand is getting more diversified and versatile with the invention of advanced technology. In addition to writing characters by hand on a piece of paper, handwriting, in a new sense, can also be done with a mouse, on an app, or on a digital whiteboard or notebook. Using a mouse to write characters on screen is not highly recommended as a major means for character learning since it is slow, inconvenient, and cannot generate the type of characters we need to fulfill pedagogical functions.

The following summarizes three ways of producing handwritten characters in a traditional way and innovatively mediated through the advancement of technology. Handwriting on a piece of paper requires one more step for submission, whereas handwriting aided by technology tools can be readily submitted in just seconds.

1. Handwrite Chinese characters on the regular piece of paper and then take a photo or scan to submit it. Learners can submit it within the LMS or upload it to the Google Drive folder created by the teacher.
2. Handwrite on any app with a draw function. The draw function is popular for some instructional apps, such as Nearpod, Pear Deck, and Padlet. However, these apps may be appropriate for novice learners only, due to the limited number of characters that can be written in the available space. The big advantage is that the teacher can view the student's work directly from the apps, which is convenient for both teachers and learners.
3. Handwrite with a draw function on a digital whiteboard or digital notebook, such as

Google Jamboard, Microsoft Whiteboard, Evernote, OneNote, etc. Many new computers have built-in touch-screen functions that allow users to write characters with a fingertip or a wireless stylus pen on the screen. Learners could share the writing assignments directly with teachers using a shareable link. The digital whiteboard or notebook is good for learners at any level because of its unlimited space, and learners can type longer essays with more characters.

While handwriting on a piece of paper remains a core and fundamental practice for the initial stage of character learning, it is worth exploring the pedagogical values of handwriting through other technology-enhanced mediums such as handwriting on an app, a tablet, a digital whiteboard or notebook, and a computer touch screen. As of today, it is unclear which of the options mentioned, or which combination of them, with or without typing, yields better results in character recognition, production, and retention. As more technological options for character learning become available, we need more studies to guide us on making solid and wise decisions.

Proctoring Online Tests

Online proctoring does seem to pose some challenges that are additional to regular F2F teaching. One convenient strategy is to have students share their screen while taking an online test, so teachers can see their screen and keep track of what exactly they are doing. As usual, instructors should clearly state the "No Cheating" policy at the onset of a course. Communicate with learners, with full transparency, that cheating and plagiarism will result in negative consequences such as expulsion from school, which is consistent in courses regardless of delivery mode. Although online proctoring tools are available, the choices are very limited and come at a cost. Even if budget is not an issue, using these tools to condition learners' behavior can feel demoralizing, humiliating, and distrustful of learners' integrity and honesty. Reinforcing positive behavior and maintaining learners' self-esteem, instead, respects what they can do and can do well. Pledging and adhering to honor codes are a good example of positive reinforcement.

Prepare and Observe Teaching

The following checklist has dual purposes. It offers categorized effective strategies for preparing for the delivery of online teaching and observation. Category A on the top shows summative reflections that are keys to success in online teaching. Under this category are seven categories of principles for effective online teaching, with a good number of strategies rolled out in each category. It has been consistently observed that Category D — using the target language to provide comprehensible input and generate productive output — is the most challenging area for UVA STARTALK teacher participants. Skillsets required for effective use of the strategies in this category take longer to develop and use with full, mature competence in comparison with others. Constant practice sharpens skills. A reflective mindset is the best way to keep improving and growing. While teaching online, ask your colleagues to join a session to observe your teaching and give you feedback. Or take some time to watch the recorded video and analyze your strengths and weaknesses in accordance with the strategies in the checklist. Reflective and critical self-analysis of the recorded teaching video complements the feedback from a colleague. Following this self-evaluation and self-reflection, take the time to summarize a list of things that are working well and not working well and incorporate these in your future improvement plan. With a growth mindset and self-reflective practice, you will thrive as a high-performing Chinese language instructor in the online world.

Checklist for Teaching Preparation & Online Class Observation

Instructor:_____ Observer:_____

Date:_____ Time:_____ Location:_____

Daily topic: _____Level: _____ Number of students: _____

Instructions

1. Take notes on what you observe during the class in chronological order. Please use the last page to help you keep track of the instructional flow.
2. Check and/or comment on the following categories to organize your observation notes.
3. For each criterion, check the appropriate box to indicate the degree observed and add observational evidence for each criterion as appropriate. (FO= Fully Observed; PO=Partially Observed; NO=Not Observed)

A. Summative reflections that are keys to success of teaching

1. Were instructional objectives fulfilled?

　☐ FO　　　　☐ PO　　　　☐ NO

2. Did students generate expected language output?

　☐ FO　　　　☐ PO　　　　☐ NO

3. Total amount of time for student's talk?

4. Total amount of time for teacher's talk?

5. Total amount of time for student-centered activities (3 modes)

B. Implementing a standards-based and thematically organized curriculum
The statements that follow are indicative of the planning that occurs prior to the development of an individual lesson plan.

1.1 Interpersonal	1.2 Interpretive	
2.1 Practices of cultures	2.2 Products of cultures	
3.1 Making connections	3.2 Acquiring new information	1.3 Presentational
4.1 Language comparisons	4.2 Cultural comparisons	
5.1 School & community	5.2 Lifelong learning	

FO　　　　　PO　　　　　NO

C. Facilitating a learner-centered classroom (create 2–3 student-centered tasks during 1-hour teaching).

Teacher			
Criteria	Degree Observed		Observed Evidence
1. Good time length/management	☐ FO	☐ PO	☐ NO	
2. Clear instructions	☐ FO	☐ PO	☐ NO	
3. Modeling prior to pair/ group work	☐ FO	☐ PO	☐ NO	
4. Opportune assistance/ Monitoring	☐ FO	☐ PO	☐ NO	
5. Culturally responsive strategies	☐ FO	☐ PO	☐ NO	

6. Strategic grouping	☐ FO	☐ PO	☐ NO	

Student				
Criteria	Degree Observed			Observed Evidence
7. Engagement & participation	☐ FO	☐ PO	☐ NO	
8. Satisfactory language output	☐ FO	☐ PO	☐ NO	
9. Learning objective(s) achieved	☐ FO	☐ PO	☐ NO	

D. Using target language and providing comprehensible input (to generate productive language output)	Degree Observed			Observed Evidence
Use the target language almost all the time	☐ FO	☐ PO	☐ NO	
Strategies for making language comprehensible (NOTE: Body language/gesture/facial expressions and visual aids/real or concrete objects are effective strategies for F2F teaching. They are still applicable in online teaching but much less frequently used)	Degree Observed			Observed Evidence
1. Language modification/ simplification	☐ FO	☐ PO	☐ NO	
2. Contextual clues	☐ FO	☐ PO	☐ NO	
3. Modeling for pair/group work	☐ FO	☐ PO	☐ NO	
4. Age-appropriate language use	☐ FO	☐ PO	☐ NO	
5. Level-appropriate language use	☐ FO	☐ PO	☐ NO	

Teacher scaffolding in other aspects	Degree Observed			Observed Evidence
6. Vocabulary/grammar taught in meaningful contexts	☐ FO	☐ PO	☐ NO	
7. Meaning/communicative drills	☐ FO	☐ PO	☐ NO	
8. Frequent invitations of students' responses	☐ FO	☐ PO	☐ NO	
9. Appropriate error correction	☐ FO	☐ PO	☐ NO	
10. Effective elicitation techniques	☐ FO	☐ PO	☐ NO	
11. Quality input flood	☐ FO	☐ PO	☐ NO	
12. Sentential-level pushed output	☐ FO	☐ PO	☐ NO	

E. Integrating culture, content, and language	Degree Observed			Observed Evidence
1. Cultural products appropriately used	☐ FO	☐ PO	☐ NO	
2. Cultural practices appropriately addressed	☐ FO	☐ PO	☐ NO	
3. Cultural perspectives appropriately introduced	☐ FO	☐ PO	☐ NO	
F. Adapting and using age-appropriate authentic materials	Degree Observed			Observed Evidence
1. Use different types of authentic materials	☐ FO	☐ PO	☐ NO	
2. Age-appropriate	☐ FO	☐ PO	☐ NO	
3. Level-appropriate	☐ FO	☐ PO	☐ NO	
4. Appropriate selection for meeting instructional objective(s)	☐ FO	☐ PO	☐ NO	

G. Conducting performance-based assessments	Degree Observed			Observed Evidence
1. In-class frequent comprehension checks	□ FO	□ PO	□ NO	
2. Use different types of in-class formative assessments	□ FO	□ PO	□ NO	
3. Use different types of after-class assessments	□ FO	□ PO	□ NO	
4. Connect to real-life experiences	□ FO	□ PO	□ NO	

H. Through the learning tools, have the instructional objectives been achieved?	Degree Observed			Observed Evidence
1. Use a variety of learning tools to help learners ACCESS language, culture, and content to meet performance objectives in three modes.	□ FO	□ PO	□ NO	
2. Use a variety of applications to help learners PRODUCE language, interact with culture and content to meet performance objectives in three modes.	□ FO	□ PO	□ NO	
3. Use available technologies, via the Zoom online platform and Nearpod, to help learners engage and meet performance objectives.	□ FO	□ PO	□ NO	

Zoom: Interactive whiteboard; annotation; recording; livescreen/application sharing; nonverbal feedback; breakout rooms; hand-raising; in-meeting chats

Nearpod: Test and assessment; collaborate activity; polls and surveys; web contents

Others: Google Forms & more tech tools that are applicable

Instructional flow

A. Implement a standards-based and thematically organized curriculum

B. Facilitate a learner-centered classroom

C. Use target language and providing comprehensible input

D. Integrate culture, content, and language

E. Adapt and using age-appropriate authentic materials

F. Conduct performance-based assessments

Time	What teacher & students did	Comments
Before Class		
Class Begins		

References

Mishan, F. 2005. Designing authenticity into language learning materials. Intellect Books. Oregon: Portland.

Tseng, M. 2014. The Handbook of Tasks and Rubrics for Teaching Mandarin Chinese (Volume I). Beijing Language and Culture University Press.

Tseng, M. 2018. The Handbook of Tasks and Rubrics for Teaching Mandarin Chinese (Volume I with added e-version). Beijing Language and Culture University Press & Phoenix Tree Publishing Inc.

Tseng, M. 2020. The Handbook of Tasks and Rubrics for Teaching Mandarin Chinese (Volume II). Phoenix Tree Publishing Inc.

Tseng, M. 2020. The Handbook of Tasks and Rubrics for Teaching Mandarin Chinese (Volume III). Phoenix Tree Publishing Inc.

Willis, D., & J. Willis. 2007. Doing Task-based Teaching. Oxford University Press.

Chapter 8
Frequently Asked Questions

Some misconceptions or misbeliefs prevail in online teaching. With its rapid rise, language educators and administrators continue to hold assumptions about online teaching, assumptions with varying degrees of truth and of such a range that they sometimes contradict each other. Some issues are disputable, while others may be more clear-cut problems that need explanation or resolution. It is encouraging that as more and more language teachers gain experience in virtual teaching, belief and trust in this mode is growing, while being shaped, formed, and verified. Online teaching has the potential to improve and expand the field of teaching Chinese as a foreign language, and so it is best to confront the assumptions and misconceptions about it now.

This chapter is meant to illuminate some points, unravel some myths, and provide a practical guide to questions that Chinese language educators frequently ask about online teaching and learning. It is structured by a list of fifteen questions pertaining to beliefs and widely circulated hypotheses that language educators might continue to hold and to bring up in many professional development venues — often leading to heated discussions and expressions of skepticism about online teaching. The responses to the questions that originate from these discussions are intended to unpack knowledge and understanding of what online language teaching and learning should be. Some responses are generated to disclose the unexplored or underexplored, and others may corroborate existent ideas or thoughts and re-affirm some common grounds. While in this chapter, *online teaching* in most cases refers to F2F virtual teaching, it also applies to remote teaching featuring asynchronous learning most of the time, if not all, or blended learning with a mix of F2F and self-paced independent learning.

1. Can online teaching replace F2F teaching?

Many language educators have asked this question repeatedly. Fear of job insecurity is prevalent. Online teaching in whatever form is an alternative to F2F onsite teaching and cannot fully replace it. However, there are populations of students who are unable, for various reasons, to attend onsite F2F classes.

Online learning, in whatever form, is a good option for the following groups of students.

1. Students who need to work, and whose part-time or full-time job is during a regular F2F class.
2. Students who cannot attend a regular F2F class due to personal health or family issues.
3. Students who cannot attend a regular F2F class due to other excused or unexcused reasons.

It is not true that creating an online class costs much less than teaching a F2F class. An online language course cannot be created by simply moving practice items in conventional textbooks and exercise workbooks for online self-paced learning. Indeed, setting up an online course in alignment with research-supported best practices, whether asynchronous, synchronous, or a mix of both, is likely to cost more — roughly triple the amount of time, effort, and budget for F2F teaching in the initial year of development. The initial setup is much more costly, time-consuming, and labor-intensive than F2F teaching. After the initial stages, including pilot testing, the demands in terms of time and budget decrease, and the instructor and students will start to witness its worth in outcomes and efficacy in following years. The setup of an online course that is purely or mostly asynchronous for self-paced learning requires team effort to ensure that curriculum design, pedagogy, and technology are well-connected and supportive to achieve the best outcomes. An ideal setup cannot be done by a language instructor alone, but relies on consultation with a technology specialist, instructional designer, graphic designer, and even learners' feedback. After the initial setup of an online course, the necessary support group gets smaller, but well-trained instructors, assistants, coaches, and tutors remain key personnel, to ensure that students who need immediate assistance and tutorials are not left alone or helpless. Even though social connection is possibly achieved by virtual meetings or social gatherings through whatever social media, it is never equivalent to F2F social interaction, and for this reason, students in online classes may need extra attention.

2. Does online teaching require a teaching certificate?

All qualified teachers that are hired to teach in K-12 schools, whether certified or not certified in teaching a foreign language, can teach online courses. This is the same as instructors teaching at colleges or universities in the United States. With increasing demand for online courses, more institutions, programs, and educational centers will offer training and certificates for online language teaching. A certificate in online teaching will be a winning point to add to one's teaching credentials and professional profile. At present, though, this is not officially required. As online teaching continues to gain popularity in the teaching and learning of world languages, more schools will likely prefer to employ certificate holders to teach online language courses. As the job market in online teaching becomes more competitive, certificate holders will be at an advantage. Even for those who do not hold a certificate, prior experience or relevant professional training will create more opportunities for career development. It is likely that online language teaching will become a must-take course in a robust and well-established teaching preparation program in graduate schools in the foreseeable future.

3. Is anxiety and tech-phobia normal for online teaching?

Having a certain level of anxiety and tech-phobia is not unusual, and indeed is quite normal. Even experienced instructors have felt this way and have outgrown it. Indeed, one of the authors of this book had technology phobia! The thought, "I am a slow learner in technology", has been lingering in many minds for years. As observed, veteran faculty tend not to cope with new technology as flexibly as young employees. Accept the reality and instill a "can-do statement" for yourself that will send fear and phobia swiftly away. Thinking positively and realistically, people with middle range of intellectual ability can learn technology: it is really just about a matter of time and degree of familiarity. Set a reasonably achievable goal and seek help from technology specialists or colleagues who are more familiar with the technology. No one is good at everything, but practice makes skills perfect. Fostering a growth mindset leads you to learn new things and incrementally build competence in what you can do and what challenges you are willing to take, big or small. Taking a positive angle will make you feel better.

As new technologies evolve and advance so rapidly, college students seem born adapted in the E-era. New graduates are required to demonstrate their competence in the use of technology before graduation. But they, even as savvy technology users, do not know as much pedagogy as language professionals do. They have much less expertise in language teaching and have not had the time or experience to cultivate a good sense of what excellence in teaching means. In fact, a moderate level of anxiety leads to greater productivity and high performance. And even seasoned teachers have a certain level of anxiety or pressure when they take on a new task or a new role. You do not need to know it all, just to learn several tools that closely align with your course objectives.

Let technology specialists or instructional designers help you. Seek their advice and consultation first, and avoid indulging in unnecessary worries. Also, you do not need to do everything alone. If budget allows, seek resources to hire an assistant, either undergraduate or graduate, to help create some technology-based tasks for your course. The most important thing is to figure out which technology tools can fulfill the central instructional objectives you have in mind for your curriculum, not vice versa. Never let technology scare away or mitigate your confidence. Do it for a pleasure or even for leisure. Start small.

Keep in mind that like instructors, students also have a certain level of fear and anxiety before attending the first online class. Even if the instructor offers technology-supporting workshops or tries ice breakers or activities before a semester begins, the first online class may have a mix of feelings among students. Some students may worry about whether online learning of Chinese, a language so different and foreign, is the right choice; others may anticipate that their first online Chinese lesson will turn out to be a welcoming experience. Being empathetic and compassionate about what students feel adds human touches that students sense and are grateful for. Students will appreciate your kindest intentions to put yourself in their shoes and be thoughtfully considerate.

4. Is online learning appropriate for all ages of learners?

Not really. Not all students in K-16 educational settings are ready for online learning. Even if some are, K-12 learners need constant parental guidance, including reminders about eye protection and avoiding long-time exposure to the computer. Online learning is good for those who are mature, highly motivated, self-disciplined, truly independent, and have a strong desire to learn. In general, adults and college students are more mature, self-disciplined, and independent than secondary school students, and their attention span is longer. Elementary school students are perhaps the group of learners that needs the most support and supervision to get the most out of online education. Online classroom management poses additional concerns across different levels for teachers. Considering physical and psychological maturity and constraints, online modules must be balanced and adjusted between synchronous and asynchronous learning and well monitored by teachers' online presence.

5. Can one create an online course alone?

Yes, but this is not recommended. Creating an online course takes much more effort and time commitment than a F2F course. Doing it alone is possible but formidable. An online course with great potential to be a success involves extensive collaborative work within a team composed at minimum of an instructor, an instructional designer, and an assistant. The instructor has expertise in curricular design and pedagogy but needs advice and assistance in translating F2F teaching experience and delivery models into the online mode. A smooth transition relies on an instructional designer's guidance to identify, select, and finalize technology tools and applications that are best suited for fulfilling course objectives. Choosing technology tools and applications that are existent and available is a good strategy that will make the process more feasible and satisfactory. Creating tools or applications from scratch, by anyone on the team, is too ambitious, time-consuming, and costly unless it is a wide-scaled project substantially funded with strong budgetary support. Ideally, the instructional designer should have several years of experience in teaching a foreign language in general and a certain level of understanding of the language that you teach. It would take more time to communicate what you need if the instructional designer provides technology advice and support in general fields that are not related to language. Lacking knowledge of research-endorsed best practices in effective online language teaching would prolong the preparation process.

After determining technology tools and applications, the next step is to hire one or more student assistants to help you key in materials, such as vocabulary, word expressions, and sentences, or even a text or lesson into the tool or app to get them well tested before running. Doing all this on your own is possible, but it may take time you need and should be using to think bigger and more holistically for the entirety of course design. If funding is limited, then prepare for the course a bit earlier, as you need to avoid exhausting yourself with intensive work and too pressing a timeline. Remember that creating an online course takes at least triple the effort it takes to create a F2F course. Many teachers who transition from F2F to online teaching do not initially sense this but will come to realize it later after experiencing laborious and tremendous amount of work in need.

6. Is technology more important than curriculum and pedagogy?

Technology alone without solid professional training in curriculum design and pedagogy does not make an effective online language teacher. Technology tools and applications for online language teaching can be learned in short courses. But building knowledge, skills, and competence in a teacher preparation program takes much more than one or two courses on technology. Normally, it takes one to two years to complete a professional teacher preparation program, including an internship or teaching practicum in real classrooms. Professional development for pre-service teachers takes much more training time than the time it takes to get familiar with tech tools needed for online teaching. A language educator's job is technology user and evaluator, not the creator of technology tools.

It is best to select pedagogically appropriate technology tools and applications in consultation with instructional designers. Even if not taking courses on technology use in relation to language teaching, seeking advice from an experienced instructional designer in foreign language teaching is also a viable time-effective option. Technology is supplementary to the overarching curricular and pedagogical goals. Course design and instruction are first and foremost, and technology plays a supporting role to help fulfill course objectives. To put it more precisely, technology is the way to facilitate good online teaching, but not the wholeness of what accounts for good online teaching. It is important to distinguish learning to use technology from learning to teach online or remotely. The former places technology at the center, whereas the latter puts effective online teaching at the heart of training. And the latter is far more important than the former in achieving effective real-time online teaching.

7. Who can be an excellent online language teacher?

In UVA STARTALK, we consistently observed that the effectiveness of online teaching is not significantly correlated with prior online teaching experience. The effective principles for model instruction in F2F settings apply equally in online teaching, and in fact successful online teaching depends on the same principles as successful in-person teaching does. Prior experience in effective F2F teaching resonates with the overarching principles necessary for online teaching. Online teaching is in a vacuum if it is not grounded in the proven principles of F2F teaching. The major difference is that technology has more weight in online teaching than in F2F onsite teaching.

In four years of observation of teachers in UVA STARTALK, those with prior online teaching experience did not necessarily outperform those without prior online teaching experience. This seemed counterintuitive and puzzling, so we took a closer look. Individual interviews and analysis of teacher participants' backgrounds revealed that most teachers with prior experience in online teaching worked as coaches or graders, and as such, did not contribute to online course design and materials development. Their major responsibilities were to create pre-recorded lectures, mostly in English, for self-paced learning in grammar or vocabulary. Of those who had taught online before attending UVA STARTALK, very few had received solid training in applying effective elicitation questioning strategies to engage learners in communicative and immersive settings. Therefore, they lacked significant (and sometimes any) real-time teaching experience in virtual settings, so did not have existing skills transferable to synchronous teaching, which was the aim of the UVA STARTALK teaching training program.

I vividly remember one of teacher participants sharing her immeasurable excitement about the program: she confessed to me that her role was simply as a grader in an online language program and that the training in online real-time teaching at UVA STARTALK was exactly what she had been looking for. And indeed, most instructors who are hired to work for K-12 online language programs are indeed graders or coaches. They do not determine instructional goals or finalize materials, nor do they need to teach virtually or interact with students. Most K-12 online language programs rely on asynchronous learning. Students mainly self-learn pre-uploaded materials and pre-recorded teaching videos. This further explains why some teacher participants in UVA STARTALK were used to lecturing and explaining and needed to learn how to create opportunities for students to talk and perform. It took several rounds of teaching practice and reflection for them to realize the importance of performance-based teaching. Teachers used to a great proportion of teacher-talk in online teaching needed to buy into the rationale that it is student-talk that makes learning happen. After developing awareness of this principle and modifying a deeply rooted mindset, they develop the skills and resilience in creating a student-centered class.

8. Can an online virtual class fully cover what is covered in a F2F class?

The material covered in an online virtual class is either as much as or less than that in a F2F class. More likely, it will be less. What matters is "how much less is less". This will be determined locally. Any robust Chinse language program will not manage courses at the expense of instructional quality. Imagine the negative impact on accumulative "less" at each level of course. Altogether, this may be detrimental to programmatic goals and the development of language proficiency in each course and among individual learners. The key question to think on profoundly is how to teach less and still manage to help learners achieve predetermined can-do statements. We cannot stress enough the importance of instilling a "can-do" mindset in each learner. Strategically, consider cutting down busy work and keeping core content essential for the mastery of language functions. Revisit curricular design and instructional strategies and plan innovatively for ways to translate them into effective learning online.

9. What is the ideal class size for an online synchronous language? course?

With all factors equally monitored and well controlled, the smaller the class size, the better. The UVA STARTALK training program in 2016–19 offered a very small class size for each F2F virtual class. Each class had two to four students, taught by a homeroom teacher and facilitated by a supporting teacher. When the homeroom teacher delivered synchronous teaching, the supporting teacher helped by troubleshooting technology, taking attendance, responding to questions posted in Chats, and so on. All teachers unanimously expressed their preference of teaching only two students in a session. No one favored the idea of teaching four or more. The undisputable consensus among all 48 teacher participants was that smaller class sizes resulted in better instructional quality and effectiveness, namely, the achievement of can-do statements and instructional objectives. Keeping instructional materials and in-class time the same, a student in a two-person class proportionally gets more opportunities to practice the target language and interact with his or her peer than a student in a four-person class. Similarly, a small class with few students is much easier to manage online than a larger class.

In general, a class of twelve students is likely to constitute a better-managed online class than a class of twenty students, even without taking into account the frequency of technology troubleshooting or individual learners' inappropriate behavior that may interfere with normal instructional flow and disperse the attention for the instructor and learners. Grouping is more manageable in a physical class than in a virtual setting. Online breakout rooms in Zoom are a smart device for group work, but they have limitations: students in Zoom breakout rooms are unable to receive instant feedback from the instructor, and verbal or nonverbal cues are more difficult to read or nonexistent during group discussion. These limitations do create constraints that a F2F class is not likely to have. And even in unfavorable situations that pose some potential problems in a F2F class can be much more quickly resolved by the instructor's quick response to mitigate or minimize any potential negative impact on learning.

Considering the inherent limitations and potential problems in F2F online teaching settings, the majority of teachers would do better with a small class size. However, many other considerations factor into the actual size of class for online teaching. To name a few, issues of funding, personnel, technology support, and space, all come into play in the decision-making process. Academic standards and instructional quality are key to the core mission of education, but the limitations of administrative resources and allocation of funding may not provide enough support to serve learners as much as teachers would like. How to leverage resources to achieve the most and best is a central issue for educators and administrators.

10. What is the ideal time length for a F2F online class?

The ideal time length for a F2F online Chinese language course is no longer than 50 minutes or one hour. Sitting in front of the computer and staring at it for longer is bad for physical and mental health. The longer the online lesson, the more fatigue it will cause and less effective it will be. An online course that lasts for 75 minutes or more is not likely to achieve better outcomes than a course of 50 minutes or less. To keep learners engaged in active learning, group projects that require frequent interaction should be created; these minimize fatigue and energize learners at the end of the course. A longer online session is doomed to fail, especially if it consists of entire-class interaction that is not alternated with other types of interactive activities. It is best to create meaningful tasks that invite learners to use all five senses and keep multiple intelligences: this is always a salient strategy to guide instructional flow and meet different learners' needs.

Be reminded that learners' attention spans in an online setting are shorter than in a F2F class. Heavy reliance on information shown on the screen as the sole medium or stimulus causes exhaustion for eyes and cognitive constraints on information processing. This is true for college learners, and even more so for younger learners such as middle- or high-schoolers, who have a hard time staying attentive anyway. An overarching principle for lesson design is to divide one hour of content into several small segments, and connect them from small to larger segments to conclude with an integral summative assessment. This allows activity design to include three communicative modes and make them as diversified as possible. Do frequent ongoing comprehension checks to elicit learners' immediate responses to promote active learning and genuine communication. Limit each small communicative task to five to ten minutes to keep learners focused and to maximize interaction to yield full engagement and participation. This can never be understressed for teenaged learners and is also true for college learners.

11. Is handwriting required for an online course?

YES, definitely. Handwriting cannot be replaced by typed characters and must be included in online teaching for several reasons. First, writing a character by hand is a production skill, but typing a character is not the same. The former involves writing a radical and its associated component to make a complete character in most cases. But the latter requires learners to cope with word processing software to type Pinyin, recognize characters, and choose the right and discard the wrong. To put it concisely, typing characters tests a learner's mastery of Pinyin and character recognition skills, but not production skills. Second, typing characters loses the clues of stroke order and the balanced proportion of different strokes and components that together exhibit the esthetic beauty of character writing. Third, handwriting yields long-term retention, but typing does not. The retention of Chinese character learning involves cognitive loading and information processing. Learners who know how to write characters on a piece of paper can easily demonstrate competence in typing, but not vice versa. Writing characters wins over typing as a sole means to character learning, retention, and long-term memory effects.

Research in effective strategies for learning Chinese characters has yielded insights, but when and how to make progressive changes to the proportional balance between handwriting and typing at different levels of instruction remains unclear and needs further study. For elementary learners, learning to write radicals and understanding their meaning are key for building the foundation of character learning. Knowing how to pronounce a character does not seem to correlate with the production of character writing. To ensure long-term memory, experienced instructors usually encourage learners to associate meaning with different parts of a character, in addition to frequent handwriting. But there are no clear guidelines for when, what, and how to do to incorporate both handwriting and typing in different levels of language instruction for F2F in-person teaching, let alone online teaching.

As we await more research-supported pedagogical recommendations, a feasible option that is currently endorsed by the majority of Chinese language instructors is to start introducing handwriting in beginning courses and gradually increase the proportion of typing as proficiency increases. It would be dangerous to completely disregard handwriting and resort to typing only in elementary and intermediate Chinese, whether taught remotely or in a traditional classroom. AP Chinese, which is equivalent to the fourth semester of a Chinese language course at the college level, recommends a combination of handwriting and typing in the curricular framework even though the AP exam is completely online. Even advanced learners need opportunities to practice character handwriting to partially fulfill curricular requirements at the college level.

With the invention of advanced technologies, learners can also practice writing characters on a tablet, a smartphone, and an interactive white board. Using a keyboard to type and a mouse cursor or fingers on the screen of an online platform can also produce characters, although online settings lose the art and beauty of character writing. These technologies provide viable and welcome options for character writing and add practicality and convenience for character learning. The demonstration of online animated characters can to some extent restore the artful realization and cultural heritage of Chinese characters. Exposure to different ways of character writing in addition to traditional paper-and-pencil handwriting is inevitable in any mode of online learning. As computer-assisted character learning emerges as a new area for exploration in innovative pedagogy, there is a lot to explore and test through well-conducted research projects and empirical studies.

12. Does online teaching pose more challenges for elementary Chinese?

Elementary Chinese can be taught online as well as at other levels, but Chinese language teachers of such a level do face more challenges than those of intermediate and beyond. The following briefly summarizes different challenges for teaching elementary Chinese online synchronously.

1) Using the Target Language to Create Immersion Experience

According to ACTFL's position statement, an elementary class should be conducted with at least 90% of discussion in the target language. While this immersion experience can be fully implemented for F2F teaching, whether it is fully transferrable to online learning for true beginners at the initial stages of learning is questionable and needs profound thinking.

In a F2F teaching scenario, creating a linguistically and culturally enriched immersive setting is made possible through appropriate use of gestures, facial expressions, body language, physical movements, here-and-now contextual clues, posters and materials on the wall of the classroom, realia and tangible objects, and many other types of authentic materials as teaching aids. Admittedly, online teachers are still able to use these techniques in front of the webcam, but the effects are not fully comparable to the same actions live in a four-walled classroom that is spacious, movable, dynamic, and multifunctional. Even as animated images, 3D videos, and virtual reality and augmented reality can add a high degree of authenticity to online learning settings, creating an authentic learning setting alone does not ensure the production of the target language: it requires appropriate use of teaching strategies for verbal expression.

Assuming learners stay attentive and technology is fully supported, verbal expressions can be strategically used to help create an immersion learning experience for learners. Using language simplification strategies, here-and-now techniques, and contextual clues coupled with a slower speech pace whenever needed should work as well as in online as in F2F teaching. A precaution for online teaching at the novice level: set practical and reasonable expectations about the use of the target language after introducing the course syllabus. In a F2F in-person classroom, Lesson One on greetings and simple self-introductions can proceed smoothly and quickly, entirely in the target language. But when converting such an experience to an online environment, some adjustments to instructional techniques are necessary. To explain more concretely, shaking hands in action and holding or pointing to one's name tag are not doable virtually and need to be replaced by other visual clues and creative techniques. A good recommendation for the first several days of class is to prioritize building the bonding and rapport that make for an online community and ease learners' pressure and anxiety. The use of the target language in 90% of class time is achievable after observing that learners are gaining confidence and establishing their comfort zone. Before this happens, the pace of instruction may need to slow a bit, requiring patience, and materials to be covered should adhere to the "less is more" principle. This means teaching less content, compared to what is covered in a F2F class, but recycling it more to ensure that genuine learning is really happening and that increasing competence is being built within learners' comfort zone, so students are not overwhelmed, scared away, or forced to drop the course in the first two weeks. It is worth reiterating that effective factors play a far more significant role in online learning, and this is particularly true for the first couple days of an online course.

2) Coping with a Non-alphabetical Language Virtually

Learners of Romance languages are less willing to pursue studies in non-Roman languages online. This is due in part to the distinction between alphabetical and non-alphabetical languages. Unlike Romance languages, Mandarin Chinese is a non-alphabetic language characterized by tone and pictograph. Pronunciation and writing do not correspond to each other as in English, and beginning learners are therefore unable to pronounce based on decoding written cues. This linguistic uniqueness poses some challenges for the development of new learning strategies online.

For those whose native tongue is an alphabetical language such as English, different tone marks may sound merely different in pitch or intonation. A pronounceable unit, in principle, is composed of a tone mark, a consonant, and a vowel, resulting in a syllable that shapes meaning. A set of must-learn initials and finals includes *zhi, chi, shi, ri, zi, ci, si, ri* distinguishable from *ji, qi, xi*: online learners might experience delays and difficulty in identifying the right from the wrong, whether practicing individually or chorally. The vowel "ü" sound, made with rounded lips, more or less similar to a German umlaut, is more easily taught in a F2F class where the instructor can see each learner's face and lips on site to provide immediate feedback. It is certinaly possible to do this in online teaching, but techniques as simple as switching from a PowerPoint slide to an entire class mode, in which the teacher and students see all the faces on the computer full screen, takes one more step of planning and in-action technical operation during teaching. And even with extensive planning and practice, technology glitches are possible.

Pertinent to familiarity with the pronunciation system in the Chinese language is competence in literacy skills. The lack of direct correspondence between the writing of characters and pronunciation complicates the learning process and remains one of factors detrimental to maintaining good enrollment. Reading non-alphabetic written scripts can be facilitated by decoding strategies and evolving technology tools. There are animated websites of character writing showing correct stroke order and calligraphy and linking to proportional distribution of different stokes and esthetic representation. With the aid of advanced technology, the decoding of a radical and its accompanying part in a character can be acquired and systematically recycled for initial fundamental learning that begins the building of incremental skillset. In-class online teaching, enhanced by pre-class learning and reinforced by after-class learning, is one of the most effective strategies to make sure learners are well-prepared before class. The invention of new technologies has made this highly achievable and feasible.

3) Adapting to a Multifaceted New Learning Environment

Novice language learners are challenged by more complex factors associated with their adaptation to a completely new learning environment. Elementary Chinese language courses normally have a greater percentage of first-year high schoolers or college first-years than other levels of courses. In addition to coping with the new language, they are also adapting to a new phase of life experience. With so many new things clustering at one time, learning Chinese online may add complications to their first-year experience in a new school. Online learning induces anxiety among learners, and this is especially true for lower-level learners.

Many first-year Chinese language instructors admit that a minimum of one month is needed to get the class on the right track in a F2F class, meaning, for example, setting up a class routine, establishing an attendance policy, clearly communicating expectations, clarifying many Do's and Don'ts, establishing grading criteria, and so on. And it may take longer for virtual learning even if some learners have prior experience in online learning.

Adjusting to online learning also reveals different layers of complications socially and psychologically. New learners not only strive to meet instructor's expectations academically, but they simultaneously deal with the shaping of many new roles, such as a new identity, a new agency, and a new method of social interaction and engagement in the online community, to be created by the instructor and defined by the real undertaking of in-class and outside-class interactive behavior. All these new experiences can be daunting or even disorienting for beginners in pursuit of Chinese language study, especially if the new experiences not well guided.

To ease the adjustment process, instructors of elementary Chinese must make extra efforts to carefully organize and sequence course materials to best prepare for clear presentation of online lessons for true beginners. This, however, adds to the workload, which some administrators may not fully understand. In theory, it is possible to create meaningful and rewarding experiences for online learners, but it is just a reality that time commitment matters. Realistically, elementary Chinese language instructors, with multi-leveled responsibilities in the high-demand working environment, may not have sufficient time to meticulously plan for the three stages of materials needed for pre-class learning, during-class synchronous learning, and post-class reviews. This leaves online teachers somewhat underprepared in most cases. Satisfaction and success can be achieved, but they need strong support at the academic, administrative, and budgetary levels.

13. Is flipped learning necessary for an online course?

Most institutions do not mandate flipped learning, but it is highly recommended. Flipped learning is incorporated into F2F, blended, and online learning. It takes place before learners enter a class, so it is characterized by pre-class learning through which learners self-acquire knowledge and skills before class and get ready to apply them in class. Flipped learning has several advantages. It helps save in-class time and fills the class with active and engaging learning. Students who have done the pre-class learning are well-prepared to bring questions to class for thorough discussion. This is beneficial for the development of problem-solving skills and analytical and critical thinking abilities.

Flipped learning can be created innovatively and diversely to engage learners in fun and meaningful learning before class. For example, before entering a F2F class, either onsite or online, students can do the following: watch a YouTube video, complete interactive video learning by typing comprehension check responses, engage in vocabulary learning through Quizlet, post several sentences on Padlet to comment on a news or comic strip, or upload a photo, recording, short essay, or PowerPoint slides via VoiceThread.

Secondary schools do set limits for homework time. Some even remove homework time for certain subject areas. Flipped learning, if embedded in a language curriculum, can be as short as ten minutes. An effective preview task does not have to be long, and it is expected to potentially exert learners' incentive to want to do it and do it well. In principle, making a pre-class task interesting, visually appealing, and most importantly, meaningful and communicative, is likely to get learners hooked on what they are doing. Since online learning promotes independent learning, instant feedback and scoring are essential for flipped learning. Making pre-class preview works as interactive as possible is a welcome feature.

14. Can online learning be playful and meaningful at the same time?

YES. Online learning can be playful and meaningful at the same time, and this is pivotal in reaching the end goal for online learning. Playfulness in online learning is no less important than being meaningful. Adding colors, animation, visual graphs, acoustic effects, and the like are favored by all ages of learners. Language professionals know what accounts for meaningful learning but have little experience in making meaningful learning playful. Instructional designers and technology specialists can contribute here. Technology tools that can be used to create a welcome environment of playfulness that will have a prevailing positive impact on reinforcing learning. Adding playfulness to online task design is critically needed to sustain interest and motivation. Making learning fun and interesting, in such a way as to trigger a genuine desire to do more and well emerges as a central area to explore further. This centers on human needs, not monotonous or mechanical learning, and will lead online activity design to thrive in the foreseeable future.

15. Can an online language course keep a satisfactory student completion rate?

It depends. In general, an online course whose learning components are all or mostly asynchronous tends to have a higher dropout rate and a lower level of satisfaction. Conversely, an online course featuring more genuinely productive interaction, both quantitatively and qualitatively, is more approachable and likely to keep students engaged in learning and active till the last day of course. As in F2F classes, students need immediate support and assistance in language learning while learning remotely. Responding to questions posted by students in the online discussion board in lieu of a F2F meeting, virtually or physically, is unarguably less effective because of the necessary delay. This can be remedied by F2F tutorial or coaching sessions in whatever form to better connect the instructor with the learner and enable the instructor to offer what the specific learner needs. Unsatisfactory and delayed responses to questions and appeals for help can account in large part for the rise of the dropout rate.

It is not easy to keep a 100% student completion rate for remote learning, but it is possible. The Virginia STARTALK Chinese Student Academy (VSCSA) in conjunction with Virginia STARTALK Chinese Teacher Academy was able to maintain a 100% student completion rate in four consecutive years, the entire length of the online learning program. Recognizing the high dropout rate for online language courses, the VSCSA team established a goal of 75% student completion rate while planning the student online learning program. Thus it was surprising to achieve the miraculous completion rate of 100%. Constant in-program and after-program analysis and reflections disclose the reasons why this can be achieved, as outlined below.

Learners in the Student Program

Well-implemented pre-program technology orientation and program overview
Successful recruitment of a group of highly motivated learners for online learning
A three-stage learning cycle featuring flipped learning, in-class synchronous learning, and post-class learning
Quality interaction in afternoon tutorial sessions, individually or in groups

Core Administrative Team

The constitution of a dedicated administrative team
Well-defined responsibilities among core team members
Detailed planning before the program and carefully implementation during the program
Constant reminders and positive reinforcement with students on asynchronous learning

Online Real-time Instructional Delivery

Well-sequenced and closely monitored synchronous online teaching
A strong instructional team with high standards for teaching
Curriculum well-guided and supervised by leading trainers, leading instructors, practicum facilitators, and technology coordinator
Multifaceted practicum starting from lesson planning in close alignment with best practices, and rehearsals to refine lessons
A seamless process contributing to productive online instructional delivery
Sufficient and immediate online and onsite support whenever needed

Strong Team Building

The building of a vibrant and productive teaching community

The nurturing of a growth mindset
Striving for excellence among individual teachers

In any class, there are nuances and intricacies conducive to learners' satisfaction and attainment of language proficiency. A good starting point for online program design is the research-endorsed concept or rationale that frequent quality interaction is key to the success of an online learning program. The three-stage learning cycle is well proven: it features productive synchronous learning, reinforced by pre-class preview (flipped learning), in connection with the in-class online synchronous learning, strengthened by post-class review tasks. This model has great potential for the success of online learning and deserves full consideration and future replication for online Chinese language teaching.